The Vanishing Frame

Border Hispanisms
Jon Beasley-Murray, Alberto Moreiras, and Gareth Williams, series editors

The Vanishing Frame

Latin American Culture and Theory
in the Postdictatorial Era

EUGENIO CLAUDIO DI STEFANO

University of Texas Press ◆ Austin

Requests for permission to reproduce material from this work should be sent to:
Permissions
University of Texas Press
P.O. Box 7819
Austin, TX 78713-7819
utpress.utexas.edu/rp-form

♾ The paper used in this book meets the minimum requirements of
ANSI/NISO Z39.48-1992 (R1997) (Permanence of Paper).

Library of Congress Cataloging-in-Publication Data
Names: Di Stefano, Eugenio Claudio, author.
Title: The vanishing frame : Latin American culture and theory in the
    postdictatorial era / Eugenio Claudio Di Stefano.
Other titles: Border Hispanisms.
Description: First edition. | Austin : University of Texas Press, 2018. | Series:
    Border Hispanisms | Includes bibliographical references and index.
Identifiers: LCCN 2017056778| ISBN 978-1-4773-1618-4 (cloth : alk. paper) |
    ISBN 978-1-4773-1619-1 (pbk. : alk. paper) | ISBN 978-1-4773-1620-7 (library
    e-book) | ISBN 978-1-4773-1621-4 (nonlibrary e-book)
Subjects: LCSH: Spanish American literature—20th century—History and criticism.
    | Politics and literature—Latin America—20th century. | Dictatorship—Latin
    America—History—20th century. | Chilean literature—20th century—History
    and criticism.
Classification: LCC PQ7081 .D483 2018 | DDC 860.9/980904—dc23
LC record available at https://lccn.loc.gov/2017056778

doi:10.7560/316184

To my father, Francesco Di Stefano

Contents

Acknowledgments

This book has taken many years to write and has involved the continuous support and love of countless family members, friends, and colleagues. I am deeply indebted to two extraordinary scholars, Margarita Saona and Walter Benn Michaels. Both provided constant guidance and critical input, which pushed me to become a sharper thinker and a better writer. Margarita's extensive knowledge of, and engagement with, Latin American literature continues to be an inspiration. And Walter's insight and critical perspective have marked many pages of this book. I was lucky enough to have taken classes and conversed with some excellent minds: Jennifer Ashton, Nicholas Brown, Rosilie Hernández-Pecoraro, Steven Marsh, Dianna Niebylski, Cristián Roa-de-la-Carrera, Rebecca Saunders, Leda Schiavo, and Bill Van Patton. Cristián and Rebecca were instrumental in my journey to understanding the political potential of theory. A special thanks to Lennard Davis, who was invaluable in my understanding of disability studies and central to the first stages of this project.

I must also acknowledge the formative and intellectual origins of this book. When I was an undergraduate at the University of Missouri–Kansas City, Rafael Espejo Saavedra, Louis Imperiale, and Alice Reckley Vallejo were the first to suggest that I pursue graduate school in Hispanic Studies. In particular, after finishing my dissertation, Louis urged that I see this project through and complete this book. I am grateful to him for this encouragement, and for so much more.

Many of the ideas expressed herein emerged from conversations with three brilliant scholars, Steve Buttes, Eduardo Ledesma, and Emilio Sauri. I consider myself very fortunate to have benefited from their discerning eyes, but much more importantly, to have their uncompromising friendship. I would also like to thank Susana Domingo Amestoy, Mathias Nilges,

Magnus Nilsson, and Charles Hatfield for their insight and comments at various stages of this work; a special note of thanks to Charles, whose input at every point of this process has been essential.

I am grateful to have crossed paths with and received important feedback from various scholars and artists: Hugo Achugar, Abraham Acosta, Txetxu Aguado, Jens Andermann, Jon Beasley-Murray, Alex Beaumont, Ericka Beckman, Caitlin Benson-Allott, Todd Cronan, Patrick Dove, Susana Draper, Stanley Fish, Ben Gest, Andrew Hogan, Lori Hopkins, Rachel Jacobson (and those at Film Streams in Omaha), Adam Kelly, Justin Kemerling, Annabel Martín, Jeff Menne, Toril Moi, Alberto Moreiras, Charles Palermo, Dierdra Reber, Adolph Reed, Djurdja Trajkovic, Myka Tucker-Abramson, Richard Van Heertum, Robert Wells, Daniel Wuebben, and Daniel Zamora.

Since 2012, I have considered myself very fortunate to have an amazing group of colleagues at the University of Nebraska at Omaha: Melanie Bloom, Ana Carballal, Gwyneth Cliver, Adrian Duran, Claudia García, Dan Hawkins, Brett Kyle, Marie Lee, Arturo Miranda, Tatyana Novikov, Juliette Parnell, Patrice Proulx, Thomas Sánchez, Cecilia Tocaimaza-Hatch, Steven Torres, Tara Toscano, and Laura Walls; faculty and staff at the Office of Latino/Latin American Studies, including Jonathan Benjamin-Alvarado, Juan Casas, Yuriko Doku, and Lourdes Gouveia. At the University of West Georgia, my gratitude goes to Lisa Connolly, Julia Farmer, Robert Kilpatrick, Euisuk Kim, Felix Tweraser, and Jeffery Zamostny, who read earlier drafts of this work.

Other dear friends who were important during the writing process include Paolo Alessi, the Ballone family, Leonardo Campos Salcines, Sancho Campos Salcines, the Caldara families, the Clark family, Hugo Liberal Fernandes, Edurne García, the Groppi family, Alice Haisman, Larisa Homarac, Jill Jegerski, Ana Martín Sagredo, Giovanni Mazza, Laura Pereira, Laura Salcines Torre, and Jacob Sayre. In research related to Uruguay, I owe my deepest gratitude to Gabriel Abend, Lali Aguiar, the Barbeito family, especially Daniela, and to Alejandro Lazar, Antonio Montalbán, Josefina Repetto (de la biblioteca de la Facultad de Humanidades y Ciencias de la Educación de la Universidad de la República, Montevideo), Elina Ricciardi, and Alejandro "Cano" Viera Varoli. A very special thank you to the Trajtenburg family, who opened their home in Montevideo to *un pibe americano* who was interested in Uruguayan literature—in particular to the extraordinary Isabela Pareja: you are deeply missed.

Part of this book was made possible with generous funding from the National Endowment for the Humanities in 2015 and with a UCRCA summer stipend from the University of Nebraska at Omaha in 2014. I would also like to express gratitude to the Border Hispanisms series editors, Jon Beasley-Murray, Alberto Moreiras, and Gareth Williams, who showed not only initial interest but also unrelenting support in the development of this project. I am appreciative of the invaluable feedback provided by the two anonymous readers. Thank you to Kerry Webb and Angelica Lopez-Torres at the University of Texas Press, who have been truly delightful to work with.

All of this means very little without the support and love of my family: my sister, Sandy Di Stefano Serowka, who always led the way, Patrick Serowka, Patrick "Little P," and Alex Serowka; my brother, Leopoldo Di Stefano, who at an early age showed me how to think critically and socially; my mother, Giulia Di Stefano, and my father, Francesco Di Stefano, who provided me not only with the opportunity to pursue my studies but also with the strength to pursue them uncompromisingly; and the Toscano family, who have become a second family, in particular Peggy Brennan for her delightful questions, comments, and genuine interest. Finally, I want to thank my partner, Tara Toscano, who accompanied me in every moment of this process and who worked even harder than I did to see this book's completion. Your absolute love, and now Beatrice and Emilo's, make this not only possible, but worth it: vi voglio tanto bene.

Earlier versions of material contained herein were published as "From Revolution to Human Rights in Mario Benedetti's *Pedro y el Capitán*," *Journal of Latin American Cultural Studies* 20.2 (2011): 121–137; "Reconsidering Aesthetic Autonomy and Interpretation as a Critique of the Latin American Left in Roberto Bolaño's *Estrella distante*," *Revista de Estudios Hispánicos* 47.3 (2013): 463–485; "What Can a Painting Do? Absorption and Autonomy in Fernando Botero's *Abu Ghraib* as a Response to Affect and the Moral Utopia of Human Rights," *Modern Language Notes* 129.2 (2014): 412–432.

The Vanishing Frame

Freedom at the End of the Postdictatorial Era

Released almost forty years after Augusto Pinochet's 1973 coup d'état, Pablo Larraín's *No* (2012) immediately sparked controversy in his home country of Chile. The film would go on to garner critical acclaim throughout the globe, including an Oscar nomination in 2013 for best foreign film. This controversy and success, if anything, shows that the most recent dictatorship in Chile, which officially ended in 1990, is still a deeply divided subject, one that also continues to draw interest beyond national borders. *No* opens with the adman René Saavedra (played by Gael García Bernal) pitching a marketing campaign for Free Cola, which includes images of the pop group Engrupo singing about the cola as teenagers and a mime blissfully dance and drink the beverage. The Free Cola commercial will serve as a model for political ads that will reappear later in the film, after Saavedra becomes one of the architects behind the No marketing campaign for the 1988 plebiscite to determine whether Pinochet will rule for another eight years. Previous attempts to end the dictatorship have failed, though Saavedra's savvy market-driven approach eventually succeeds, ending over sixteen years of military rule in Chile.

No, however, is about not the triumph of democracy but rather its failure, a failure linked to the consolidation of neoliberalism in Chile, where redemocratization is largely the result of Chileans' desire for a society that looks more like the world in a Free Cola commercial than a democracy that comes to terms with a legacy of human rights violations. Thus Larraín's film offers an account of the transition to democracy that is a result of some clever marketing that ignores or sidesteps human rights justice. The film, in other words, is an account of how neoliberalism, which was first implemented in the mid-1970s under Pinochet, goes democratic. That is, if Chileans had neoliberalism before redemocratization, what they want now—and what the victory comes to stand for—is a democracy that upholds this neoliberal economic agenda rather than a dictatorship that imposes it. What they want, and what they get, is neoliberal freedom.

But, as the film makes clear, neoliberal freedom—much like the Free Cola commercial—is not very good. One of the last scenes of *No* confirms this point. As a crowd joyously celebrates the No victory, ecstatically singing the campaign jingle "Chile, la alegría ya viene" (Chile, happiness is coming), the camera pans and then focuses on a concerned-looking Saavedra, who walks through the crowd protectively holding his child's hand. The contrast between Saavedra's protective gesture and the jubilant crowd celebrating democracy's return suggests that the promise of happiness would not be fulfilled. And, in fact, it has not been for the majority of Chileans. Almost thirty years after the triumph of the No campaign, Chile ranks among the most economically unequal countries in the world. This should not come as a surprise, however, given that the transition to democracy did not challenge the neoliberal economic policies that were first put in place by Pinochet's regime. Contrary to the upbeat jingle, for many today, Chile is not a very happy place.

Importantly, the film's focus on the campaign and the happiness it failed to produce also raises questions about the intersection of affect, aesthetics, and politics, questions that I argue have been essential to Latin American dictatorial and postdictatorial literature and visual art since the late 1970s. More specifically, artists and critics have sought to mobilize affective responses, such as sorrow and pain, in order to produce an ethical/moral response often aligned with human rights advocacy. To be sure, human rights today has become the primary lens through which global citizens frame questions of justice. But in the early 1970s, the discourse of human rights had little political resonance inside or outside of Latin America. As Samuel Moyn suggests, for much of the twentieth century, human rights had been overshadowed by other political utopias, including nationalism and communism. By the mid-1970s, however, these projects were, for various reasons, including decolonialization and the USSR's loss of credibility, understood as failures. As a response to this new political reality, human rights would emerge on the world stage as a "moral alternative to bankrupt political utopias" (Moyn 5). And yet, part of what I hope to demonstrate in this book is that if human rights can be considered an "alternative," it is an alternative that, unlike socialism, is deeply compatible with capitalism. In the following pages, I contend that human rights discourse comes to obscure an anticapitalist project that was at the center of leftist mobilization in the 1960s and 1970s by replacing it with a political project that centers primarily on an injustice done to the body by the state.

Insofar as human rights erase an anticapitalist politics, they do so in part by mobilizing an aesthetic project as well. As I examine later, the logic of human rights in Latin America manifests itself aesthetically in two fundamental ways. First, it focuses heavily on representing torture, mutilations, and other corporeal injustices; it does so, undoubtedly, to draw attention to, and raise awareness of, the atrocities perpetrated by the dictatorships in countries like Chile, Argentina, and Uruguay. But while this logic raises awareness, it rarely explains—when it does not entirely disregard—the ideological and historical reasons that motivated these dictatorships. That is, while making violence visible, the discourse of human rights also renders invisible the reasons behind that violence. Second, by highlighting corporeal injustice, the discourse seeks to eliminate the division between art and life (or art and politics) so that the pain of the victim can somehow become that of the reader or the spectator. In other words, human rights want to render invisible the work's aesthetic status so the reader can be transformed into a kind of witness of a horrific event. In short, insofar as the logic of human rights imagines the violence and the pain of the other as our own, it does so by vanishing the aesthetic frame that divides the textual witness and the reader or spectator.

No represents a departure from this human rights discourse to the extent that it is more interested in critiquing neoliberal freedom than in endorsing a project where the pain of the victim is shared with the spectator. That is, *No* offers a response to the discourse of sorrow and pain by noting that their emotional opposite, happiness, does not present a contradiction to neoliberalism. Thus, while the film highlights the link between the politics of human rights and the happiness that "is coming," it also shows how this emphasis on affect is intimately connected to neoliberal freedom. And yet, *No*'s rejection of human rights is made visible in other crucial ways. In one of the more controversial scenes in the film, members of the No campaign are viewing a potential ad. Saavedra did not create this particular ad, but he has been asked to provide feedback. The ad shows images of the coup and the abuses that followed. There is footage of the bombing of the Moneda Palace, of military tanks rolling through Santiago, of bodies lying in the street. Numbers flash across the screen: "34,690 tortured," "200,000 exiled," "2,110 executed," "1,248 disappeared." These images clearly echo many of the political concerns that emerge in the dictatorial period, and they undoubtedly have an emotional impact on those in the room who watch. But the images do not provoke an emotional reaction in Saavedra; or, at least, this reaction is not relevant to him, as he dismissively asks if there is another ad to watch, since "this doesn't sell." In another meeting with campaign members, Saavedra shows one of his own ads, one that apparently does sell. The ad is very much in the style of the Free Cola commercial presented at the beginning of the film; any mention of the regime's crimes is now absent.

This depoliticized ad upsets the members of the No campaign. One man reacts by saying that "this is a campaign to silence what really happened" as he declares that he will not be a part of the campaign and storms out of the room. Perhaps some audience members feel the same as the man, but these violations, and whatever reaction the viewer has to the violent images, are not necessarily central to the film's political critique. For Saavedra, these violent images are simply not as interesting, since they do not sell; and the same can be said for *No*'s director, who is more intent on chronicling the triumph of this market logic in the 1980s and how this triumph affects Chile today. Larraín notes that "the movie's not just about what happened before the referendum, it's about what happened after. Since 1988, we've been living in a shopping center. *No* is not just about defeating Pinochet, it's about where Chile is going—and what's going on *now* is terrible" (Romney 32; emphasis added). For Larraín, the recent past has become a mechanism for achieving a shopping center reality in which everything, including democracy, can be bought and sold. In this way, *No* is a response less to the dictatorship than to "what's going on now" and how the dictatorship has gotten us there. "What's going on now" is a world in which neoliberalism has gone unchallenged and everything has become quite "terrible."

Crucially, however, Larraín addresses the *now* by making a film that not only looks old but, in a certain material sense, is old. Larraín does this by using the very same "U-matic" videocassette technology that the 1988 campaign employed. The result is a blurred image that takes some time to adjust to and has been described as "ugly" or even off-putting (Dargis). According to Caetlin Benson-Allott, this blurriness is meant to critique the "blurred principles of the campaign" and to frame the transitional process as a "mixed moral victory" (61). In her account, a moral assessment is created by muddling the line between different mediums as well as the line between art and politics. She puts it this way: "By matching his video medium to that of the original No campaign, Larraín emphasizes that both are constructions and suggests that there can be no unmediated access to the history of the No campaign, because No itself was a media creation. By making his fiction archival, he underscores the fictive quality of the archive and of politics in general" (62). For Benson-Allott, Larraín's usage of the U-matic produces a critique by suggesting that both "his fiction" and "politics" more generally are "constructions." As will be seen throughout this book, this type of reading that reduces art and politics to constructions will be deployed in order to create a moral claim that often comes at the expense of an economic critique.

Yet, *No* is more interested in breaking with, rather than creating, a moral claim. Instead, and to contradict Benson-Allott, the objective of U-matic video is less to blur the lines between and art and politics than to use this blurriness as an opportunity to assert a distance between an aesthetic world and our own. Larraín underscores this point when addressing the utilization of this old technology: "It breaks my illusion when I'm looking at a film that is shot in high resolution and they cut to archival footage that is made in video or old resolution film stock. [In *No*], we were able to create the illusion in a way that fiction became documentary and documentary became fiction" (Wilkinson 3). Larraín does indeed attempt to make fiction look like documentary in *No*, and to make documentary look like fiction, but Benson-Allott's account notwithstanding, the point is not to blur the divide between art and politics but rather to insist on it. Larraín's contention with contrasting "high resolution" and "old resolution" is that it "breaks" the aesthetic "illusion," which, in turn, returns the spectator back to the real world. Instead, by *not* contrasting—that is, by blending—the old and new resolutions, Larraín insists on creating an autonomous aesthetic space that is unlike the world that is outside of it. That is, the old technology functions not to erase the line between the aesthetic world and the real world but rather to create an aesthetic world that stands apart from the real world. As already noted, part of the problem with the real world is that it increasingly envisions all injustices through the lens of human rights, and thus the desire for an autonomous aesthetic space is, in part, to turn away from this dominant worldview. Which is just to say that while the break with the illusion and the return to the real world would be considered a triumph for human rights politics, since it brings us back to the question of human rights morality (and the demand that we envision the world through its lens), for *No* it's understood as a failure, since this real world stresses a commitment to an affective vision of justice rather than one that is aligned with a critique of economic inequality.

Unsurprisingly, then, much of the controversy surrounding the film has revolved around human rights. Some believe that the film mischaracterizes the campaign because it ignores the human rights activism that played a part in No's victory. For example, former cabinet minister Fran-

cisco Vidal decries that "to believe that Pinochet lost the plebiscite because of a TV logo and jingle is not to grasp anything of what occurred"
(qtd. in Howe 424). Vidal's critique of *No* is strikingly similar to that of
the man in the film who accuses Saavedra of trying "to silence what really
happened"—a criticism that is quite valid if *No* were not, in fact, fiction.
Addressing these accusations, Larraín declares that "[Chileans] have a
problem with fiction and I think it's one of the most hidden legacies of the
dictatorship: not being able to understand fiction, to believe that everything works in the realm of reality, where abstraction is not possible" (qtd.
in Howe 424). Bracketing for a moment the arrogant tone of the claim,
what is important about what Larraín calls "fiction"—or what can also be
understood as a desire for aesthetic autonomy—is that it functions less as
an excuse than as an opportunity to think toward abstraction and beyond
the human rights world we now live in. Or, said differently, the assertion
of the aesthetic frame in *No* makes the critique of capitalism primary and
its morality secondary.

The Project

I began this book with Larraín's *No* because the film offers the opportunity for viewers to reexamine the political and aesthetic concepts that
have been associated with freedom in the postdictatorial period. These
concepts center principally on a politics of human rights and an aesthetics that seeks to eliminate the division between art and life, or art and
politics, in order to produce a more direct experience between the textual
subject (often a victim) and the reader or viewer. In this book, I propose a
counternarrative to this postdictatorial notion of freedom by examining
a number of contemporary artists, like Larraín, who have begun to create a
type of art that identifies the assertion of autonomous form with the possibility of thinking beyond the logic of human rights and neoliberalism.

This insistence on aesthetic autonomy is a critical departure from postdictatorial discourse, which has tended to ignore the aesthetic object in
the name of memories, trauma, mourning, melancholy, bodies, and affects relating to both the victims of state-sponsored terror and the readers and beholders who experience those texts. I posit that these dominant
forms of postdictatorial thought, although initially productive in addressing abuses, are ultimately conservative in scope, facilitating the continuation of unjust practices in Latin America that previous anticapitalist
projects sought to alleviate. Thus, I set out not only to reframe the conver-

sation of contemporary Latin American theory and culture, especially its emphasis on remembering or forgetting human rights violations, but also to suggest that this reframing begins with a reconsideration of aesthetic autonomy in relation to contemporary postdictatorial politics, neoliberalism, and the larger global economy. Said differently, I contend that the aesthetics and politics of human rights in Latin America have given way not to freedom but rather to its opposite: unfreedom.

Thus, in *The Vanishing Frame*, I provide a timely intervention in the study of Latin American postdictatorial culture and theory by arguing for a reconsideration of aesthetic autonomy in Latin American literature and art today. Making this claim requires addressing the paradoxical relationship that literature—and art more generally—has maintained with literary studies in the last several decades. Since the end of the recent dictatorships—and increasingly in the era of the postdictatorship—Latin American literary studies has abandoned what defines it as a field: literature. What this means more specifically is that the theorization of literature and art more broadly as an autonomous space has vanished from contemporary conversations. By autonomy I simply mean an aesthetic space that is not determined by the reader's experience or position, a space, more specifically, that treats the reader's position as irrelevant to the meaning of the text.

The commitment to aesthetic autonomy in this book challenges the dominant approach to Latin American literary studies, which has become largely interested in theorizing the experience of the reader and his or her relationship with the victims of state-sponsored terror. More specifically, in *The Vanishing Frame*, I set out to question the works of contemporary critics, from John Beverley to Alberto Moreiras, through Nelly Richard and Francine Masiello, to Idelber Avelar and Jon Beasley-Murray, who not only have insisted on the significance of readerly experience but also have endorsed, to varying degrees, the idea that bourgeois individualism, reactionary politics, and even authoritarian logic are intimately connected to literature and to the autonomy of the text in particular. Instead, by engaging with recent works from a mostly new generation of artists (literary, visual, interdisciplinary), I suggest that aesthetic autonomy, far from supporting a reactionary position, offers an opening to think beyond postdictatorial politics—especially those of human rights (which factor heavily in the first several chapters of this book)—a politics that has ignored, at best, and is complicit with, at worst, Latin American economic injustices that exist today.

As noted, the waning importance of aesthetic autonomy in the postdictatorial period is doubled by the increasing effort to imagine aesthetic and political projects in Latin America as determined by the reader's experience. One version of this account appears in the discussion of *No* by imagining that the division between art and politics is eliminated so the reader or spectator can be transformed into a witness who relays what he or she sees, hears, or feels. As I discuss in chapter 4, this account of political art is meant to prompt an "ethical and political response" in the beholder, by which one can testify to and denounce a form of injustice that has often been associated with the author, authoritarianism, and official history (Beverley, "Margin" 31).

For now, however, it is paramount to point out that the primacy of the reader in criticism and theory is not at all new; neither is it always aligned with human rights politics. One of the first articulations of this commitment to the reader can be found in Roland Barthes's landmark essay "The Death of the Author" (1967), which argues that the meaning of the text is determined not by the author but rather by the reader's experience, since it is the reader, and not the author, who now writes the text. Although not quite a witness, the reader, for Barthes, is imagined as a political actor whose newfound recognition undoes the aesthetic constraints of the author whose "reign" will "impose" his or her meaning upon the text ("Death" 147). Insofar as each reading takes on a new meaning—that is, a new text—freedom for Barthes is imagined by the insistence on the reader and the proliferation of readers' experiences. In other words, Barthes locates a fundamental problem in the author's intended meaning, and he finds a solution to that problem in the multiplication of positions and perspectives. Here, I challenge Barthes by suggesting that this conceptualization of aesthetics is symptomatic of a larger political project that renders ideological disagreements irrelevant—disagreements that may, in fact, serve to undermine the neoliberal world order. Indeed, I contend that this commitment to the reader's subject position (for which a politics of human rights is one version) replaces an ideological critique that sought to eliminate class inequality with a commitment to difference that renders that economic critique impossible.

Insisting on the primacy of a reader's position eliminates the possibility of disagreement because it imagines that we are not arguing about different interpretations but rather seeing, hearing, and feeling different experiences. It is worth briefly examining what I mean by (the elimination of) disagreements and how it differs from a description of what one experiences. Consider for a moment Barthes's critique of the author who "imposes" his meaning on the text ("Death" 147). Barthes's critique is meant to undercut a conception of art based on authorial intent, one in which the author writes and the reader interprets what the author means. Accordingly, each reader will have an interpretation of that intention, and, undeniably, disagreements among readers will emerge about what is the true meaning of the text. If I argue that, say, Larraín's *No* is a critique of neoliberal freedom, and you argue, instead, that it is an endorsement of that freedom, we have a disagreement about what the author intends the meaning of the text to be. Furthermore, a disagreement is predicated on a difference of beliefs about what is right or wrong—a difference, no doubt, that does not allow for two interpretations to be right: either I am right that it is a critique of neoliberalism or you are right that it is an endorsement of that freedom; it cannot be both. At the same time, and this is equally important, if my reading of *No* is right, it is right precisely because my position or experience is irrelevant. Why even argue if I truly thought the contrary? That is, why argue about Larraín's film (or any text for that matter) if you are only registering different experiences that are uniquely yours?

Barthes's "The Death of the Author" has had a profound and lasting impact on cultural and theoretical production, so much so that one would be hard-pressed to find scholars today who consider differences as disagreements about the author's intended meaning, to say nothing about how these disagreements about authorial intent can be aligned with a progressive politics. Instead, scholars think of the difference between such beliefs as the difference between the various identities and experiences one can claim as one's own. Consider once again Barthes's critique of the author, which is meant to give rise to the "birth of the reader" ("Death" 148). This "birth" must incorporate the reader's position, a position that includes not only what one sees, hears, or feels but also the identities or other cultural markers that inform who one is. Although subject positions cannot always be reduced to identities, today identities are the primary way we think through claims about subject positions. Regardless of whatever cultural marker one chooses, the point of the primacy of the subject position is that it will be informed chiefly by a series of experiences that will determine how one sees the text.

Following Barthes's logic, then, we will have different experiences, and those experiences will be informed by who we are, but it would be wrong to imagine that we are disagreeing, since whatever we see is grounded in our experiences. There is no claim to right or wrong beliefs because what you register and what I register are determined by our positions. *No* may make me think about my childhood, and it may make you thirsty for some

Free Cola, but regardless of what it makes you experience, it would be wrong to say that we disagree about the meaning of the film. In fact, once one begins to imagine disagreements about the text as differences in perspectives, then the status of the text also comes under scrutiny, since the text is regarded less as something that is interpreted and more as an occasion for registering one's responses, reactions, and experiences. Indeed, once your experience is the most important consideration, the text becomes tangential to that experience. One person can see a text, and another can see something entirely different. The experience is what counts; the text, less so.[1]

Barthes's 1967 essay is not simply theoretically but also historically relevant; and part of this historical project is informed by, if not a reaction to, a highly divisive Cold War reality that was framed around a fundamental disagreement about two belief systems: liberalism and socialism. The rise of human rights politics, as we will see later, is very much a consequence of the demise of this divided Cold War reality. For now, however, we should take into account that ideological disagreements, much like aesthetic disagreements, are structured around right and wrong beliefs; they are disagreements that transcend the subject and his or her experience. For example, if you are a socialist, you believe that socialism is right, and you think that liberalism is wrong, not because it is right for you, but because it is right for everyone, irrespective of who you are (gay, straight, etc.), which is to say, irrespective of your position. (Ultimately, you could be wrong about that truth, but insofar as you are wrong, it serves to reaffirm its relation to right; that is, it serves to reinforce the conceptual structure of disagreements between right and wrong beliefs.) In the postdictatorial period, however, political claims relate to our subject positions, suggesting that what we see, hear, and experience is essential, which, in turn, renders disagreement irrelevant. Again, if you stand in one place and I stand in another, it would be theoretically illogical to suggest that what you see is wrong (or even right), since whatever you see is inextricable from your position.

The idea here is less to suggest that Cold War politics were always ideological and all postdictatorial politics are always reduced to subject positions than it is to stress that these respective commitments are always structurally different. In other words, insofar as there is a structural difference, the way society values and desires these differences has been historical; that is, in the postdictatorial period, while disagreements and ideology are largely regarded as polemical, subject positions are almost universally considered politically productive and are often aligned with an aesthetics and politics of freedom and resistance. The primacy of the subject position can be located in a wide range of names, theories, and fields that include reader response, memory studies, hauntology, identity politics, cultural studies, disability studies, deconstruction, and affect theory. Perhaps the most common name this commitment to the subject position goes by in the postdictatorial period is postmodernism. I share Idelber Avelar's idea that "Latin American postmodernity is postdictatorial—that is, the continent's transition to a postmodern horizon is carried out by the dictatorships—because the old populist or liberal states could not usher in the new phase of capital, because they were global capital's prospective victims themselves" (*Untimely* 79). The point here is to understand how this "new phase of capital" emerges in Latin America as well as to suggest that postmodernism in Latin America takes on different aesthetic and political characteristics in order to both usher in and register this new era.[2] For instance, as noted above, the elevation of the subject position to a principal concern has usually been associated with identity politics (especially within the United States), but in Latin America in particular, such claims have become enmeshed with the dictatorships and the emergence of a human rights politics. In some narratives, however, identity will be understood as the crucial motivation for committing these human rights abuses; that is, people are raped, tortured, and disappeared not for what they believe about socialism or capitalism but for who they are. Thus, human rights logic becomes a dominant framework to ground political agency in the subject position, one that is no less compatible with neoliberalism.

In the first part of *The Vanishing Frame*, I trace the beginnings of this politically inflected Latin American postmodernism, exemplified by resistance narratives that many consider to be crucial to transitional justice, memory politics, and political inclusion. I challenge the politics of highly acclaimed works such as Diamela Eltit's *El padre mío* (Father of mine; 1989), Ariel Dorfman's *Death and the Maiden* (1990), and Albertina Carri's *Los rubios* (*The Blonds*; 2003) by demonstrating that while these and similar works conceive of justice in terms of recognizing the torture, disappearances, and death that victims suffered at the hands of the dictatorships, they also tend to ignore the injustice of economic inequality and exploitation.[3] At the same time, this insistence on torture, disappearances, and death—as we saw with the images of abuses in *No*—functions as a technology to overcome the distance between the textual subject and the reader so that the experience of the victim and the reader can be blurred. These texts demand that the aesthetic frame vanish in order to better mobilize a politics of experience. I argue here that these narratives make their contribution to contemporary Latin American politics by replacing the critique of economic inequality that had been at the center of the revolutionary politics of the 1960s and 1970s with the recuperation of the experience of the body and identity that comes to underlie the emergence of neoliberal postdictatorial politics.

Neoliberalism may have an aesthetic project, then, but so too does its critique. I have already begun to show how this happens in Larraín's *No* by the assertion of the frame as a project that rejects the reader's position in order to make a political claim. Larraín's film is not the only work to do so. In the second half of the book, I explore the resurgence of conversations about aesthetic autonomy, prompted by a series of innovative works such as Roberto Bolaño's *Estrella distante* (*Distant Star*; 1996), Fernando Botero's *Abu Ghraib* (2005), and Alejandro Zambra's *Bonsái* (*Bonsai*; 2006). Undoubtedly, these works maintain a more complex relationship to the dictatorships as they reveal a certain irrelevance to questions that were central to the narratives of the 1980s and 1990s, including the means by which the text is meant both to testify to and affect our bodies, identities, or subject positions on behalf of a postdictatorial politics. As such, it should come as no surprise that some scholars have argued that these more recent narratives have forgotten the dictatorship or can even be considered reactionary.[4] Instead, by insisting on the aesthetic frame, I argue that these texts not only reject an aesthetics of experience (and the politics it entails), but also, and perhaps more significantly, insist on the work of art as a point of departure for an anticapitalist politics today. The assertion of the frame in these texts, and recalling Larraín, may make the abstractions (of a system) visible in a way reality or experience cannot. In other words, what I am calling "the frame" is vital to the aesthetics of these works, and for this reason, they allow us to look beyond the immediacy of experience to the larger economic structure that postdictatorial forms of freedom have failed to make visible.

The question of the aesthetic frame is a critical trope not only to the film *No* but also, as the title of this book makes clear, to the overall understanding of theory and culture in the postdictatorial era. The claim here is that the postdictatorial narrative has always been a question of the frame, but it has been an attempt to make the frame disappear on behalf of a moral/ethical claim. The idea for this book began very much as a response to the sense in which the aesthetic frame had—aesthetically, politically, and discursively—vanished from contemporary postdictatorial art and criticism. And the hope for *The Vanishing Frame* is to make the aesthetic frame visible again and to argue for its centrality in understanding the relationship of art to politics in the postdictatorial era.

At this point, it will be useful to elaborate a bit more on what I mean by the frame and its relation to aesthetics today. I suggested that in *No*, for example, the assertion of the frame gives rise to what Larraín calls "fiction" or what I have called a politics of autonomy. This means that *No* is committed to an aesthetic project that, by insisting that it has a form and meaning, marks a division between art and nonart. Indeed, whether the object is a painting, a novel, or a film, the assertion of the frame distinguishes the work from everything that is outside of it, including the reader. Thus, when referencing this assertion, I am speaking about a work that is more interested in creating an aesthetic space—a space of aesthetic autonomy—that treats the reader's experience as irrelevant to its meaning and form. In this way, the assertion is at once a turn toward literature's autonomous space and a turn away from the reader and the politics that have long been attached to an emphasis on experience.

Thus, this assertion openly challenges the postdictatorial account of the frame, which has sought to problematize this division between art and nonart by suggesting that the frame reflects the idea of liminality. More specifically, the frame reveals an indeterminacy at the heart of any attempt to distinguish art from nonart, an inability to be either one or the other. Jacques Derrida puts it this way: "Deconstruction must neither reframe nor dream of the pure and simple absence of the frame" (*Truth* 73). Patrick Dove elaborates on Derrida's claim by noting that the "frame [. . .] is a border that does not belong inside or outside, and whose proper ontological status (belonging or not belonging, inside or outside, work or nonwork, being or nonbeing) cannot be resolved once and for all" (*Literature* 15). For Dove, the frame becomes "a synonym for 'literature' understood as a deconstructive limit for ontological inquiry" (*Literature* 15). In this sense, the frame is always marked by an indeterminacy that leaves the limits of art and nonart forever frustrated.

But, as we will see, an insistence on the liminality between art and nonart is also a means toward treating readerly experience as a primary concern for criticism and theory. That is, such indeterminacy offers up an account that is less concerned with the object than with the reader, whose experience will in turn determine what the object is. And yet, the insistence on the aesthetic frame central to works like Larraín's *No* or Botero's *Abu Ghraib* problematizes this liminal reading of the frame by suggesting that if indeterminacy is what counts, then the aesthetic frame ultimately cannot, since this suggests that the reader's experience will be regarded as essential to the meaning (or nonmeaning) of the object. Indeed, it's the primacy of the experience that is valued over everything else. By giving primacy to the reader's experience, the attempt is *not* to affirm but rather to undermine the frame because it is less the object (whether that object is a work of art, a frame, a table, or a rock) that counts than one's response to that object. The commitment to experience, in other words, turns Derrida's account of the liminal frame into a vanishing one.

These concerns about the aesthetic frame are not limited to Latin America, and the questions and consequences that emerge from *The Vanishing Frame* follow a small but growing body of work in other disciplines, such as art history and English—and include Todd Cronan's *Against Affective Formalism* (2013) and Lisa Siraganian's *Modernism's Other Work* (2012)—that rethink the political and aesthetic potential of form and autonomy in literature and art. My account of the frame is very much indebted to the work of Walter Benn Michaels, who envisions the assertion of the aesthetic frame primarily in relation to North American neoliberal politics and art. According to Michaels, the contemporary moment is "coterminous with the rise of neoliberalism and with two sets of social and economic conditions"; the first is the social emphasis on discrimination, and the second is the increase of economic inequality ("Force"). For Michaels, these projects are intimately intertwined, as the identification of the text's meaning with the reader's experience involves a related emphasis on identity discourses and a politics of antidiscrimination. Put differently, the vanishing frame is not only a mechanism to affirm the subject's experience but also a politics that imagines injustices as centrally concerned with excluding people for who they are. Michaels describes the commitment to the subject position and discrimination in this way:

> What we see, how we feel, become crucial components of the work and thus it's possible for the normativizing gaze (white, male, straight/racist, sexist, homophobic) to become a crucial object of both aesthetic and social critique. After all, the problem of discrimination is in its essence nothing but a problem about how we see and respond—no racism without racists, no homophobia without homophobes. The appeal to the viewer produces the principle of neoliberal justice. ("Force")

The point here, of course, is not that discrimination is actually good, or that denouncing discrimination is a futile act; nor is the point to argue that discrimination is never informed by exploitation. Rather, the point is that today discrimination has become a mechanism to ignore, if not (implicitly) promote, exploitation. One only needs to think about how corporations and multinationals fully endorse diversity projects while completely disregarding concerns about economic exploitation. And this disregard is equally manifest in Latin American theory and criticism that has emphasized the question of identity often at the expense of exploitation.[5] In Latin America, this type of identitarian justice has been endorsed by leading scholars such as Antonio Cornejo Polar, Doris Sommer, and Diana Taylor, to name only a few. In his brilliant book *The Limits of Identity* (2015), Charles Hatfield takes to task this form of identitarian criticism in Latin American literature and culture by convincingly arguing that identitarianism is both theoretically unsustainable and politically aligned with neoliberalism today. I am indebted to Hatfield's work, as I wanted to explore in *The Vanishing Frame* this commitment to subject positions in the more politically inflected version—that is, the postdictatorial politics of human rights—where readers are transformed into witnesses who must experience the pain of others. What makes human rights a primary form of neoliberal justice is that they identify equality and freedom with a recognition (or repudiation) of who we are rather than with the elimination of the gap between rich and poor.

Freedom at the End of the Postdictatorial Era

The argument in the second half of the book is meant to point to the end of the postdictatorial era, an argument that is anticipated in part by a series of critics who have scrutinized this predominant form of liberal thought (e.g., human rights, identity) in the postdictatorial era. I thus share with Susana Draper the objective to challenge the limited view with which we talk about the dictatorships, one that sees "redemocratization as an opening up and passage toward neoliberal modes of freedom" (*Afterlives* 6). This same scrutiny of neoliberal modes of freedom can also be found in the work of Latin Americanists such as Alberto Moreiras, Gareth Williams, and Brett Levinson, who critique dominant identitarian positions of the 1980s and 1990s that imagine the developing world as "not only an area to be studied but [also] a place (or places) from which to speak" (Mignolo, qtd. in Moreiras, *Exhaustion* 134) and were endorsed by scholars such as Néstor García Canclini, Mary Louise Pratt, or Walter Mignolo. Against such identitarian thinkers, scholars like Moreiras, Williams, and Levinson propose more productive approaches to criticism that move beyond stagnated political concepts such as the people, the nation, and hegemony. At the same time, I depart from these same scholars' accounts insofar as I maintain in this book that aesthetic autonomy does not represent a return to past political iterations but offers an opportunity to think outside of postdictatorial aesthetics and politics.

I also address the period that follows the postdictatorial era in Latin America, one that is associated with both the political rise of the Marea Rosada, or Pink Tide, governments and the critical turn to affect theory. Jon Beasley-Murray's important work on affect theory in some ways continues the postdictatorial criticism of Moreiras and Williams, while also seeking to move beyond them. For example, Beasley-Murray rejects locational/identitarian thinking, but he also attempts to reposition critical thought toward an ever-expanding market horizon and commodity form. At the same time, although anti-identitarian, Beasley-Murray's commitment to affect theory entails a continuation of the postmodern logic that I set out to critique in this book. In her essay "The Turn to Affect," Ruth Leys keenly notes that affect is "independent of, and in an important sense prior to, ideology—that is, prior to intentions, meanings, reasons, and beliefs—because [affects] are nonsignifying, autonomic processes that take place below the threshold of conscious awareness and meaning" (437). By insisting on "autonomic processes that take place below the threshold of conscious awareness and meaning," I suggest that affect theory renders invisible the aesthetic frame, which distinguishes art from nonart as well as art's meaning from other commodities. I contend herein that the assertion of the frame today presents an opportunity to interrogate the status of literature in relation to affect theory and the growing sense that there is no outside to the market and art's commodification.

To be sure, while affect theory does share with postmodernism a critique of identitarianism, it also maintains some differences. For instance, by focusing on corporeal differences, senses, and experiences, affect theory seeks to avoid being reduced to past moralisms of feelings and emotions, which include those aligned with human rights. Indeed, if affect locates its importance in the "autonomic processes that take place below the threshold of conscious awareness and meaning," it also should not be understood in the same way as any moralism, or even any emotional or sentimental manifestation. Another difference is that affect theory sees itself as prior to and beyond *all* political ideologies and beliefs—not only liberal but all socialist beliefs, even when these beliefs have sought to critique economic inequality. Whether these differences (i.e., preconscious and preideological) should be called postmodern or something else is less the point. Rather, these differences reveal a deepening, rather than a rejection, of the idea that beliefs, ideologies, and disagreements have no place in challenging the growing gap between rich and poor. Instead, affect imagines a more productive world appearing once ideologies are replaced by bodies, sensations, and movements. Or as Beasley-Murray puts it, "The key to social change is not ideology, but bodies, affects, and habits" (qtd. in Fernández-Savater). In *The Vanishing Frame*, I contend that the assertion of the frame is an argument for the reconsideration of intentions, meanings, reasons, and beliefs, as well as an opening to question the post-ideological conception of the world that affect theory wishes to endorse.

The Vanishing Frame, in short, reengages with art (and particularly its ontology) in a period in which the political concern with art (and its value) is increasingly defined in relation to the market. This reengagement requires us to explicitly address the rise of cultural studies during the 1980s and 1990s when Latin Americanist literary criticism began to embrace cultural critics such as Richard Hoggart, Stuart Hall, and Raymond Williams. The work of Pierre Bourdieu, especially for North American scholars, became essential as it sought to show how questions of taste are neither natural nor entirely legitimate, but determined and defined by social positions (Sarlo, "Cultural" 118). Within Latin America, the appropriation of cultural studies by literary scholars such as Ángel Rama, Antonio Cornejo Polar, and Julio Ramos represented a significant shift away from aesthetic formalism and New Criticism toward a critique that made aesthetic and social concerns paramount. Furthermore, by drawing attention to social critique, cultural studies made visible the relationship between art and other commodities, as well as the market logic that both art and commodities shared. This type of social analysis, however, often comes at the expense of the aesthetic object. I agree with Beatriz Sarlo that "cultural studies is perfectly equipped to examine almost everything in the symbolic dimension of the social world, except art" ("Cultural" 122).[6]

Thus, the vanishing aesthetic space in the postdictatorial era should be understood in connection with the rise of cultural studies, as it, too, attempts to elide the difference between art and nonart. From this vantage, it is important to end this introduction by briefly noting that my insistence on the ontology of the work of art (i.e., the distinction between art and nonart) and the (progressive) politics it entails today marks a departure from past conceptions of aesthetic autonomy that began to emerge at the end of the nineteenth century with *modernismo*. In his excellent book *Rubén Darío y el modernismo* (1970), Ángel Rama notes that autonomy was predominantly framed as a separation from colonial authority. Rama begins with this point:

> The objective that Rubén Darío proposed was practically the same as the last neoclassicists and the first romantics of the independence period: the poetic autonomy of Spanish America as part of the general process of continental liberation, which means establishing its own cultural orb that could oppose peninsular Spanish ["el español materno"], with an implicit acceptance in the participation of this new literature in the overall conglomeration of European civilization that had its roots in the Greco-Latin world. (5)[7]

The desire for much of the nineteenth century, according to Rama, is one of cultural autonomy from Europe; that is, autonomy is a form of independence from colonial domination and a search for Latin America's own cultural uniqueness. In his account, in other words, the politics of autonomy is less a concern with what the work of art is than an affirmation of Latin American identity.

Julio Ramos's *Desencuentros de la modernidad en América Latina* (1989) similarly explores the idea of autonomy, though with an emphasis on modernization projects at the turn of the nineteenth century. For Ramos, however, autonomy is largely a response to a new division of labor that is constitutive of the market rather than to Latin American identity. This new division of labor marks an important shift from an earlier moment in the nineteenth century when writers and intellectuals (i.e., *letrados*) served as functionaries of the state and could not live solely from their profession as writers (54). This new moment of specialization instead provides a professional space where a writer can live principally by means of his work. For Ramos, this process remains uneven and incomplete. Nevertheless, the politics of autonomy, from his position, reflects this new status of a writer who is emerging from the constraints of the state.

Several points about Ramos's account of autonomy should be highlighted here. First, questions about ontology (i.e., the difference between art and nonart) are generally disregarded in his book. That is, although his conception of autonomy has a connection to what the writer writes—there is no doubt that, for example, José Martí critiqued Spanish colonialism and US imperialism—the primary concern for Ramos is the professional specialization of the writer due to the expansion of capital in Latin America. Second, far from revolutionary discourse, autonomy is intimately linked to liberal aspirations and Latin American modernization projects.[8] Third, and perhaps most importantly, for Ramos, though there is an ontological account of art within a restrictive field of production, this account is overshadowed by an interest in the social field's relationship to the professionalization of the writer. From this standpoint, and like Rama's account, the difference between art and nonart remains mostly unquestioned.

No doubt, there is a critical shift in the twentieth century, as the ontological status of the work of art is not only scrutinized but attacked (for example, during the historical avant-garde) until it presumably vanishes in the postdictatorial moment. Today, the idea of the vanishing aesthetic object finds fodder in conversations about the commodification of the social field in the dictatorships' aftermath. In his book *The Untimely Present*, Idelber Avelar declares that the "dictatorships' *raison d'être* was the physical and symbolic elimination of all resistance to implementation of market logic," and today "every corner of social life has been commodified" (*Untimely* 1). On this account, contemporary artistic production is marked by its real subsumption under capital, as its status as art can now be reduced to a commodity form. To put this differently, the ontological difference between art and nonart vanishes in the insistence on art's reducibility to a commodity. I explore in this book the implications of this dominant narrative in which the significance of art is found in its commodification.[9] For now, however, it is fundamental to recognize that whereas at the end of the nineteenth century the ontological status of the work of art goes unquestioned, at the end of the twentieth century, it is art's commodification that largely does.[10]

Today the commodification of art is regarded as a given, and it is here that the assertion of the frame can be understood not as a politics in itself, but rather as making a certain kind of politics imaginable. Indeed, in the works of Bolaño, Zambra, and Larraín, I argue that contemporary conversations about the commodification of art not only prompt a reconsideration of aesthetic autonomy but also offer a new reading of political potential that was unavailable in previous periods. For this same reason, the assertion of the frame in this book is not meant to be read as a return to the idea of art for art's sake (*modernismo*), identitarian autonomy (Rama), or professional freedom (Ramos). Nor is it meant to be read as a rejection (or reaffirmation) of the literary institution that was integral to the various avant-garde projects of the twentieth century.[11] As Moreiras puts it, this "space-in-resistance" that was aligned with the "strengthening of the national-popular state and against monopoly capital" has now passed (*Exhaustion* 5, 14).

The project of *The Vanishing Frame*, instead, is meant to be a historical and conceptual construction of the postdictatorial era, from its inception to its end. Each chapter roughly spans a decade of this era, building on certain themes and arguments from previous chapters. For this reason, I do not consider the entire opus of individual authors or the aesthetic and political differences (especially in the case of Benedetti, Botero, and Zambra) that could emerge from this engagement, but rather focus on individual works that best represent the logic of the period. Chapter 1 examines the shift from revolutionary politics to human rights in the dictatorial period by way of a reading of Mario Benedetti's *Pedro y el Capitán* (1979), a play that provides a glimpse into a world that preceded what Moyn calls the "last utopia"—the utopia of human rights—that would define the 1980s and 1990s (10). Chapter 2 explores the discourse of disability, and the body more generally, as a framework to understand the period of redemocratization and transitional justice in Ariel Dorfman's *Death and the Maiden* and Diamela Eltit's *El padre mío*. Chapter 3 investigates the postpolitical world of the 1990s and the rise of memory as a means to redescribe the past as an affirmation of who we are in Mauricio Rosencof's *Las cartas que no llegaron* (2000) and Albertina Carri's *Los rubios*. I argue that the discourse of memory, along with other postdictatorial technologies discussed in the first half of the book, both allegorize and bear witness to the transformation of revolutionary socialism into the consolidation of neoliberalism by privileging one's subject position at the expense of a critique of economic exploitation and the assertion of the aesthetic frame.

In the second part of *The Vanishing Frame*, I consider a series of recent artists whose works are marked by an increasing attentiveness to the question of the aesthetic frame. By analyzing this assertion of the aesthetic frame, I reevaluate the aesthetic movements and theoretical positions that have been at the center of Latin American cultural studies in the postdictatorial era. In chapter 4, I argue that the absorptive techniques of Fernando Botero's *Abu Ghraib* are a rejection of the human rights aesthetics found in the Latin American *testimonio*, a genre that seeks to elide the distinction between art and life on behalf of political action. Vis-à-vis a reading of authorial intent and autonomy in Roberto Bolaño's *Estrella distante*, chapter 5 suggests that the theoretical approaches to the Chilean neo-avant-garde (often understood as in opposition to *testimonio*) are equally committed to the vanishing frame and to the beholder's experience. The work of Bolaño, especially in *Estrella distante*, represents a transitional moment in Latin American aesthetics and politics. Chapter 6 moves beyond the postdictatorship as it examines Alejandro Zambra's *Bonsái* and the role of literature in the aftermath of the Pink Tide. Lastly, the coda returns to Larraín's *No* as a film that addresses historical referents of the dictatorship and the question of neoliberal freedom, but does so by critiquing the structure of capital rather than its moralism.

On a final note, it should be stressed that the assertion of the frame today is not a return to a class politics that led up to the dictatorships. It is not, for example, a call for the revolutionary world that is represented in Benedetti's *Pedro y el Capitán*. Rather than a class politics, the emergence of the aesthetic frame is closer to the creation of what Michaels calls a class aesthetics, one that proposes a vision of society that is *not* organized by subject positions. As noted above, this particularly pervasive vision can be found in the national and regional accounts of Latin American society; it is a vision that imagines identitarian exclusion as the problem and sometimes as the solution. Instead, this class aesthetics provides a vision of society organized by "the conflict between labor and capital" that frames exploitation as the problem and economic equality as the solution (Michaels, "Force"). The assertion of the aesthetic frame in works like Bolaño's, Zambra's, and Larraín's is where this class aesthetics is made visible, since these works provide a space to think not only about literature but also about the possibility of a world ordered by a structure that demands class and economic inequality. *The Vanishing Frame* offers a first intervention in class aesthetics in Latin American cultural studies by proposing the assertion of the frame as a key concept to examine the recent dictatorships and to imagine forms of freedom and equality that move beyond neoliberalism. This book thus provides an alternative understanding of recent developments in Latin American aesthetics and politics, an alternative that puts art at its center and the postdictatorship at its end.

PART 1

POSTDICTATORIAL AESTHETICS

CHAPTER 1

From Revolution to Human Rights

If we admit that the big question right now, the only question possible, is democracy or totalitarianism, then we won't have freedom. We must be convinced of this, because this option is the option structured by the adversary. If you think from this category, you are in the terrain of the adversary.
ALAIN BADIOU, "LA ÉTICA Y LA CUESTIÓN DE LOS DERECHOS HUMANOS"

In this sense, the theory of the communists may be summed up in one sentence: Abolish all private property.
KARL MARX AND FRIEDRICH ENGELS, *THE COMMUNIST MANIFESTO*

No one pays attention to these killings, but the secret of the world is hidden in them.
ROBERTO BOLAÑO, 2666

Immediately following the attacks of September 11, 2001, the United States began an aggressive and brutal campaign to eradicate terrorism. The campaign included wars, unlawful detentions, and torture. In 2002, and then in 2004, criticism and protests against this campaign intensified after the opening of the Guantánamo Bay detention camp and the release of photos and videos taken at Abu Ghraib prison that showed Iraqi prisoners naked and forced into humiliating positions. For the Latin American critic Idelber Avelar, these events were a clear sign that the Universal Declaration of Human Rights (UDHR) "continued to be trampled on" and that "few documents [. . .] are so widely recognized while being almost universally disrespected" ("Unpacking" 25). Furthermore, for Avelar, these events, especially in Guantánamo, revealed the "culmination of a model that systematically used Latin America as a laboratory of cruelty and a location for the production of bare life ("Unpacking" 26–27).

Almost seventy years after the adoption of the UDHR (1948), the fact that injustices and violence continue (and that the United States continues to engage in these acts) is both unfortunate and perhaps not so surprising. What is surprising is that—even though human rights continue "to be trampled on"—the contemporary discourse on human rights has become universally accepted as the framework through which we understand injustices, especially when, as will be shown below, one considers that the rise of such rights as the dominant guiding moral lens is a recent phenomenon. As noted in Avelar's essay cited above, the significance of human rights is registered not only by referencing the Universal Declaration of Human Rights but also by drawing comparisons between the events and abuses at Abu Ghraib and Guantánamo and those in the Southern Cone during the dictatorships of the 1970s. Later in this chapter, I suggest that using this human rights framework to comprehend the dictatorships that took place in countries such as Argentina, Chile, and Uruguay needs to be complicated; for now, however, it is crucial to suggest that the rise of human rights ideology today has prompted contemporary Latin American literary and cultural critics to recover texts that engage with the theme of torture and pain in order to make links between both periods.[1]

In this chapter I address one such case of recovery, Mario Benedetti's 1979 play *Pedro y el Capitán*, which has been studied as a condemnation of torture and as a testimony to human rights abuses taking place in the writer's home country of Uruguay and in Latin America more generally. What I argue here, however, is that this more humanitarian reading of Benedetti's text is not only misinformed but comes at the expense of the ideological project that is at the play's center. To this end, I first consider some of the text's most influential readings, which make the question of torture central to Benedetti's play while pushing aside its commitment to the primacy of the conflict between competing ideologies: namely, the conflict between socialism and liberalism. Second, I take up the ways in which the emergence of human rights discourse in Uruguay (and Latin America), and the various forms of literary criticism associated with this discourse, have themselves been part of the conceptual framework through which the Left has become increasingly disengaged with its past commitment to economic equality. Thus, in this chapter I lay the foundation for many of the claims that follow in this book, as I examine the relationship between the loss of the socialist project and its replacement with the moral utopia of human rights as well as interrogate the aesthetic and political mechanisms through which the emphasis on human rights becomes both absolute and problematic.

Published in Mexico in 1979 during the Uruguayan military dictatorship (1973–1985), Benedetti's *Pedro y el Capitán* centers on a "conversation" between a "torturer and his prisoner," in the course of which the cruel Captain attempts to persuade Pedro to name the names of his fellow comrades (xiii).[2] Each act of the play concludes with Pedro, despite the torture that he experiences, still declaring "No" to the Captain's demands. The effects, however, of this "conversation" seem more devastating for the Captain, so much so that in the final pages of the play, the Captain will declare to Pedro, "You are meaner than I am" (92). The play ends with the prisoner's death but also with the unequivocal understanding that Pedro has triumphed. The Captain will survive, yet his survival will serve as a testament to his ultimate defeat.

While *Pedro y el Capitán* concludes with a clear sense of victory over the Uruguayan military regime, the outlook for the Left in this small Southern Cone country in 1979 was not nearly as promising. The armed forces, which had seized power after the legislature was dissolved in 1973, constituted one of the most authoritarian in Latin America, detaining over 600,000 and forcing another 400,000 of its 3 million citizens into exile. Yet what is striking, and somewhat puzzling, about Benedetti's text is that although torture was ubiquitous in this period and clearly takes place in the play, it is never directly represented. Indeed, although one in every five Uruguayan men was tortured, the Captain, who represents those who torture, has no interest in beating or even hurting Pedro. Instead of representing the relationship between "a monster and a saint," the play focuses on what Benedetti describes as a "conversation" between "two flesh and blood beings," a conversation in which one human attempts to convince the other that he is "wrongheaded, but human" (xiv, 28). Why does the text give primacy to the verbal argument between Pedro and the Captain rather than show the Captain beating, prodding, and sodomizing Pedro? Why is Benedetti more interested in the conversation between the torturer and the tortured subject than in the act of torture itself?

What gives these questions their critical force is the widespread consensus that Benedetti's text is above all about torture. Marjorie Agosín, for example, has argued that Benedetti's play is a "human rights" text that reveals the absolute "uselessness of torture" (65). She explains further that because "Pedro does not speak: he refuses to confess, to denounce his friends," this proves that torture is nothing more than "a futile act of self-indulgence" (66). This view is shared by others, including Beatriz Alem-Walker, who adds that "with regard to the status of Uruguayan collective memory, Benedetti's work is first and foremost about the denunciation of torture" (74). Other critics, however, have argued that the text, far from denouncing torture, actually legitimates its practice. Avelar, for example, believes that Benedetti's text indirectly endorses the use of torture because it perpetuates the misguided idea that a torturer can in fact extract information. For Avelar, then, the problem with Benedetti's text (and, in turn, both Agosín's and Alem-Walker's claims) is that instead of condemning torture, it implicitly perpetuates what he calls a certain epistemic "lie" about torture wherein truth can be reached by "confession" (*Letter* 31, 39).[3] But even though Avelar sees himself as strongly disagreeing with the traditional reading of the text, as exemplified by Agosín and Alem-Walker, he continues to see torture as essential to *Pedro y el Capitán* and to ignore the conversation that stands at the play's center. Indeed, virtually all recent criticism places torture at the center of the text. Thus, the question I began with—Why is Benedetti more interested in the "conversation" than in the torture?—is mirrored by another: Why has the reception of the play emphasized torture rather than the conversation?

As indicated above, for Benedetti, the play is crucially about something more than the desire of one man to brutalize another. It is, instead, about the desire of one man to persuade the other that he is "wrongheaded" (28). In other words, the play represents the difference between two men, understood not as a difference between a torturer and a tortured subject but as a difference between two people with profound disagreements; more to the point, it is about why, as the Captain puts it, "we're enemies" and why "in this war [. . .] you put us down, we put you down" (23). More specifically, the reason they are "enemies" is because Pedro is a communist and the Captain is "anticommunist" (72). Although the Captain says to Pedro that he can appreciate how "you commit yourselves to a cause, the way you'll risk everything for it; how you'll give up your creature comforts, your families, your work, your lives even" (23), what distinguishes him from Pedro is that he does not believe in "doing away with private property" (21). The Captain can appreciate Pedro's dedication and is even envious of his willingness to sacrifice everything for a cause, but he fundamentally disagrees with the communist's commitment to class warfare. Thus, the essential antagonism between the two is political, or, as Benedetti himself puts it, "the distance between the two of them is ideological, and this perhaps holds the key to their other differences—the moral, the spiritual, [and] the sensitivity to human pain [. . .]" (xiv).

Insofar as the play centers on an "ideological" disagreement between two men, then, it also illustrates the reasons why these two men find themselves in the interrogation room. The Captain wants Pedro to give names; he wants to know the "real names and addresses" of "Gabriel, Rosario, Magdalena and Fermín" (26). That is to say, what the Captain wants is "to get information" (50), information he needs in his battle against communism. If he were there for any other purpose than to try to extract information, he would, as the Captain himself suggests, be forced to regard himself as "a sadist, or a monster. I'd have had you tortured for nothing. And that's disgusting. I can't bear it" (50).

The distinction to which the Captain points here is first and foremost a difference between goals, since the goal for a sadist is not information but pleasure. Likewise, the Captain does not want to be viewed as a person who orders people to torture for no reason at all, because to torture without reason would transform him into a "a sadist, or a monster"—a person who tortures because he is evil. From the Captain's perspective, then, what is wrong with being a sadist or a monster is that both categories function to disconnect him from the reasons he is fighting this war; or to put this in slightly different terms, anticommunism is not sadism.

The same logic, of course, holds true for his political prisoner. Pedro never distances himself from the Left's political objective, steadfastly supporting a movement that sought to defeat the "Yankees," destroy the bourgeois state, and eliminate the division between the classes (23). For Pedro, then, to identify himself as either a victim of the Captain's sadism or a mere tortured subject who is beaten "for nothing" would not only displace the basis for his imprisonment but also, and more importantly, displace the reasons why the Uruguayan communists are fighting in the first place. Thus, what is important about naming names is not that it makes Pedro into what Agosín sees as a "victim" of his perpetrator's malice or even a kind of "traitor," as the Captain would have it; nor is it important that the confession is linked to an epistemic fantasy, as Avelar argues, that reveals the complicity between democracy and torture more generally.[4] Rather, the point is that the confession would signify a strategic setback for the movement as its supporters fight against the bourgeois nation-state. In other words, obtaining information and refusing to give information not only register the motives behind why both men are in the interrogation room but also serve to underscore that torture is never an end in itself in Benedetti's play. Rather, torture is a means to win a war and an ideological conflict.[5]

But though the end of the play does reveal why Pedro is in the torture chamber, it does not immediately explain the absence of torture in the interactions between the Captain and Pedro. Indeed, Benedetti's play is not about an interrogator who brutalizes in order to get information, but rather about an interrogator who dislikes torture and goes so far as to call torturers "animal[s]" (22). Rather than torture for its own sake, the Captain believes in changing the tortured subject's mind: "I totally trust the power of persuasion" (27). No doubt, his confessed disgust for violence and his preference for "persuasion" function as a means to convince Pedro to reveal the names of his comrades. But these assertions also highlight the fact that the difference between the Captain and the "animal[s]" lies not in the political ends of their acts (both want to obtain names) but rather in the means used to reach these ends. The Captain, according to his own words, will not use torture, "no beatings, none of that waterboarding or forced standing or hanging by your wrists, no, just a reasonable conversation" (22).[6] My point here is not that the Captain is somehow dishonest about his position on torture—undoubtedly, he is playing the "good cop" and is a torturer. The point is rather that in the play, the Captain's primary means to get information is not by torture but by persuasion. Of course, the Captain's investment in the "conversation" may appear suspect, since the playing field is coercively tilted to one side. Even Pedro comments on the absurd nature of the Captain's claim: "How can there be any communication [. . .] between a person who is being tortured and his torturer?" (39). Nonetheless, Pedro himself supplies a kind of answer to this question by also using the "power of persuasion" ultimately to defeat the Captain.

To the extent that Benedetti's play counts as a victory for Pedro over the Captain, it is not simply because Pedro never gives names, but rather because he refuses to remain silent. Simply put, to triumph, Pedro must speak. Pedro will not remain silent, but rather, as Marta Morello-Frosch puts it, will "annihilat[e] his interrogator with his questions" (90). In other words, Pedro will forcefully interrogate the Captain until he reaches his political objective: the Captain's own confession. In questioning the Captain, however, Pedro focuses not on the advantages of a classless society but rather on the Captain's own way of living. It is no coincidence that Pedro chooses to question the Captain on his own lifestyle, since it reveals what Pedro is willing to sacrifice for the cause ("your creature comforts, your families, your work, your lives even") and the Captain cannot (23). This interrogation—in particular, questions about his job as a torturer— will ultimately lead to the Captain's breakdown (his defeat), when he finally confesses to Pedro the worthlessness of his bourgeois beliefs. I will return to this breakdown later, yet what is important to highlight now is that to the extent that the power of persuasion is central, it is due both to Pedro's ability to persuade the Captain to confess the emptiness of his bourgeois beliefs and to the Captain's inability to persuade Pedro to let go of his socialist beliefs.

This is why I argue that Benedetti's play gives primacy to the verbal conflict between the interrogator and the subject of interrogation and not to the physical battle between the torturer and the tortured subject. Indeed, in a period and place where repression and torture are everywhere, how else can Pedro win the ideological battle? And, as indicated above, this is also why Benedetti insists in the prologue that "the distance between the two of them is ideological, and this perhaps holds the key to their other differences—the moral, the spiritual, the sensitivity to human pain [. . .]" (xiv). My point thus far has not been to deny that Pedro is treated very badly; rather, it is that this terrible treatment is not what the play is primarily interested in. It is the difference between Pedro's and the Captain's political beliefs that is paramount for the play, the insistence that its action—that is, the Captain's interrogation, Pedro's refusal to name names, and his counterinterrogation, as well as the Captain's defeat and Pedro's ultimate death—be understood in ideological terms. Yet, as will be shown, there is a significant difference between the conflict that produced the play and stands at its center and the conflict in which the play will come to perform such a crucial role during the period of redemocratization.

Of course, the historical conflict that produced *Pedro y el Capitán* was the conflict between the state and the guerrilla movement in Uruguay's civil war that began in the mid-1960s (Aldrighi 143).[7] The guerrillas were the MLN (Movimiento de Liberación Nacional)-Tupamaros, who, according to US declassified documents, were the "most sophisticated urban guerrilla group in Latin America" and who, despite their own knack for "theatricality," wanted to destroy the bourgeois state and replace it with a socialist one (Markarian 80). The Tupamaros had quickly gained a reputation through a series of spectacular attacks (including, robberies, kidnappings, and bombings) dating as far back as 1963.[8]

Beginning in 1967, however, the government of President Jorge Pacheco Areco began implementing the "Medidas Prontas de Seguridad" (Prompt Security Measures), which not only censored newspapers but also led to the arrest and torture of Tupamaros in order to eradicate Marxism.[9] By 1973, the year of the coup, repression had increased, as most of the Tupamaros were already incarcerated and sentenced to long prison terms. Furthermore, statistics reveal that one in every fifty people was detained for interrogation—almost every interrogation included torture—and of those interrogated, one in every five hundred received a long prison sentence for political offenses. At the height of the repression, Uruguay could claim the disgraceful honor of maintaining the highest per capita rate of political incarceration on the planet. Within a span of only twenty years, Uruguay had drastically (and sadly) transformed itself from one of the most democratic societies in South America to one of the most authoritarian, from being known as "the Switzerland of South America" to "the torture chamber of South America."[10]

Yet during the military regime (as well as following the return to democracy) the conflict between communism and capitalism, fundamental to both the Tupamaros' struggle and Benedetti's text, was being replaced by a different antagonism, between liberal democracy and the dictatorship. The emergence of human rights organizations like Amnesty International (AI) in the early 1970s is crucial to understanding this new political reality.[11] In 1976, AI made Uruguay its flagship country in a new "campaign against torture," which proposed "to impress upon the government, with purely humanitarian arguments, that it does not need torture. We want them to stop using torture, not more but definitely also no less than that" (Markarian 88). But though many recognized the importance and success of AI's campaign and consequently began to deploy "purely humanitarian arguments," some leftists were strongly opposed to both the language and the logic of human rights discourse. AI defined itself as a "nonpolitical" organization that focused primarily on "grave abuses" of torture and political imprisonment. Needless to say, the Tupamaros had never defined themselves as a "nonpolitical" organization. Indeed, from the perspective of the Tupamaros, the fundamental problem with AI's crusade for the elimination of torture was that it was fighting the wrong crusade. Eradicating torture did not translate into the eradication of capitalism, and for this reason, torture was a secondary issue at best. Instead, the primary objective, as one Tupamaro put it in a 1968 interview, "was socialism" (Gilio 138). For the Tupamaros, the humanitarian discourse functioned not as a way of fighting for socialism but rather as a way of eliding the reasons to fight in the first place.[12]

This elision is also at play in the use of the "humanitarian" terms "victim" and "perpetrator."[13] For example, during a 1975 meeting of the Comité de défense des prisonniers politiques en Uruguay, "two conceptions about solidarity" emerged, which stemmed from a disagreement about the term "victim" (Markarian 102). The disagreement, of course, was not about whether these political prisoners were being threatened, injured, or killed. Rather, the difference of opinion centered on how the term was being used. For those who rejected "purely humanitarian solidarity," it was not enough that a political prisoner was recognized as a victim; they thought it was necessary to "know not only *how* but *why* there was repression in Uruguay" (Markarian 102). Those who supported "purely humanitarian solidarity" believed that focusing on the historical background of the Tupamaros and their methodology of armed action would only make it difficult to gain support for political prisoners. What is more, they viewed appropriating the term "victim" as a short-term solution that did not translate into abandoning their radical ideology.[14] Yet, for those who criticized this position, the terms "victim" and "perpetrator" rendered irrelevant the beliefs of both the communists who were tortured and the anticommunists who tortured them. Put differently, and in the terms of Benedetti's play, the terminology of victim and perpetrator denied the centrality of the disagreement between the Captain and Pedro about "private property" (Benedetti, *Pedro* 21).

The language of victimhood was not the only way the political commitments of the tortured were pushed to the margins.[15] Human rights documents of the period center overwhelmingly on the "physical integrity of the body," in a way that, as Vania Markarian observes, stood in stark contrast to a "previous conception of political activism that demanded immolation for the common cause" (104). Where "political activism" in the 1960s focused on the revolutionary's willingness to sacrifice his or her life for socialism, activism in the 1970s turned, as Markarian points out, to protecting the body from human rights abuses. I would argue, however, that Markarian's observations about this shift do not go far enough to uncover the logic behind this shift. My idea here is that insofar as the 1960s were defined by the commitment to fighting for the "common cause" (i.e., socialism), the representation of the body—even the immolated body—proved to be secondary.[16] This is not to say that discourses about the body were entirely absent in Tupamaro manifestos and communiqués, but it held no intrinsic political value in relation to the "common cause." That is, if the Tupamaros understood that their ideology was worth dying for (thus rendering the body irrelevant), human rights activists imagined that the protection of the body was the only politics worth living for (thus rendering the body central). For the revolutionaries, in other words, the chief conflict during the 1960s is not between "immolation" and the "physical integrity" of the body but rather between socialism and liberalism, that is, between competing political ideologies.

In contrast, during the 1970s (and, as I show in chapter 2, in the 1980s), the difference between recognizing and denying the body became the essential conflict. The reinscription of a politics of ideology into a politics of the body can clearly be seen in the marked distinction between Tupamaro communiqués, which stressed class warfare and the destruction of the bourgeois nation-state, and AI documents (post-1974), which focused primarily on the perpetrators' gruesome techniques and the effects on victims' bodies. For example, in a 1976 "Letter to the Editor," the chairman of Amnesty International USA, Ivan Morris, quotes a Uruguayan military officer who declares, "All of them will 'sing' here or we will break every bone in their bodies."[17] Despite the revolutionaries' own hostility, this representation of the body bereft of reasons and actions was very effective: "The general strategy worked well in a mass-media world," writes Markarian, "where the sight of a torture victim could rouse great sympathy and enlarge support of human rights organizations without much knowledge about local history and context" (89).

But though both the "victim" and the body are essential to Morris's claim and to human rights politics more generally, they are largely irrelevant to socialism and to Pedro's politics in Benedetti's play. This is what it means for the conflict between socialism and liberalism—rather than the conflict between the torturer and the tortured subject—to be at the center of the play. The whole point of Pedro's ideological victory is that his ideas are vindicated whether or not his body survives. Of course, my idea here is not an ethical-moral claim, but rather a logical one. From this perspective, if socialism is valuable, it is valuable whether or not an individual socialist lives or dies. Or to put this more precisely, socialism does not die simply because Pedro does. And this ought to be true for liberalism as well. But as we have already begun to see, Benedetti's text complicates this. Where the body means nothing to Pedro (it's his ideology that he cares about), it certainly means something to his interrogator. In the final scene of the play, the Captain confesses that while Pedro can withstand torture precisely because he is committed to an ideology, he himself could never endure it because he doesn't have anything to "believe in" (98). That is, the Captain does not have the same commitment to bourgeois liberalism that Pedro has to socialism, and this is precisely why he fears torture. Clearly, the Captain recognizes his lack of commitment as problematic. And it should come as little surprise that the Captain functions as the first critic to focus on the body, since he understands his own lack of ideology as symptomatic of his commitment to his body. For Benedetti, however, the Captain's investment in his body (or family or job) does not signify the absence of ideology but rather serves as the definition of what it means to be committed to bourgeois liberalism. And, of course, the Captain is fundamentally invested in upholding rather than rejecting liberalism. In this way, the body becomes irrelevant the moment Pedro makes a gesture toward ideology, whereas the logic of the body (of survival) be-comes essential the moment the Captain abandons the commitment to his ideology. Thus, while Pedro's ideology functions as a call to destroy capi-talism, the increasing commitment to both Pedro's and the Captain's body in the postdictatorship puts the question of socialism in the background and begins to function instead as the celebration of democratic liberalism.

Or to put it another way, if Benedetti's text is about a kind of victory, it is a victory not primarily over torture and for human rights, but rather a victory over capitalism and for socialism. Even though Benedetti's text is committed to the logic of the socialist cause, its reception is equally symp-tomatic of the growing irrelevance of that logic to the human rights move-ment. The play was met with almost universal acclaim in Latin America when it was published, winning an award for best foreign play in Mexico, and was subsequently translated into nine languages. Amnesty Interna-tional even championed the text, awarding it the Golden Flame Award in 1979. The fact that AI praised the play, of course, should come as no sur-prise, since it raised awareness about the repression and torture that was occurring in Uruguay, which was desperately needed to further the Uru-guayan case. As a transitional text, *Pedro y el Capitán* did present a strong argument against the practice of torture as a method of interrogation.[18] In short, Pedro's incarceration, torture, and death, as well as the Captain's psychological torture, his lack of empathy, and his self-serving actions at the expense of Pedro's interrogation, all pointed to the complete "use-lessness of torture," stressing precisely the cruelty, irrationality, and in-humanity of torture made visible in the text (Agosín 65). In this way, as the discourse of human rights took firm root in Latin America, the United States, and Europe, Pedro's ideological commitment was pushed aside, not just by Amnesty International and by the play's critics but also more gen-erally by a humanitarianism seeking to "document and denounce" the tor-ture that was taking place in Latin America (Sikkink 66).[19]

And this displacement of the ideological discourse, as I demonstrate in the following chapters, has become even more powerful with the end of the dictatorship and the arrival of liberal democracy, to the effect that critics urge readers of the play to address and confront the legacy of hu-man rights violations in the Southern Cone. Agosín argues, for example, that Benedetti's play "compels the reader-accomplice" to think about the torturers in present-day Latin America who have been forgiven by gov-ernments for their crimes (65). As noted above, Agosín's analysis gives pri-macy to torture in Benedetti's text, but here, more pointedly, she places special emphasis on the reader-accomplice who needs "to think about" the crimes of the military. For Julio Cortázar, who coined the term, the "reader-accomplice" was an "active reader" who stood in direct opposition to what he identified as a "female" or "passive reader"—a compliant and intellectually inactive reader. The point of the "reader-accomplice" is imagined not simply as the difference between a reader's active or passive role in relation to the text; rather, it is about the text's precise ability to "compel" the reader to act outside of the literary realm. This is what Cortázar means when he suggests that "to write and to read is increasingly a possibility of acting extraliterarily" (Agosín 64). Cortázar here is underscoring the effect that the text has on the reader, which moves beyond the literary into the political sphere. Following Cortázar's lead, Agosín employs the idea of acting extraliterarily to suggest that the reader should not only be active vis-à-vis the text but also and more importantly, actively engage questions that deal specifically with past military crimes. In other words, for Agosín, Benedetti's text is not simply a vehicle through which the reader is informed about military abuses, but rather a technology that compels the reader to engage in human rights activism. Crucially, however, the action it is supposed to produce is entirely focused on human rights mobilization and the support of democratic liberalism, as opposed to the kinds of actions in which Benedetti's text and the Tupamaros were most interested, which involved fighting capitalism. Indeed, it is worth remembering that in the 1960s and 1970s, the Tupamaros themselves saw a human rights agenda as a function of "bourgeois legality" and human rights groups like AI as "tools of U.S. imperialism" (Aldrighi 76). Thus, though in Benedetti's text socialism is fundamental, it has been read as a kind of *testimonio* that urgently reminds the reader of the civil and political rights lost during the years of military rule.

Of course, the Latin American *testimonio* (see chapter 4) raises the point about the question of the aesthetic frame and the "extraliterary" desire to eliminate it. As I noted above and will explore in more detail later, the logic of human rights demands that we see novels, books, and films less as art than as "extraliterary" objects that allow readers/viewers to share the pain of those who have been violated. To put this point differently still, this logic tends to eliminate the divide between art and life not only to disarticulate ideology but also to make human rights vital. *Pedro y el Capitán* challenges this logic not by ignoring the issue of torture but by insisting that torture is always meant to be read through the lens of ideology. This is, of course, what Benedetti means when he says "the distance between the two of them is ideological, and this perhaps holds the key to their other differences—the moral, the spiritual, the sensitivity to human pain [. . .]" (xiv).

If torture in *Pedro y el Capitán* is meant to be read through this ideological distinction, this objective is doubled by an assertion of aesthetic space that negates the immediate identification between characters and spectators. More specifically, Benedetti insists on an aesthetic distance that provides the opportunity to think of torture not simply as a question of pain and horror that must be shared between the characters and the public. Adding to this point, Benedetti notes that he always felt that "in theater [torture's] aggression is felt too directly, and this makes it difficult for the spectator to keep a needed distance. If the torture is there only indirectly, however, as an evil yet unseen presence, then the audience is able to be more objective, and if what we are judging is the degradation of a human being, objectivity is essential" (xiii–xiv).

Benedetti's point is not new and can be seen, for example, in Bertolt Brecht's theorization of estrangement in theater, in which the German playwright insists on a distance between characters and the audience so the latter doesn't identify or empathize with the former. For Brecht, the problem with identifying or empathizing with the characters is that it mystifies the political reasons behind their pain and suffering. For this same reason, torture is never directly produced in Benedetti's play. Torture overwhelms the spectator and thus negates an aesthetic space (the play) that allows the viewer to think about the ideological question at the play's center. In this way, the absence of torture is meant to be understood as an affirmation of this aesthetic space and a rejection of an aesthetic politics that attempts to dismantle the division between art and life. That is, what we see in Benedetti's play is not the elision between art and life, but rather the opposite: the assertion of aesthetic autonomy in order to think beyond our empathy—beyond our realm of reality—to the structure that produces our shared misery.

The assertion of an autonomous space in for questioning an ideological position conceptually disappears during the 1980s in order to promote a human rights world. As can be seen in the chapters that follow, part of this ideological displacement will be found in the emergence of memory politics during the 1980s. Andreas Huyssen suggests that "the issues of memory and forgetting have emerged as dominant concerns [that] [. . .] determine, to varying degrees, the cultural and political debate [. . .] in *post-dictadura* societies in Latin America, raising fundamental questions about human rights violations, justice, and collective responsibility" (26).

What is important to highlight here is that the marrying of "memory" with human rights gives rise to a form of cultural analysis that is primarily enlisted in the service of remembering "human rights violations, justice, and collective responsibility."[20] Or, as Agosín puts it, "The theme of human rights is intrinsically linked to a literature that does not forget and that refuses to be silenced" (65). But if it is the commitment to memory that keeps alive for us the violence done to the bodies of the tortured victims of the dictatorship, it is at least as important a fact that what gets remembered above all is violence without revolutionaries, torture without motives, and bodies without beliefs. And it is equally important to see what the ongoing commitment to memory forgets. And once we begin to focus on the forgotten, we can also begin to see the role that the memory of Pedro's tortured body and the forgetting of his socialist politics have played in the victory—in Uruguay specifically and Latin America more generally—of a neoliberal politics.

Redemocratization, Neoliberal Transition: A Uruguayan Example

At the turn of the twenty-first century, human rights continued to be a central issue in Uruguayan politics and would become—especially when linked to the discourse of memory—a defining issue for the Left. Above, I cited Huyssen's observation as evidence that "issues of memory determine" present-day readings of Benedetti's *Pedro y el Capitán*. Now, however, I want to use it to argue that "issues of memory" have also become increasingly connected to the political sphere, shaping how the Left envisions political conflict and action. What has disappeared, both from Uruguayan politics in general and from Uruguayan leftist politics in particular, is the commitment to class equality, not to mention to a social revolution.[21] In fact, the dominant economic trend in Uruguayan politics—on both the Left and the Right—has been the shared commitment to neoliberalism.

Beginning in 1985, President Julio María Sanguinetti, a strong supporter of the neoliberalization of the Uruguayan economy, introduced market reforms in Uruguay that sought to privatize state entities and grant long-term concessions to private interests in the areas of gas pipelines, forestry, and water.[22] By the end of the 1980s, Uruguay was well on its way to ensuring its role in the new millennium as the new "financial center" in Latin America, a "future Hong Kong or Singapore" (Weschler 160). The effects of the conservative government's neoliberal agenda were clearly making themselves felt throughout the country, including a steady decline of public services, a weakening of the quality of life of the popular sectors, and the increasing rise of poverty (Chávez 158).

The more recent rise to power of the Left, marked by the so-called Pink Tide, however, has done little to fundamentally alter this trajectory. For if Uruguayan politics throughout the 1980s and 1990s were about the Left— first resisting and then grudgingly coming to terms with neoliberal policies—the beginning of the twenty-first century is fundamentally about the Left enthusiastically executing these policies. Following the 2004 victory of Frente Amplio's Tabaré Vázquez—the first democratically elected leftist president in Uruguayan history—there has been no substantial shift away from the neoliberal policies first introduced by the conservatives in the 1980s.[23] Daniel Chávez explains that since the Left took power, "in practice, there are no significant changes in the great lines of political economy, in monetary politics, in the gestation of international commerce" (177). Frente Amplio not only continues to uphold past International Monetary Fund (IMF) agreements to manage debt payment but also makes it a top priority to seek out new free market agreements. Since Frente Amplio's victory, for example, the coalition has endorsed a Trade and Investment Framework Agreement (TIFA) with the United States, hoping to increase exports in Uruguayan beef and software as well as gain a stronger foothold in the international market. Federico Leicht sums up the consequences of this commitment to finance capital, explaining that "after 15 years of experiences within the free market laboratory, poverty has increased 108 percent, affecting more than 40 percent of the population. Unemployment has reached figures that were once never imagined, salaries have dropped and emigration has reached the same level as during the military dictatorship" (190). Thus, insofar as the Left has continued to defend neoliberal policies, it has intensified economic inequalities, precisely the inequalities the Left before the dictatorship was centrally committed to challenging.

If, then, the radical Left of the 1960s and early 1970s sought to eliminate or at least minimize economic exploitation, the Uruguayan Left today has sought to incarcerate torturers and memorialize their victims—while leaving the political and economic mechanisms of class inequality virtually untouched. Indeed, what the Left has done when confronted with this intensification of inequality has been to insist on the importance of memory and justice. As a result, since Frente Amplio's victory in 2004, "human rights is where the Left government has had its greatest impact" (Chávez 171). The administration of President Tabaré Vázquez represented a radical break with the past regimes' stance on human rights as the new government shifted its position on not only "truth-telling" but also prosecuting human rights violators, including the monumental 2005 arrest of the former president and leader of the 1973 military coup, José María Bordaberry, and the 2009 sentence of the military ruler Gregorio Álvarez.

Memory discourse (discussed in chapter 2) is entrenched in an opposition between remembering and forgetting human rights violations. Or, as Adriana Bergero and Fernando Reati succinctly put it, "If the 70s are the years of terror [. . .], then the 80s and the 90s are the years of a conflict between the will to remember and the will to forget" (11). Bergero and Reati's claim underscores the ongoing rift that runs throughout the postdictatorial period between those on the Left who demand that the abuses of the past never be forgotten and those on the Right who want to look forward and not reopen old wounds. Yet, what is interesting here is that regardless of whether it is the Left remembering or the Right forgetting, what is being remembered or forgotten is only the "years of terror." The political struggle that produced the years of terror and torture has largely been ignored. Thus, the commitment to remembering torture has effectively served as a vehicle for forgetting the socialist political agenda for which the Left once stood. In other words, the politics of memory not only functions as a technology through which socialism is foreclosed, but in so doing, successfully—albeit inadvertently—concludes the military's political project of eradicating socialism begun in 1967.[24]

This foreclosure didn't happen all at once, and it happens not only in politics but also in the cultural sphere, informing, as I have shown, the reception of Benedetti's text. In the following chapters, I show how in the postdictatorial period the question of human rights, which was found in the audience's reception of *Pedro y el Capitán*, now becomes a dominant concern in the content of novels, films, and plays, such as Ariel Dorfman's *Death and the Maiden* and Mauricio Rosencof's *Las cartas que no llegaron* (*The Letters That Never Came*). What this means is that the ideological commitment that was fundamental to *Pedro y el Capitán* becomes less so; it also means that the claim to an autonomous space as a vehicle to promote this message fades as well. In this way, it will be productive in what follows to think that both aesthetic autonomy and ideology today are part of the same project, just as the critique against them has been crucial to mobilizing human rights cultural criticism, a form of criticism that attempts to eliminate the aesthetic frame so that human rights violations can be seen everywhere. Thus, part of the argument of this chapter has been to think of Benedetti's play today as an attempt to speak to a world of repression (to document and denounce) as well as an effort to represent an ideological world that no longer exists. That is, the project of Benedetti's play becomes one of insisting on an aesthetic world that memory politics will soon forget.

I will return to this point later, but for now the argument has been that the emergence of human rights and the various forms of literary memory associated with it have themselves been part of the imaginative apparatus through which the Left has forgotten about its past commitment to economic equality. My analysis of Mario Benedetti's *Pedro y el Capitán* has sought to show how a text in which this ideological conflict is central has been reinscribed as a human rights text, and thus redeployed, even if unwittingly, as a tribute to neoliberalism. Hence, Adrianne Aron, in the book announcement for her translation of *Pedro y el Capitán*, notes that the play "captures the essence of this dehumanizing practice [of torture] [. . .], which speaks to the universality of the abomination, whether in Uruguay's La Libertad [prison] or the USA's Abu Ghraib."[25] Yet in contrast to the Uruguayan political prisoners in Libertad Prison, the Iraqis imprisoned in Abu Ghraib were not there because of their socialist beliefs, and to make the ideological commitments of those who were tortured irrelevant to their torture is to obscure both the history and ideology that produced Benedetti's text in the first place. Aron's "dehumanizing" claim promotes rather than problematizes the predominant reading that insists that we remember the body, torture, and incarceration while ignoring the ideological causes that give rise to these effects. But, of course, the more fundamental claim here is not just that Benedetti's text has undergone a critical revision, but rather that this revision and the human rights logic that sustains it—in Uruguay, the United States, or elsewhere—do not serve to challenge the logic of neoliberalism. The idea of this chapter has been to reveal that the relationship between literature and criticism devoted to the question of memory and the free market is clearly not one of contradiction but of deep compatibility. Or to put it more simply, my point has been to show that human rights literature and criticism function not as a vanguard for real social change but as the kinder, gentler face of neoliberalism.

CHAPTER 2

Disability and Redemocratization

In an article from 2013 in the University of Chile's newspaper, the journalist Carolina Pérez asks these two questions: "¿Qué pasó con las Personas con Discapacidad en la dictadura?" (What happened to disabled people during the dictatorship?) and "¿Cuántas de las personas torturadas quedaron con algún grado de Discapacidad?" (How many of the people who were tortured were left with some degree of disability?) (Pérez n.p.). Those who study the recent dictatorships and the period of redemocratization in the Southern Cone will find these questions somewhat surprising, because "disability" as a term is rarely associated with the recent past. And yet this virtual silence regarding the term is strange, since not only do we come across words like "wounds," "trauma," "schizophrenia," and "amnesia" in cultural production from this period, but we also study the dictatorship through disability-inflected fields such as trauma studies and memory studies. We think disability, but we don't say disability.

Perhaps the reason for this silence has to do with a certain bias that sees mental and physical impairments as individual, deeply experiential, and ultimately apolitical and therefore irrelevant to the political context of the dictatorships. The recent rise of disability studies, however, has done much to show that this idea of disability is quite limited, driven more by a lack of awareness than by any rigorous examination of the term.[1] Other scholars will accept that disability can be political, but they will resist applying it to the recent past, since the term may obscure the lens through which we understand the dictatorships. The politics of disability, in other words, are not always concerns of the dictatorships. Nevertheless, as we are already beginning to see, disability *is* a critical lens through which the authoritarian period is envisioned (e.g., trauma, schizophrenia, amnesia, trauma studies), despite rarely calling it disability. Thus, the question that will guide this chapter is not, What will a disability reading reveal about the dictatorship? but rather, What does the incorporation of this disability lens tell us about postdictatorial (specifically transitional) politics and art?

In the previous chapter, I argued that the fundamental conflict in *Pedro y el Capitán* is one between ideologies; I also addressed how the rise of human rights at the end of the 1970s and 1980s produced a new discourse that emphasized the body. That new discourse, however, imagines a very specific type of body, a body that is victimized, traumatized, raped, tortured, and debilitated: a disabled body. In this chapter, I explore in further detail the emergence of human rights in the transitional period, and the centrality of the disabled figure in cultural texts such as Ariel Dorfman's *Death and the Maiden* (1990) and Diamela Eltit's *El padre mío* (1989). At the same time, I suggest that human rights (with the disabled figure as their representational marker) function to construct a new national discourse that identifies inclusion/exclusion as the central social antagonism, but that, in so doing, paradoxically, treats questions about what we believe as irrelevant. I also address scholarship that challenges this type of human rights framing of inclusion and exclusion. More specifically, I explore Nelly Richard's reading of Diamela Eltit's *El padre mío*, a reading that promotes a more radical form of exclusion that not only critiques human rights discourse but does so by deploying disability as a device that deconstructs representation. As the chapter ends, I argue that this so-called radical form of exclusion is far from radical, since it replaces an anticapitalist project that challenges neoliberalism with a corporeal project that is compatible with neoliberalism.

The Emergence of Disability Discourse in the Dictatorship

Although the word "disability" is rarely mentioned in the dictatorial context, one can still see its presence in political, social, and aesthetic discourses. The discourse is visible in three primary ways: first, people with disabilities were incarcerated, tortured, and disappeared; second, the military used the discourse to characterize so-called subversives; and finally, there were those people who became disabled at the hands of the military.

Regarding the first, the military regimes did torture and disappear people with disabilities. For example, the Argentine junta drew much international attention surrounding the disappearance of Claudia Inés Grumberg, a paraplegic sociology student. In Argentina's report from CONADEP

(National Commission on the Disappearance of Persons) entitled *Nunca más*, we find other narratives of disabled people who were tortured, including the Chilean José Liborio Poblete, who used a wheelchair and who was disappeared along with his wife and child. Although there has been a tendency to think of these regimes principally as versions of previous eugenics regimes devoted to the extermination of undesirables, especially in Argentina, where these tendencies have been most present, their raison d'être was not primarily to purify the blood of the nation (see chapter 3). I don't mean to suggest that these regimes did not murder disabled people. Instead, these regimes above all sought to exterminate the ideology to which they subscribed.[2]

Concerning the second, beyond torturing and disappearing people with disabilities, the military regimes deployed metaphors of disability to describe their adversaries. These military regimes attempted to brand anticapitalist revolutionary groups, such as the MLN-Tupamaros in Uruguay, the Montoneros in Argentina, the MIR in Chile, and the MR8 in Brazil, first as terrorists and then as cancers of a sick nation.[3] For instance, Saúl Sosnowski notes that the Uruguayan military regime used "the common metaphor of health and disease to interpret and justify policies against the guerrilla movement and, more extensively, against those who challenged or disregarded their parameters for political life" (522). The military saw themselves and the nation as normal and healthy, while Tupamaros were described as a cancer that needed to be excised from that healthy body. By redescribing anticapitalist ideology as disease, the military imagined a precise surgical intervention to remove this cancerous tumor from the nation.

Finally, military regimes not only disappeared disabled people and used disability as a metaphor; they also disabled people. Although these regimes were especially cruel in their disappearing and killing, they also beat, burned, raped, mutilated, terrorized, and traumatized many more of their citizens, who survived and bore the marks of the ordeal on their bodies. As discussed in chapter 1, in Uruguay one in every five men was tortured; in Chile, over 30,000 were tortured; and the same could be said about Argentina, where up to 30,000 were disappeared and many more were tortured. Those who survived would have to live with the effects of this reality. Some of the most pressing questions during the period of transition centered on how to come to terms with people who were disabled by the regime. Undoubtedly, such questions addressed the types of truth and justice projects that would be taken on by transitional democracies; whether perpetrators would be prosecuted or given amnesty;

whether these victims would be politically and symbolically incorporated back into the nation. It will be this last discourse (i.e., how the military disabled its citizens) that will also largely mark the transitional texts discussed in this chapter, as the disabled figure remained excluded from the newly formed democratic governments.

Disability in Transition: A New Imaginary

For the Left, this political conversation about the (disabled) body and the nation represents an important shift away from the ideological conflict that marked the dictatorship. Arguably, the film that inaugurates this new discourse in Argentina is Adolfo Aristaráin's *Tiempo de revancha* (*Time for Revenge*; 1981), which centers on an ex-syndicalist who feigns muteness after an accident in order to win a civil suit against a copper mine. Avelar has suggested that the film is a "multi-layered political allegory" in which muteness is intended to critique (*Untimely* 52), but what is most interesting about the film is not just the use of muteness but also its adamant rejection of what Avelar calls "normality" (52). Indeed, after winning the suit, the main character (played by Federico Luppi) "find[s] himself unable or unwilling to return to normality" (52). This rejection of normality is dramatized in a rather disturbing final scene, in which the main character takes a razor blade and slices off his tongue. While this self-mutilation represents a rejection of the military regime's image of a healthy nation, it also aligns the main character with citizens who are physically and mentally impaired by the dictatorship. The slice, in this way, becomes an act of solidarity.

And this act of solidarity marks not only a difference from the military's rhetoric but also a distance from the conflict that was at the center of Pedro and the Captain's conversation, since a sliced tongue politically speaks during the transition in a way that would only count as a failure in Benedetti's text. That is, for Pedro to win the ideological battle, he must persuade the Captain, and if he can't speak because his tongue has been sliced, then he will lose. The act of solidarity in *Tiempo de revancha*, instead, gestures to a new political reality whereby the disabled figure becomes integral to the postdictatorial imagination and its relation to the military's official history. Where for the regime the disabled body before carried a negative meaning of disease, or where for the Tupamaros or Montoneros it was even considered irrelevant, for the Left in the transitional period, and increasingly in the postdictatorial era, it signifies a form of resistance to the type of nation that wishes to ignore these bodies as they move toward democracy.

Mutilation in *Tiempo de revancha* presents one way for disability to interplay with the formation of a new national imaginary. A quick overview of narratives that appeared during the transition offers up other examples: amnesia in Luisa Valenzuela's 1982 short story "Cambio de armas" (Other Weapons), mental health in Cristina Peri Rossi's *La nave de los locos* (*Ship of Fools*; 1984), schizophrenia in Diamela Eltit's *El padre mío* (Father of mine; 1989), and PTSD in Carlos Liscano's *El furgón de los locos* (*Truck of Fools*; 2000), among others.[4] While all these novels were published at the tail end or even in the aftermath of these brutal regimes, what makes them noteworthy is not only that disability appears at the center of the narratives, but that at the core of the transitional imaginary itself is a disability that exists, a disability that won't simply be forgotten or reconciled away by the transitional government. In other words, if the military wanted to ignore or exclude corporeal difference from the nation, the new form of solidarity insists that disability be made visible and included in the nation.

To be sure, the argument can be made, as Susan Antebi does, that disability is found everywhere in Latin American literature and "plays a significant role in narrative, even [. . .] when readers may have failed to notice it" (1). One can easily point to numerous disabled figures that appear, for example, in Boom narratives, such as the disfigured boy whose pigtail signals the end of the Buendía lineage in *Cien años de soledad* (*One Hundred Years of Solitude*; 1967) or even the many disabled characters that populate the imbunche's world in José Donoso's *El obsceno pájaro de la noche* (*The Obscene Bird of Night*; 1970). But to place disability in this light is also to recognize how, for Boom writers, disability marked something that had to be exercised, or even erased from the nation.[5] Instead, in the transition, disability directly confronts (even challenges) a history that wishes to erase it. And the idea promoted in texts such as "Cambio de armas" and *La nave de los locos* is that if readers also wish to ignore (or to deny) disability, then they are closer to the military regime than they are against it. Thus, in the transitional period emerges a corpus of texts in which disability not only appears but must be assertively insisted upon. Insofar as disability denounces a past regime, it does so to imagine a better one.

The transitional period revolves around a battle waged between those who want to include certain bodies within the new democracy and those who want to exclude them. Perhaps the most commercially successful work of the transition, Ariel Dorfman's play *Death and the Maiden* (1990), frames this battle around the character of Paulina Salas, who, during the dictatorship, was interrogated, raped, and tortured by a doctor who played Schubert's String Quartet no. 14, *Death and the Maiden* (a musical piece, incidentally, inspired by Schubert's own struggle with disability in the form of acute syphilis). The play begins fifteen years after her rape and torture, or as the first stage directions note: "The time is the present and the place, a country that is probably Chile but could be any country that has given itself a democratic government just after a long period of dictatorship." In the present, Paulina is still traumatized by this experience, a point that Dorfman also wants to make clear by characterizing her as a person with "hysteria" (10). But let's call it what it really is, PTSD. Her husband, Gerardo Escobar, fared better, both during the period of the dictatorship and in the present climate of postdictatorial compromises. While Paulina stopped studying medicine because of her traumatic experience and has done "nothing" since then, Gerardo continued to study law and was then appointed to the country's Truth and Reconciliation Commission, taking on a task that places him squarely within national debates on responsibility, guilt, and punishment or reparations (38).

The play's pivotal conflict takes place in Gerardo and Paulina's home and revolves around the encounter between Paulina and Dr. Roberto Miranda, whom she believes to be the doctor who raped her during her interrogation. What Paulina demands is some form of retributive justice, justice that shifts throughout the play, from the desire to rape Roberto to putting him on trial, from obtaining a confession to finally killing him. The desire to exact punishment and revenge is complicated by two important factors: first, the uncertainty (for Gerardo and for us as readers) that Roberto truly tortured her, an uncertainty born of the fact that Paulina was blindfolded when she was victimized and can base her accusations only on Roberto's voice, his peculiar expressions, and his "smell" (44), and second, Gerardo and Roberto's incessant attempts to undermine her account and accusations; both men, for instance, attribute her accusations to products of a "diseased mind," one that is "sick" and "prototypically schizoid" (44, 23, 32). From a certain position, then, Gerardo, who represents the newly formed democratic government, stands closer to the dictatorial regime of "normalcy" than to those who, like his wife, suffered at the hands of that regime.

Paulina's "hysteria" is therefore anything but secondary to the plot (10). Her PTSD creates a tension in the play by problematizing the sense of certainty, normalcy, and justice that the two able-bodied men are attempting to impose. This can be seen in several ways. Her disability, for example, introduces uncertainty that is internal to the structure of the play, since the play's open ending means that we never quite know if, in fact, Paulina's accusations against Roberto are true or misplaced. And this becomes all the clearer in the differences between Dorfman's play and Roman Polanski's Hollywood adaptation of *Death and the Maiden* (1994). Throughout both the film and the play, the viewer oscillates between two extremes, unsure whether Paulina is correctly identifying her assailant or simply delusional. The film, however, ends with Miranda's confession that he did rape her and with the certainty that he is guilty. That Roberto is guilty in the film means that Paulina is correct in identifying him, in spite of her disability; that is, Roberto's guilt ultimately renders the question of disability irrelevant to the film's point. The play, instead, ends with no real confession, and with a certain unease about Miranda's guilt. This uncertainty—as Dorfman wants us to believe—means that Paulina may still be wrong precisely because of her disability. Unlike the film, the play uses disability as a means to create doubts and critical tension that we as readers are left to consider.[6]

And this critical tension in the play, unlike the film, better captures the national uncertainty that is taking place during the transitional period in Chile, an uncertainty that prompts us to again ask questions that are directly related to the social and political context of transition, including: What will happen to people like Paulina in the transition to democracy? How can the country reconcile, or how can justice even be considered, when people like Paulina are left out? Will people like Paulina be included or excluded from this new democratic moment?

These questions are no doubt significant because the transitional government has been unable to recognize and reconcile them. To this point, Paulina's erratic behavior is clearly related to Gerardo's recent appointment to the country's Truth and Reconciliation Commission, which, like the Retting Commission in Chile, had clear restrictions; or, as Gerardo admits, those heading the commission are "limited" (10).[7] The problem with the play's fictional truth commission, like the Retting Commission, is that although its purpose is to gather information—or what Gerardo calls the "truth" (15)—about those who died or disappeared, it cannot enforce real "justice" (15).[8] That is, the commission could not try or convict any of those who committed crimes. Nor could it address those victims like Paulina who are still living and suffering because of these crimes. The commission, in this sense, is constructing a new national imaginary of justice, one that will include citizens like Roberto and Gerardo and exclude victims like Paulina. Thus, the political problem that the play frames is one of transitional justice between those who are included in the nation and those who are rejected.[9] It asks who will be embraced by the democratic nation and who, perhaps more importantly, will be denied that opportunity.

Death and the Maiden is as much a critique of exclusion as it is a disregard of an anticapitalist project that marked the dictatorship, since those who are included—and who also excluded—are from both the presumed Left (Gerardo) and the Right (Roberto). Said differently, Dorfman's play is less about the difference between socialism and liberalism that we saw in *Pedro y el Capitán* than about the corporeal politics of human rights that seek, in part, to undermine such political differences. Indeed, as the play signals, it wasn't just the military who wanted to exclude these disabled bodies like Paulina, but also those on the Left, including Gerardo, who represents the Concertación in Chile, the leftist coalition that came to power in the transition.[10] When Gerardo desperately pleads with Paulina that "we'll die from so much past, so much pain and resentment," the point couldn't be clearer that in *Death and the Maiden*, the Left in power is as committed to a politics of forgetting as the Right (54). In Dorfman's play, then, the emergence of a transitional politics seeks, on the one hand, to render irrelevant an ideological divide that had in a previous period defined the difference between Gerardo/Paulina and Roberto, and, on the other, to insist on the inclusion and exclusion of the disabled body that would, in *Pedro y el Capitán*, have been considered beside the point. Or to say this differently, in the transitional period, the discourse of inclusion and exclusion becomes indispensable insofar as it renders irrelevant a past political project that sought to eliminate the divide between rich and poor.

Disability and Human Rights: From Exploitation to Exclusion

Disability in *Death and the Maiden* speaks to the inability to come to terms with the legacy of state-sponsored terror, or at least the inability to fully incorporate human rights justice into the state. The incorporation of a human rights agenda into the nation, in other words, is bound to produce political limitations, limitations that are embodied by Paulina's disability. Or as Tobin Siebers suggests, disability is a "resource for thinking about fundamental democratic principles such as inclusiveness and participation" (93). But insofar as there are limitations, they reflect the interest in questions about which bodies are included and which are not. Daniel Zamora has shown that exclusion and inclusion become a vital conceptual framework in the United States and Europe during roughly the same period of the 1980s, a framework that disarticulates a critique of economic exploitation. Zamora argues that terms such as "unemployed," "the poor," or "the precarious" are "disconnected from being understood in terms of the exploitation at the heart of capitalist economic relations"; these terms instead "find themselves and their situation apprehended in terms of relative (monetary, social, or psychological) deprivation, filed under the general rubrics of 'exclusion,' 'discrimination,' or forms of 'domination'" ("When Exclusion"). Rather than point to "capitalist economic relations" that pin labor against capital, the problem with such "rubrics," instead, is that they pin labor against itself; that is, they create divisions in labor in order to obfuscate the shared exploitation of these groups. In this obfuscation, capitalism thrives, in part, because a critique of exploitation disappears. A similar point can be made about the discourse of human rights, and, as we saw in chapter 1, terms such as "victim," "tortured," and "wounded" transform the conversation from a critique of capitalist economic relations to a critique of exclusion from the state. In Latin America, in other words, human rights appear as a conceptual and political discourse that allows for the economic restructuring of the state to occur without any critique of capital.

Read as a human rights play, *Death and the Maiden* makes this paradigm of inclusion and exclusion visible in several ways. Perhaps the most visible is through the play's construction of justice. In *Pedro y el Capitán*, justice is imagined as a critique of private property. In *Death and the Maiden*, justice instead cannot be imagined without private property. And this becomes all the clearer when one considers that the national debate that *Death and the Maiden* stages takes place in Gerardo and Paulina's home, a home that is allegorically meant to stand in for the nation. This means not only that the play portrays the home as inseparable from a conception of the new nation but also that both the nation and the home are inseparable from the question of private property. That the home (and *not* the courtroom) makes Paulina's form of justice, if not possible, at least accessible suggests, at the very least, the limitations of the state in its relation to justice. This means that justice in the play, or what she calls a "private trial," renders private property essential (37).

The centrality of private property in the play should not be surprising, especially when considering that the function of the neoliberal state in the transition to democracy, especially in Chile, is both to become more like a corporation and to facilitate the free flow of capital on behalf of corporations. As Rob Van Horn and Philip Mirowski suggest, "neoliberalism is first and foremost a theory of how to reengineer the state in order to guarantee the success of the market and its more prominent participants, modern corporations" (161). The result is not only the further selling of national resources to private investors but also the restructuring of the state's conception of justice to benefit private enterprises. What is lost in this conception of justice is the critique of the class system that divides those who can afford to buy a home from those who cannot, or to put this more simply, a class system that divides the haves from the have-nots. This class critique is replaced by an idea of justice that imagines injustice principally as a form of exclusion from the market. Importantly, then, the paradigm of exclusion and inclusion is as much a diversion of a class critique as it is a reflection of a moment when the separation between the state and the market is compromised, that is, when the state is imagined as a private(ized) space, much like Gerardo and Paulina's home. For neoliberal logic, this means that exclusion is a problem insofar as it is a hindrance to the market's full potential to accumulate. And the neoliberal fantasy (i.e., the dominant form of injustice the market recognizes) is one that unjustly excludes people's access to the market *not* because they are exploited (that's what capitalism is supposed to do) but because they are discriminated against for who they are (whether for race, disability, or gender, as will be shown below).[11] The political force of *Death and the Maiden*, on this account, comes from its ability to defer the critique of economic exploitation. That is, the objective of the play, at least in part, is not so much to critique private property as it is to disavow that critique from Paulina's exclusion.

And this sense of exclusion in the play, as we already noted, can be attributed to a commission that only recognizes "serious cases" (9). Moreover, it intensifies this sense of exclusion by insisting that Paulina is discriminated against not only because she is a disabled "hysteric" but also because she is a woman. As Rosemarie Garland Thomson correctly declares, femininity and disability "are inextricably entangled in patriarchal culture" (27). For Garland Thomson, hysteria is not an isolated phenomenon but rather reflects "standard feminine roles enlarged to disabling conditions" (27).[12] Patriarchy, in short, deeply informs the concept of hysteria. Throughout *Death and the Maiden*, one finds numerous examples that endorse the notion of female hysteria, as well as of stereotypical gender roles. There are jokes between Gerardo and Roberto about how women are "the last mystery" and ironic assertions "that we can never possess the female soul" (14); and insults are traded between them, too, as Roberto questions Gerardo for not being able to "impose a little order in his own house?" (45). He also declares, at one point, that Gerardo, and not Paulina, is the "voice of civilization" (49).[13]

Gerardo disagrees with this last claim, but there is little else that Gerardo says or does in the text that invalidates the idea that men are the only ones who count in society. Although Paulina's desire to challenge this male-dominated world is sincere, more often than not, she validates these gender roles. For example, she sees her role in the relationship as relegated to the private sphere: "I take care of the house and you take care [. . .] of the car at least" (4); she also believes that men are in power because they have more physical "strength" (24). At the same time, and especially important to this argument, Paulina conceptualizes the dictatorship as a result of gender difference, whereby men not only create violence in the world (especially against women), but also unsuccessfully try "to fix the world (46)."[14] The point is clear that in *Death and the Maiden*, whether the country reconciles is as much a question about the disabled bodies that inform an emerging human rights politics (and the irrelevance of anticapitalist ideology) as it is about gender differences that divide men and women (the primacy of identity, for which see chapter 3).[15]

Or, said differently, the play produces numerous ways in which the question of economic exploitation can never be posed. And this even occurs when talking about the reasons why Paulina was tortured in the first place, as the play asserts that Paulina is discriminated against for who she is rather than what she believes (about class inequality).[16] To be sure, to ask what Paulina's political beliefs are when she was tortured should be considered offensive (and beside the point) because it unjustly blames the victim or implicitly justifies the act of torture. But even before the reader can ask that question, Dorfman provides an answer by insisting that she is tortured because she wanted to protect her partner. Which she does, since she declares that "I never gave them Gerardo's name" (30). To put this differently, she is tortured because she is protecting someone she loved. And, as it turns out, from Paulina's position, Gerardo's main fault is that he didn't love her enough, since after Paulina is released she finds him sleeping with another woman, or, as Paulina calls her, a "bitch" (53). The argument here, of course, is not that the play doesn't provide a political reading of the national transition, but rather that the reading it does provide redescribes a project that sought to eliminate the divide between rich and poor into a story of betrayal between men and women during the dictatorship and a (frustrated) reconciliation in democracy. In this way, Dorfman's play transforms a national history that wished to eradicate a structure of exploitation into a foundational fiction about reconciliation after a marital quarrel.[17]

Insofar as the central concern in *Death and the Maiden* becomes a corporeal difference between gendered and disabled bodies, it should also be noted that this concern is absent in *Pedro y el Capitán*. In Benedetti's play, the problem is not about a fundamental betrayal between two sides, but about a conflict between two different ideologies. Nor is it about gender difference. The Capitán wants Pedro to provide more information about "Magdalena and Fermín" (26), and, unlike in *Death and the Maiden*, the Capitán's problem is not that Magdalena is a woman and Fermín is a man, but rather that Magdalena and Fermín are communists and their beliefs (and actions) represent a threat to the regime. Furthermore, the problem that *Pedro y el Capitán* poses has nothing to do with "defending the law"; rather, it involves destroying a system of law that protects exploitation (*Death* 30). Indeed the problem is that the attention to human rights allows exploitation to flourish insofar as addressing such issues does not deal with the system that produces inequality. In *Death and the Maiden*, both those who, like Paulina, want to look back to a past that disables and those who, like Gerardo, want to look forward to Chile's bright future (as exemplified by the transitional slogan "Chile, la alegría ya viene," as discussed in the introduction) ultimately insist on ignoring the predominant economic project that characterized the politics of the Left before the 1980s. A politics of remembering or forgetting bodies leaves the economic structure untouched. Where the problem of justice before the dictatorship was fundamentally about a structure of exploitation, the problem of justice during the transition is primarily about inclusion and exclusion so the market can thrive; it's the type of justice that imagines that freedom cannot be achieved without private property.

Radical Politics? From Exclusion to Antirepresentation

As my reading of *Death and the Maiden* has shown, disability is the dominant figure through which we conceptualize the transition into democracy. More specifically, disability discourse functions on behalf of and principally within the logic of liberal democracy and human rights, where (to return to Siebers) disability is a "resource for thinking about fundamental democratic principles such as inclusiveness and participation" (93). There are, of course, other ways in which disability in *Death and the Maiden* can be read that challenge this reading of liberal democracy and human rights. For example, Randall Williams reframes the play around the idea of radical contingency and difference that is meant to reject these liberal limits; interestingly, he does so by insisting on the disabled body. Williams argues that Paulina's hysteria provides a way to move be-yond some of the restraints of transitional democracy that frame the past through human rights and Truth and Reconciliation Commissions. Wil-liams's point of departure is Avelar's criticism that the film adaptation of *Death and the Maiden* is plagued by a fetishized and hystericized pseudo-feminism that points to an affirmation of identity politics (Avelar, *Letter* 42). Dorfman's play, as noted above, is obviously meant to be about how women, like Paulina, are still discriminated against, while men, like Ge-rardo and Roberto, still rule the political landscape, a landscape where Ge-rardo and Roberto are the "voice of civilization" and Paulina is not (49). But for Avelar, the film's critique of patriarchy fails because both Paulina and Gerardo are heavy-handed caricatures that reinforce rather than re-ject gender stereotypes.[18]

Although Williams sympathizes with Avelar's criticism of this heavy-handedness and identitarian politics more generally, he still believes that hysteria produces a "persistent specter of noncovertibility" that cannot be co-opted by truth commissions and "official" state history. Despite the ob-vious stereotypical risks, Williams believes that hysteria provides a way to think beyond liberal democracy and human rights. More specifically, Wil-liams understands "incontrovertibility" as traces of the past that impede "sacrificial conversion into violence and its silenced transferred into the institutions of bourgeois culture" (89). In other words, hysteria in the text functions as a remnant that cannot be neatly incorporated into the official state version of past events. Williams explains that

> hysteria, then, serves as the incontrovertible negative force to the insis-tence of official conversion that seeks to break the present from the past in the name of a new future. Against the dictates of official conversion, it marks the uncertain outcome of the future and keeps alive the question of the past-ness of the past that renders the present (and future) as a site of contestation and struggle. It is through the figure of hysteria, and its immanent reasonableness, that the right to recall the past in the future is maintained and is not (and cannot be) handed over to the demands of transition, reconciliation, and consensus. (81)

For Williams, there is something radically "indeterminate" (81) about hysteria that not only negates the type of history that "official conver-sion" would like to impose, but also provides a counternarrative outside of "transition, reconciliation, and consensus" (81). Paulina's hysteria ren-ders both past and future radically open in a way that "official conversion" cannot. From this standpoint, Williams sees hysteria as a means to avoid the politics of identitarian exclusion and inclusion (and the limits of human rights), since the indeterminacy of hysteria cannot be co-opted by the state.

Thus, one way to frame the difference between Avelar's and William's readings is that they are disagreeing about the representation of hysteria in Dorfman's play; another way is to imagine that Avelar fails to understand that the force of hysteria is that it isn't quite like representation. This failure can best be illustrated through Ato Quayson's work on disability. For Quayson, the aesthetic representations of disabled characters produce an "aesthetic nervousness" in the reader. Disability generates an "ethical response" that other representational elements, including representations of other identitarian groups, cannot (19). Quayson states that

> aesthetic nervousness [. . .] is triggered by the implicit disruption of the frames within which the disabled are located as subjects of symbolic notions of wholeness and normativity. Disability returns the aesthetic domain to an active ethical core that serves to disrupt the surface of representation. Read from a perspective of disability studies, this active ethical core becomes manifest because the disability representation is seen as having a direct effect on social views of people with disability in a way that representations of their literary details, tropes, and motifs do not offer. In other words, the representation of disability has an efficaciousness that ultimately transcends the literary domain and refuses to be assimilated to it. (19)

For Quayson, there is something in disability—what David Mitchell and Sharon Snyder, following Slavoj Žižek, call a "hard kernel"—that safeguards it from the normal processes of representation, interpretation, and meaning (qtd. in *Narrative* 49). But unlike Mitchell and Snyder, Quayson believes this "ethical response" cannot simply be reduced to an identitarian claim (i.e., it can't just be about supposedly fixed categories like men and women as discussed above with *Death and the Maiden*). For Quayson, like Williams, fixed identities are equated with conventional liberal politics that only become more radical once those identities are understood as radically contingent.[19] I return to this idea below, but here it is interesting to note in Quayson's account that while the aesthetic frame is the point of departure for his disability reading, what is perceived to be an "ethical core" that produces a "direct effect" on the reader is constitutive of the ability to "disrupt the surface of representation." Representation, by Quayson's account, is part of the problem in that disability's "ethical core" "refuses to be assimilated to it" (81). In other words, the potential for a more radical type of politics begins once Paulina's hysteria is treated less like a representation than as the very opportunity to interrupt representation.

Although Quayson's representational claims are not directed at Latin America, a similar argument can be found in Nelly Richard's critique of the Latin American *testimonio* during the postdictatorial period. For Richard, representation—and realism as exemplified by the *testimonio* (see chapter 4)—far from political effectiveness, is deeply compatible with the consensual politics of the transition in Chile and the logic of capitalism: "Practical reason, direct language, and useful knowledge are nowadays the leading partners in this campaign of transparency (denotative realism, referential explicitness) through which powerful bureaucracies and technocracies of meaning conspire daily to erase any critical-reflexive interval that seeks to complicate communicative transaction with any suspended or dilated mode of interpretation" (*Cultural* 5). According to Richard, the objective for the transitional government in Chile is to create, under a rubric of "reconciliation," a governing reasoning that eliminates all "antagonistic" politics that might go against neoliberalism.[20] For her, the *testimonio* is perfectly aligned with neoliberalism because it reproduces a certain wholeness or totality of the subject that effectively threatens to erase the trauma, fragments, and gaps that the military regime violently created. It turns torture and trauma into an easily digestible narrative with some dramatic, even tragic turns but with an ultimately conciliatory ending. More specifically, the *testimonio* produces an "autobiographical pact" that "guarantees the confluence of narrator, author, and character" (*Cultural* 41) and presupposes a "referential continuity" that will "fill in the vacuums left by the suppressions and alienations of identity" (41). In this way, and recalling Derrida's argument in *Limited Inc*, Richard thinks that the *testimonio*—as a text that reconciles fragmented identities par excellence—is "signed" and sealed by the "signature," which once again provides the illusion of a closed text. Part of the problem with "referential continuity" is the issue of truth imposed by "powerful bureaucracies and technocracies." Consequently, the totality of the "I" in the *testimonio* fills in "the potholes of inconsistency with a line of continuity" and promotes the idea of one objective "Truth" that will "suture the wounds of memory and meaning" (*Cultural* 38). On this account, the *testimonio*—and realism more generally—is a pure mode that defends the "criteria of veracity" and neoliberal consensus by annulling the "undecidability of truth" (*Cultural* 41, 38).

And the whole point of Richard's critical project is to stress, much as

Williams does, the undecidability of truth, and for her, also like Williams, disability becomes the primary mechanism to make this point. Nevertheless, and perhaps against Williams's reading of disability, *Death and the Maiden* is still a mostly conventional realist play that, following Richard's reasoning, would present, much like the *testimonio*, a certain impasse. That is, if representation is something that we must move beyond in order to produce a more effective politics, then Dorfman's play is somewhat problematic (following Richard's logic), since it subscribes to a traditional genre compatible with neoliberalism. Against this realist form, Richard proposes a radical politics in Diamela Eltit's highly experimental text *El padre mío* (1989). The text, in part, is a transcription of a real tape-recorded interview, which consists of the erratic and altogether incomprehensible utterings of a schizophrenic homeless man. The significance of the schizophrenic man for Richard is not necessarily his relationship to the dictatorship—he was schizophrenic before the dictatorship and wasn't tortured by the military regime—but rather that as a disabled person, he cannot—according to Richard's ableist approach—be a complete, total subject. The severely schizophrenic man's shattered and fragmented identity guarantees, for Richard, that a process of recovery and reconciliation cannot take place.

This fantasy is meant to guarantee a text that radically deconstructs realism, representation, and fixed meaning, for, as Richard's logic suggests, while a neoliberal narrative like *Death and the Maiden* follows a linear and coherent trajectory, *El padre mío* would produce a "hyperbolic parade of false identifications, disconnected references, disintegrating phrases, erratic pronouncements, and crazy interpellations," all of which, in turn, give rise to a "maniacal and obsessive delirium" (*Cultural* 53, 54). According to this reasoning, then, what is wrong with *Death and the Maiden* is that it is not disabled enough, since disability is reduced only to the hysterical character of Paulina. *El padre mío* instead permeates the very structure of the text as it figuratively becomes disabled and fragmented, rejecting the production of a sense of harmony and coherency. What is released is not fixed "meaning" but something like a "convulsion of sense," "without guidance from a sociopolitical referent of action" (*Cultural* 77, 54). Whereas the affective response is obstructed by representation in Dorfman's play, Eltit's anti-*testimonio* not only transmits an effect but does so precisely because the schizophrenic man can't produce referential unity. For this reason, the schizophrenic man embodies a type of project that is "contrary to neoliberal realities" and transitional consensus (*Cultural* 58).

Thus the fantasy in Richard's reading of Eltit's text is that the schizophrenic man problematizes this commitment to aesthetic and political representation because the text can neither represent a politics nor properly be art ("hyperbolic parade of false identifications, disconnected references, disintegrating phrases, erratic pronouncements, and crazy interpellations"). And this fantasy couldn't be further from the aesthetics of Benedetti's play, which, as shown in chapter 1, is committed to representation and aesthetic autonomy, a commitment that would be, for Richard, a reiteration (rather than a rejection) of neoliberal logic. And the same type of criticism can be made of Dorfman's play.

I return to the question of autonomy in the second part of the book, but I want to highlight here that for both Williams and Richard, representation—or its critique—is perceived to be somehow more radical than human rights. Antirepresentation is considered more radical not for what it says or depicts, but precisely because it doesn't say or depict anything.[21] It is more radical, that is, because it assumes, in part, that a tragedy like the dictatorship can never be represented, and to represent it is always an unjust substitution, since it promotes a type of equivalence, restitution, and truth that neoliberalism wants to promote. What the schizophrenic man does in this regard is acknowledge how no representation could ever fix this past because this past is, in Eltit's words, "irreparable" (qtd. in Franco, *Cruel* 171).[22] But it's not just the past but also the future that can't be fixed. And this, of course, is the force of the fantasy of radical indeterminacy or contingency. By definition, it refuses to describe or choose any project oriented toward the future, whether that project is called capitalism, human rights, liberalism, or socialism. It disavows all these projects in order to remain radically open.

It is worth ending this chapter by raising several concerns that I will pursue in more detail in the remainder of the book, including the idea that radically indeterminate subjects are somehow antagonistic to neoliberalism. Indeed, if what indeterminacy does, on the one hand, is deconstruct, for example, human rights politics, on the other, it implicitly reproduces some of its same characteristics, since it not only disavows all beliefs, including the belief in any kind of alternative to the market, but also doubles down on the idea of the body. But this highlights another problem about exclusion, even radical exclusion. For Richard, the severely disabled schizophrenic man is meant to make impossible a type of reconciliation that is compatible with the neoliberal state by forever frustrating this project; in other words, since he can't heal, he will no longer be in or out of the neoliberal state. Here, the response to exclusion is not a critique of exploitation but a more radical form of exclusion. And yet, it is hard to see why this radicalization of exclusion is somehow more antagonistic to neoliberalism than human rights exclusion. Or even from the position of Benedetti's play, it is hard to see why replacing Paulina's experience with the schizophrenic man's experience can count as either historically or even politically "contrary to neoliberal realities," since neither experience—or more specifically, the attention to that experience—poses any kind of threat to a system that demands the divide between rich and poor (*Cultural* 58). The question of the subject, then, whether it is temporarily abled, mildly disabled, or severely disabled, presents no antagonism to neoliberalism. In other words, the problem is not exclusion, and the solution is neither inclusion nor a new, radicalized form of exclusion.

To return to the original question, What does the incorporation of this disability lens tell us about postdictatorial (specifically transitional) politics and art?, the answer, as I have argued here, is at once as historical as it is political. It is historical because the dictatorship did torture disabled people, did use a disability metaphor, and did disable people; and it is political because it reveals a conceptual mechanism through which a critique of capital turns into a critique of exclusion. Said differently, disability allows us to think about the dictatorship without thinking about a system of exploitation that not only brought about the dictatorship but also, and more importantly, continues today. At the same time, it is worth stressing that the argument of this chapter is not to suggest that all art should start talking about exploitation in a reenactment of social realism (the point is not that art should be a bit more like *Pedro y el Capitán*), but rather to signal how art in the transition (and increasingly in democracy) insists that politics be reduced to a question of the body, a question that is compatible with neoliberalism insofar as an attentiveness to the body seeks to obscure, hinder, and eliminate a critique of neoliberalism. Finally, it is the end of socialism as a utopian project that, in part, allows human rights to become the new utopian vision of the state (see chapter 4). What Dorfman's play highlights, then, is a tension between the end of one utopia and the frustrated emergence of another, albeit one just as questionable and fraught as the one that preceded it. The next chapter centers on the last decade of the twentieth century, a period that entails a shift from transition to full democracy and consolidation of human rights into the neoliberal state. The end of this transitional process is reflected in how the past is now imagined. What follows is an examination of how this consolidation takes place vis-à-vis a discourse of memory, a discourse that ultimately seeks to naturalize the history of neoliberalism.

CHAPTER 3

Making Neoliberal History

¿Cuánto de las ideas que movilizaron los años sesenta y setenta queda en los relatos testimoniales?
[How many of the ideas that mobilized the 1960s and 1970s remain in testimonial narratives?]
BEATRIZ SARLO, *TIEMPO PASADO*

Memory is blind to all but the group it binds. [. . .] History, on the other hand, belongs to everyone and to no one, whence its claim to universal authority.
PIERRE NORA, "BETWEEN MEMORY AND HISTORY"

The Dearly Departed

In 2000, fifteen years after the end of the dictatorship in Uruguay, the noted playwright and former Tupamaro Mauricio Rosencof published the autobiographical novel *Las cartas que no llegaron* (*The Letters That Never Came*), a text that vividly captures the brutal reality of his twelve years of incarceration and isolation from the outside world[1]—an isolation that, not incidentally, he endured precisely because of his activities as a Tupamaro.[2] Strikingly, however, even though these political activities led to Rosencof's imprisonment and torture, they play no part in the narrative. Rosencof's text, for example, never deals with his own history as a Tupamaro propagandist and leader. The text says nothing about his involvement in writing political propaganda or participating in meetings or even demonstrations. In fact, in the more than one hundred pages of the book, the word "Tupamaro" is not mentioned once.[3] More surprisingly, references that could possibly connect his imprisonment to the Tupamaros are largely suppressed; the reader never comes across typical Tupamaro revolutionary catchphrases such as a call for a "class revolution," "agrarian reform," or a "war against imperialism."[4] In short, Tupamaro ideology is largely removed from Rosencof's autobiographical novel. Indeed, even the "class enemy," which is fundamental to Tupamaro ideology, enigmatically vanishes and is replaced by an ideologically undefined "enemy" that attacks an equally ideologically undefined "us" (43).[5]

But it is not as if the reader of Rosencof's text is left without any sense at all of who the "enemy" or "us" is, because although the word "Tupamaro" doesn't appear in the entire narrative, the word "Jew" does (1, 3); and even though the Uruguayan military regime is rarely visible, there is a clear and detectable presence of the German SS (8).[6] Instead of an autobiographical novel that provides some historical information on Rosencof's political activity and his subsequent imprisonment, his text focuses on two historical events that have no explicit relationship to his torture or Uruguay's military dictatorship. The first is the story of Rosencof's early life, which primarily revolves around his relationship with his father, Isaac. This narrative is told through the innocent eyes of a child, Moishe, the author's Yiddish name. The second narrates events that happened to his aunt and speaks to her forced migration, first, to the Lublin ghetto in Poland and, from there, to Auschwitz and Treblinka. This second story is presented vis-à-vis an imagined exchange of letters between his aunt and Rosencof's father; these letters highlight his aunt's unawareness of the horrors to come as she moves closer to the concentration camps, and toward her eventual death.

As we come to learn later in the novel, these two narratives of unawareness (the child's and the aunt's) are motivated by Rosencof's desire to recuperate his father's memories: "I want to know more, Papa, I want more memories, more of your memories" (36). The reason he wants more is a response to "how little [he] know[s]" about himself (37). But, again, what he wants are not the memories of a notorious revolutionary, or even of a radicalized urban guerrilla, but the memories of his Jewish heritage. In other words, whatever else Rosencof's text is, it is certainly not the attempt to define or advocate for a socialist revolution, much less to show how his commitment to socialism resulted in his imprisonment. Interestingly, then, while his childhood and his aunt's experience in concentration camps clearly present the reader with two very separate historical events, what links both is that they are integral to what he calls the "story of our blood" (xxi).[7] In brief, they are integral to what it means for Rosencof to be Jewish. But why write an autobiographical novel in which his political imprisonment is of utmost importance to his narrative but never acknowledge the cause for which he was imprisoned? More importantly, why do away with his political affiliation as a Tupamaro and exchange it with an affirmation of his Jewishness? What does it mean to evacuate Tupamaro ideology and activities from an account of his torture and substitute them with an account of his aunt's experience during the Holocaust? Why, in other words, make your aunt's memories of the Holocaust central to the account of your own torture and imprisonment in Uruguay?

The answers to these questions must be framed in a period when neoliberal history—what will be called memory here—has fully triumphed in Latin America. In the period of transition, as explored in Dorfman's *Death and the Maiden*, remembering the past presented an opportunity to move beyond the limits that official history imposed on citizens. That is, because political transition is overdetermined by uncertainty, memory discourse, in theory, affords an opportunity to provide not only accounts that official history wishes to ignore, but also a counterhistory of a more just and equal society. But as discussed in chapter 2, this more just and equal society is pushed aside as transitional governments and transitional cultural texts offer up more conservative answers to these political uncertainties. Moving from the period of transition to full democracy in the 1990s, the politics of memory becomes the definitive story of neoliberalism. What this memory discourse will insist on is a vision of the world that turns political ideologies of the past into affirmations of one's subject position. More importantly for this chapter, it will also stress the idea of transmission as a mechanism to make that past memory present. *Las cartas que no llegaron* presents a more traditional and essentialist version of this vision, which looks to blood as a form of transmitting memories of the past. Albertina Carri's metadocumentary *Los rubios* (The blonds) provides a slightly more updated vision by imagining cultural artifacts as a means for transmitting memories. Finally, I consider the idea of the specter as a so-called radical version of memory politics; what I argue, however, is that the logic of the specter as a transmitter, far from radical, functions much like blood; it is a logic that insists on one's subject positions at the expense of an anticapitalist politics.

The Latin American Holocaust

The logic of blood is fundamental to the structure of *Las cartas que no llegaron*. The first part of the novel, titled "Wartime in the Barrio," is told through the eyes of an eight-year-old Moishe and begins with his attempt to remember the first time he met his parents, an attempt that ultimately fails: "I can't say exactly when I met my parents. [. . .] But I do remember that the first time I saw Mama, Mama was out in the patio" (1). Moishe's childhood is one of inexactitudes and doubts as he tries to make sense of the world around him, a world that's got him "all mixed-up" (9). As Anne Whitehead suggests, the use of a child's perspective produces several effects in literature, for example, "the limited insight of the child creates a hiatus in the text, which relies on the knowledge or imagination of the reader to fill in the gap and make sense of the narrative" (qtd. in Colvin 43). The critic Andrea Reiter, in her analysis of children's point of view, stresses that "in their unprejudiced and uninformed attitude, children not only notice details which escape the adult but interpret them in a way which makes them seem even more horrific" (qtd. in Colvin 43).[8] This is certainly the effect that Moishe's narrative produces in *Las cartas que no llegaron*, as the first section of the novel ends with a series of "I don't know[s]" relating to his surroundings and to the uncertain future, making his imprisonment and torture seem "even more horrific" in retrospect (21).

In this first section, Rosencof intersperses the fictional Holocaust letters between Moishe's aunt and his father; and like the eight-year-old child, the aunt's letters reflect a mixture of fear, doubt, and innocence, as she is unable to foresee the horrors to come: "We're almost there, Isaac. Thank God. And it's funny, but I'm thinking about that movie I saw in Warsaw and wondering if they'll have a glass of hot tea for us, too. Through the cracks in the wall of the boxcar, we've spotted a sign that says: 'Treblinka.' The train is slowing down. It's a relief to know we're so close" (8). These fictional letters, in particular how they problematize the division between reality and fiction, will be discussed later in my reading of Carri's *Los rubios*. Here, I only highlight that this unawareness registered in the letters serves, in part, to frame the horrors not only of his aunt's Holocaust experience but also of Rosencof's prison experience.

In the second section, titled simply "The Letter," the fictional letters between his aunt and father are replaced by one letter that Rosencof addresses to his father, a letter that "I would have written you, *Viejo*, when writing wasn't allowed" (54). Although he writes this letter—and, by extension, the book we are reading—after his release, the section focuses primarily on his prison experience and his yearning to reclaim more of his father's memories, a yearning that remains with him many years after being released. As already noted, what is most striking about this section is exactly what is missing from it, as it never mentions the preceding years as a Tupamaro or the leftist politics that put him into prison. Instead, his childhood and his aunt's Holocaust experience serve as the conceptual and structural prehistory to his imprisonment, as a way to understand the years that are skipped over. The reasons for his imprisonment become the story, much like his aunt's unawareness and their shared persecution.

In short, the reason Rosencof is imprisoned is not for what he believes in (what he thought, for example, about the class struggle) but for a certain irrelevance of these beliefs. Indeed, the horror of the Holocaust is as much about its scale as it is about the complete disregard for what Jewish people themselves thought not only about politics but about life in general. They were killed—adults and children alike—for who they were. They were killed, as Rosencof already notes, because of their "blood." But this account of genocide extends beyond the Holocaust and the SS, as Rosencof writes that these deaths can be attributed to a "miserable god who took everything and gave nothing, and made threats just to fuck with us [. . .] his Chosen People [. . .] thrashed them for no reason at all" (40, 46). Accordingly, what lands him in jail and results in his torture was his inherited "blood" and not his political reasons or beliefs. What the first two chapters of *Las cartas que no llegaron* propose, then, is the transformation of the Uruguayan dictatorship into the Holocaust by insisting on questions of Jewish identity, of Jewish "blood," above all else.

This insistence on the Holocaust means that Rosencof's Jewish identity becomes a lens through which all experiences become an affirmation of his identity. This happens in several ways in the text. If, for instance, a "miserable god fuck[s]" with all Jews, then Rosencof's prison experience brings him closer to this Jewish reality, and, moreover, to his desire to have more of his father's memories, or, as he later declares, "So I understand you, *Viejo*, because I'm reliving all that in here [in prison]" (41). At the same time, insofar as Rosencof understands his prison experience in Uruguay as "reliving" an old Holocaust experience in Europe, it allows him to turn identity into a mechanism of resistance and solidarity that unites him with both family and others who share the same "blood." As we just saw, it is his resistance against the Nazis and this "miserable god" that affords him the possibility of reliving his father's experiences. And it is his stance against both Nazism and the unyielding Jewish god that provides him with a profound sense of solidarity with other family members: "When Papa called Mama's name, he was calling others, too—all the missing names, his and *ours* [. . .] Mama's name was everyone else's: brothers and sisters, *mamele* and *tatele*, *bubeles*, nieces and nephews—any or all of them" (42). Finally, his sentiment about the Holocaust unites him and his family to Jewish people as a form of resistance: "And an Anielewicz, a whole group of Anielewiczes with a few guns, a .38, a knife or two . . ." he continues, "that's all they had, but they resisted, Papa, they resisted, it was the first uprising in all of Europe, and it was theirs, *Viejo*, it was *ours*" (57). From this position, if blood is part of the problem (i.e., blood gets Jewish people killed), it also becomes a politics of solidarity, since it provides an opportunity to form a memory project centered on identity (rather than ideology). Blood, therefore, allows him both to make sense of past violence and also to reinforce a shared identity between him and the "Chosen People" (40).

This transformation of the Uruguayan dictatorship into a Jewish Holocaust undoubtedly marks a difference from a text like *Pedro y el Capitán*, which functioned as a rejection of identity. I don't mean to suggest that Rosencof should write an autobiographical novel that is more like Pedro's life; nor that Rosencof deliberately attempts to misrepresent his past in *Las cartas que no llegaron*. My point here is less personal, or even ethical, than conceptual and historical. Considered from a historical perspective, what makes Rosencof's commitment to identity (and the concomitant irrelevance of beliefs) especially pertinent is that it is not at all unique, but is informed by a larger memory project already taking place in the period when he writes. As Andreas Huyssen suggests, beginning in the 1980s, memory becomes the critical way of framing resistance to politics and violence across the globe. But not just any memory. The predominant narrative through which memory has become global is vis-à-vis the Holocaust as the "universal trope for historical trauma" (23). Throughout the 1980s and 1990s, according to Huyssen, one finds "Holocaust memory discourse" when describing conflicts in Rwanda, Bosnia, and Kosovo, despite clear political and historical differences between them (23). These narratives undoubtedly stress issues such as the unfathomable cruelty, the absent burial rites for victims (the Antigone effect), and the undeniable existence of anti-Semitism (or, for that matter, of anti-homosexuality, of anti-Roma, and so on). Today, the Holocaust trope addresses not just contemporary violence but also past violence. By framing the past around blood and "that miserable god who took everything and gave nothing, and made threats just to fuck with us [. . .] his Chosen People" (40), Rosencof's text is less an opportunity to compare the dictatorships to the Holocaust than an insistence on seeing the dictatorships as a Holocaust; that is, the "Holocaust memory discourse" in *Las cartas que no llegaron* frames Rosencof's past (his prison experience in particular) less as a response to the dictatorship than as a reflection of a contemporary logic that is centered on identities.[9]

This turn toward identities in Rosencof not only represents a rupture from the ideological world of the 1960s and 1970s but also becomes an affirmation of the posthistorical political world that began in the 1980s and continues today. By the time Rosencof wrote this novel, Samuel Huntington's famous "hypothesis" that the primary conflicts, or clashes, of the twenty-first century would be between civilizations had already produced quite a stir in both academic and political circles (Huntington).[10] In his widely cited 1993 essay "The Clash of Civilizations?," Huntington argues that the difference between the Cold War period that ended two years earlier and the new one that then began is that conflicts would be no longer "ideological" and "economic" but rather identitarian and cultural. Indeed, for Huntington, the "end of history" would mean that liberal democracy and capitalism have triumphed (following Francis Fukuyama's well-known thesis) and, for this reason, what counts now is not "what side you are on" (i.e., your beliefs) but rather "who you are" (i.e., your identity). The eruptions of violence in Rwanda, Bosnia, and Kosovo that occurred immediately after the end of the Cold War seemed only to confirm the sense that "who you are," and not what you believe, is what ultimately gets you tortured or killed.

To the extent that who you are, and not what you believe, becomes a central political thought of this period, it also makes the real reasons why Rosencof was incarcerated in the first place seem not only politically irrelevant but even a bit passé. Thus, one way to answer the question posed above ("Why did Rosencof do away with his political affiliation as a Tupamaro and replace it with an affirmation of what it means to be Jewish?") is to respond that personally he is no longer interested in writing about this leftist past. Another way to answer the question is to argue that this personal choice is a reflection of the state of politics today (and at the time of Rosencof's writing), when ideological and economic reasons are simply no longer relevant or have been made to seem irrelevant.[11] From this standpoint, the "Holocaust trope" is useful today less because it speaks to the historical Holocaust, or speaks to what happened in the dictatorships in the Southern Cone, than because it speaks to the present commitment to liberal democracy and its complicity with neoliberalism. Or, said slightly differently still, what memory offers is a fantasy that what counts today is your identity and not your political beliefs, beliefs that might disagree with neoliberalism.

Memory politics today, in short, live in a harmonious existence with neoliberalism. Undoubtedly, my argument represents a refutation of how memory has been envisioned in the postdictatorial period. Idelber Avelar, for example, has suggested that neoliberalism signals a new reality in which "every corner of social life has been commodified" (*Untimely* 1). This commodification that is ushered in by the dictatorships implies a "passive forgetting" and the negation of "memory because new commodities must always replace previous commodities, send them to the dustbin of history" (*Untimely* 1). Part of the project for an "oppositional critic," according to Avelar, thus becomes mobilizing memory as a means of "digging" up past ruins that will "stand in the way of the accumulation of capital in the present" (*Untimely* 9). However, what memory discourse today reveals is something quite different. Memory, far from standing in the way of capitalism, takes the predominant logic of the end of history and recasts it into the past; that is, the point of memory politics is to transform the dictatorship from a story about ideology (socialism vs. liberalism) into a story about who we are, regardless of our political beliefs.

This not to suggest that identity is entirely counterproductive or that anti-Semitism didn't exist during the dictatorships in the Southern Cone. One only needs to recall the most famous *testimonio* of the transitional period, Jacobo Timerman's *Preso sin nombre, celda sin número* (*Prisoner without a Name, Cell without a Number*), to see that anti-Semitism was certainly present in the period of authoritarian rule, especially in Argentina (although perhaps less so in Rosencof's Uruguay).[12] One of the principal concerns of Timerman's text is precisely to show that Jewish people have served as scapegoats for both the extreme Right and the extreme Left. In his text, Timerman, who was arrested and tortured in 1977 during Argentina's Proceso de Reorganización Nacional (National Reorganization Process, or dictatorship), recounts several anti-Semitic episodes that he experienced during captivity. It would seem, then, that Timerman follows a logic similar to Rosencof's in the sort of insistence on seeing the dictatorship as another Holocaust. Nevertheless, what we also find in the text, unlike in Rosencof's novel, is his commitment to recognizing that there is a fundamental distinction between anti-Semitism and socialism. In one key scene, for example, he recalls that while leaving his prison cell, a guard yells, "To the gas chamber" (54). Timerman, who has been arrested because of his Left-leaning political—albeit not socialist—beliefs, is perplexed by the guard's out-of-place comment; indeed, even though a military doctor who witnesses the scene gets angry and responds that "we're not anti-Semites" (54), Timerman still cannot "understand why an Argentine soldier who was combating leftist terrorism—irrespective of his methods—could feel such hatred against a Jew" (63). The point here, again, is not to deny either that anti-Semitism did exist in Argentina or that the extreme Right and Left have often targeted Jews. Rather, the point is that Timerman understands that anti-Semitism—irrespective of its undeniable presence in the Southern Cone—is radically different from anticommunism. The two are categorically different.

They are not different, however, in *Las cartas que no llegaron*. If Timerman's 1981 text is committed to at least recognizing a theoretical difference between one's identity and one's political beliefs, Rosencof's posthistorical novel insists that we understand the primacy of one (identity) at the expense of the other (socialism): one is foregrounded as relevant, while the other is pushed to the side. Thus, if the neoliberal fantasy imagines a world where socialism ceases to be relevant, it also imagines—as we saw in Dorfman's *Death and the Maiden* in the previous chapter—a world where what puts you in jail or gets you killed is your identity and not your beliefs. Yet there are some relevant differences between *Death and the Maiden* and *Las cartas que no llegaron*. Dorfman's text, like Timerman's, represents a transitional moment when "society entered immediately into an intense contest over the meaning of its recent past" (Robben 122). Memory, during the transition, presents a problem but also an opening. Rosencof's text presents a solution to the problem (and a closing) by insisting that memory is something that one does not have to directly experience but can be transmitted through blood or through marriage: "When Papa called Mama's name, he was calling others, too—all the missing names, his and *ours*." Rosencof's text functions to ontologize beliefs, to reduce them to blood, a substance transmitted genetically and closely linked to notions of identity, ethnicity, race. In sum, the "Holocaust trope" today (and in Rosencof's text) has less to do with affirming Jewishness than with producing an account in which who you are becomes essential, an unalterable category that ultimately gets you killed.

Blood Language, Blood Memory

Rosencof's narrative is driven by the desire to find out who he is, and his childhood comes to represent the moment when the trauma of not having an identity begins, a trauma that is repeated with a reoccurring mantra: "I don't know." But what Rosencof doesn't know—that is, what divides him from knowing who he really is—is Yiddish. It is his inability to understand Yiddish as a child that represents the originary identitarian split and will cast him as an outsider in his own family. His older brother Leon, who was born in Poland, however, is the "one who knows" (24) and who will, he hopes, teach him Yiddish. But when Leon dies, the possibility to learn the language, for Rosencof, is closed forever. Language, in this way, is identified as a primary obstacle in the text, as something that impedes him not only from identifying himself with his family—and especially his father—but also from being himself: it becomes a severed connection despite the seemingly paradoxical blood link.

But language also becomes a type of answer, an answer that requires not learning Yiddish but inventing a language that requires no learning at all. In the last section of the book, titled "Days Beyond Time," a new form of language appears as a mechanism for Rosencof to communicate with his father. The chapter begins as the incarcerated Rosencof awakens from a dream in which his father transmits a message to him. He quickly realizes that it wasn't a dream, but rather something real, a moment when his father communicates a "word" that Rosencof himself cannot remember (94). For Rosencof, however, what is essential is not that he can't "remember it" or that he "never actually spoke the word," but rather that he "did speak its meaning, its translation, that sentence" (68). To be sure, language is a system of communication that represents ideas and concepts, and as communication, it assumes that the receiver of that information— if he or she commands the semantic and syntactic rules of that language— can decipher the meaning of the message. This process is universal; that is, as long as one learns the rules of the system, one could, in theory, perform the task of interpretation. But what Rosencof experiences here is something radically different, so much so that the event makes him believe it may be otherworldly. The "word" defies this process of learning or even mediation, and for this reason he defines the experience as something resembling "ghosts or bodily projects" that come to visit him (68). This new language is not a rejection of blood but, indeed, appears constitutive of it.

Blood language thus provides the opportunity to think about how this new language functions and how it distinguishes itself from conventional language. The communication of the "word" functions less as language than as a trace from father to son, since what is transmitted is neither representational nor universal. Like blood—and unlike a conventional definition of language and representation—the trace of language is transmitted without a possibility of actually interpreting its meaning. The meaning is what Rosencof instantly feels; like a blood transfusion, it is (in) him ("did speak its meaning, its translation, that sentence") (68). The outcome is that he is able not only to communicate, or to connect, with his father but also, and more importantly, to solidify the sense that "you're in me. No, *Viejo*, what I'm feeling right now is that I am you, that we're one and the same" (55). By transforming language into something that can be transmitted rather than represented, Rosencof makes his own experience part of his father's experience and redescribes history as a memory infused into his blood.

Blood into Cultural Memory

Rosencof's *Las cartas que no llegaron* is not the only text in the postdictatorial period that recuperates the memories of past relatives, especially relatives who were disappeared during the recent dictatorships. Since the mid-1990s, organizations such as H.I.J.O.S (Hijos por la Identidad y la Justicia contra el Olvido y el Silencio [Sons and Daughters for Identity and Justice against Forgetting and Silence]) have become important contributors to the process of keeping the recent past alive by "transmitting past experiences to younger generations" (Nouzeilles 265). Perhaps the most experimental text to emerge in this period is Albertina Carri's metadocumentary *Los rubios* (2003), a film that shares many of the same characteristics found in Rosencof's text. Like Rosencof's *Las cartas que llegaron*, Carri's film sets out to recover the traumatic memories of the documentarian's relatives so that they can become her own. More specifically, Carri seeks to recover the memories of her parents, who were Montoneros and disappeared during the Argentine dictatorship in the 1970s. Also, like Rosencof's fictional letters from his aunt, the documentary problematizes the lines between art and life, documentary and fiction. For example, Carri uses actors and openly stages scenes in front of the camera. This is one reason the documentary has been widely applauded for its stylistic departure from the realist mode that has defined past memory projects in Argentina, including the heroic narratives of resistance that have been endorsed by the Montoneros.[13]

Unlike those past memory projects, *Los rubios*, according to Gabriela Nouzeilles's reading of Carri's documentary, problematizes past memory politics by undermining the idea of a total history and truth. Nouzeilles suggests that *Los rubios* "is the chronicle of the impossibility of reconstructing the past and of offering a complete and reliable version of it. It also implies the impossibility of giving a final, organic narrative structure to the movie we are watching" (Nouzeilles 270). Unlike heroic narratives, which always fail to achieve the truth, *Los rubios*, much like Rosencof's imagined letters, incorporates fiction (and metanarrative) in order "to access the most painful areas of the past" (270). Carri's documentary allows for "creative memory"—memory that stresses not "historical accuracy" but a "particular recollection"—whereas both conventional memory projects and history do not (270). In short, this "creative memory" not only complicates the past but does so by insisting that all aspects of one's life are relevant, including those memories that one didn't directly experience. Indeed, complicating the past by way of fiction becomes something like the political force of *Los rubios*.

Everything that has been said about *Los rubios* up to this point could be applied to the identitarian reading of *Las cartas que no llegaron*.[14] For this reason it is somewhat surprising to note that Nouzeilles believes that Carri's documentary represents a departure from (rather than an affirmation of) this identitarian reading; she sees it as a rejection of the human rights discourse that I have critiqued throughout this book. For example, Nouzeilles correctly recognizes the risk of utilizing the Holocaust trope in relation to both the dictatorship and the *desaparecidos* (disappeared). She is aware, for example, that the Holocaust trope has been grounded in a discourse of liberal pluralism that is compatible with the world that Huntington imagines; she also understands that the trope runs the risk of turning a revolutionary subject into an "abstract victim that also characterizes the discourse of human rights advocates" (264). Following Nicolás Casullo, she suggests that the focus on the *desaparecidos*—a termed coined by the military regime—dehistoricizes the deaths of these militants. Furthermore, she finds the ethical demand of "biological identity" and "the compulsory demand of genealogical inscription" to be problematic, since, she argues, it is neither always wanted by nor entirely fair to the children of the disappeared (265, 266). That is, because of this "compulsory demand," these children come to embody their parents' political positions, and at times behave "as political literalizations" of "the living dead, the ghosts of a historical past that return to the present as the symptom of an unresolved, terrible crime" (Žižek, qtd. in Nouzeilles 266). What is wrong here, for her, is precisely this mimetic function, that children literally do not choose their actions but take on their own parents' actions. By repeating their parents' ideology and actions, they reproduce totality and closure.

For Nouzeilles, the political force of the documentary is not the insistence on blood as a transmitter of memory, but rather its ability to move beyond blood by imagining a form of transmission of memory that is located in culture. It's Carri's insistence on "creative memory"—and language as a transmitter—that presents a turn away from blood and identitarian politics and a turn toward culture and a more radical form of politics. What is more, it is this "creative memory," as both the fragmented and fictional gesture, in *Los rubios* that allows for the idea of the "living dead, the ghosts" to become a kind of cultural response. According to Nouzeilles, through the theoretical concept of the ghost, *Los rubios* challenges the "genealogical interpellation and mimetic desire, and asserts instead the necessary heterogeneity of inheritance" (272).

It is less genealogy itself than the ghost vis-à-vis genealogy that provides a response to the liberal critique against the film. Indeed, Nouzeilles believes that *Los rubios* sidesteps this "genealogical interpellation and mimetic desire" by ultimately imagining that the "spectre" delivers "a political message," one that suggests "the desirability of other kinds of communities, beyond the politics of blood and party; that is, flexible, open communities, capable of imagining still undefined, alternative political projects" (266). More specifically, what the ghost does is return to haunt society but *not* strictly on behalf of the family, identity group, or a party:

> The spectre is the return as symptom of a traumatic event, the trace of a horrible crime that remains unresolved. The trauma created by the dictatorship and its killing machine is an exemplary case of the return of the dead. The shadows of its victims continue to haunt the present as living dead until they receive decent burial, and/or the trauma of their death is somehow integrated into historical memory. The presence of the symptom, like the presence of the ghost, is a sign that the trauma is still active, still has power to wound and disrupt. (Nouzeilles 271)

For Nouzeilles, the point of the ghost is to move away from blood and pluralism to more "flexible, open communities." By no means is Nouzeilles—or Derrida, for that matter—the only one who sees the ghost functioning as a technology to produce a more radical political project.

This commitment to "alternative political projects" can also be found in Luis Martín-Cabrera's reading of the *desaparecido*, which in many ways presents a more historical and concrete reading of the dictatorships, and a more aggressive attack on ontology and subject positions, than Nouzeilles's does. Martín-Cabrera begins by examining the two primary narratives of the recent past, the "two demons" narrative of the transition and a human rights politics of the new century. The "two demons" discourse—a term penned by the writer and the president of CONADEP (Comisión Nacional sobre la Desaparición de Personas) Ernesto Sábato—frames the past as a conflict between the radical Right and the radical Left.

What is problematic about this discourse, as Martín-Cabrera rightly suggests, is the overall refusal of the state to talk about the past; furthermore, the discourse of two demons reduces both the Right and Left to a (violent) sameness, even though the military clearly killed more people than any revolutionary group. The discourse of human rights emerges instead in a more recent moment and moves away from the "two demons myth" by recognizing a multiplicity of memories. But this shift to multiplicity for Martín-Cabrera ultimately reproduces the same problem, since it "assigns equal weight" to all memories, be they fascist, centrist, revolutionary, or even apolitical (9). What is more, both of these discourses, as he correctly states, are compatible with contemporary democratic liberalism and the free market, which lay at the heart of the fraught process of transition to democracy.

To avoid the shortfalls of these "two hegemonic frames," Martín-Cabrera proposes an analysis of the figure of the *desaparecido*, which is at the "center of the struggle for the recuperation of memory" in the Southern Cone (17–18). What the *desaparecido* acknowledges, on the one hand, is that there is an incommensurability, an excessiveness that undermines the sort of calculability or idea of equivalence that is crucial for the logic of two demons. At the same time, on the other hand, the existence of the *desaparecido* represents an "insurmountable absence" that always "remains outside" of the "liberal distribution of political positions" that is paramount to the discourse of human rights (18). For this reason, the *desaparecido* can never be reduced to either of these discourses, or even to a specific ontology or subject position:

> Those who disappear are radically suspended between life and death, without origin or finality, they cannot be apprehended either by ontology or by identity politics. It is impossible to assign a subject position to subjects deprived of death, while at the same time it is equally difficult to contain the desaparecidos within an ontological framework, for they are neither dead nor alive. (19)

For Martín-Cabrera, the figure of the *desaparecido* is "suspended between life and death" and thus functions, as for Nouzeilles, as a specter that is "neither dead nor alive." Furthermore, for both Nouzeilles and Martín-Cabrera, the specter is unlike blood or family because it does not operate under an "ontological framework" but rather escapes it. It is dissimilar to blood or to family because it represents a political project that doesn't necessarily come from past politics or a definable place, but instead comes from the future or a "non-place" (Martín-Cabrera 20). Or as Derrida suggests, one cannot distinguish whether the ghost acts as the future-to-come or as the coming-back that allows for a certain political gesture "of justice where it is not yet, not yet there" (*Specters* xviii). The point about a justice-to-come, however, is not to return to a class project that existed in the 1970s. Quite the opposite: the whole force of Derrida's claim rests on its ability not to produce that "mimetic" project or any project at all; its force, instead, is its radical indeterminacy, or what Martín-Cabrera calls its "open-ended trajectory" (20).

But, at this point, it's important for us to ask, What is the logic of the haunting? How does the ghost decide what or whom to haunt? Does it haunt only those who were directly affected by the traumatic event, like the children of *desaparecidos*, or does it haunt others as well? How does it reach others? And, finally, if the ghost "does not have an origin or a destination," how does a person who is visited by it understand it to be a Montonero ghost, or a ghost of some other political group, or even some other injustice (Martín-Cabrera, 19)?[15] As I addressed above, the project of the specter is to reject identity politics (as well as revolutionary politics) and to leave open the possibility of "still undefined, alternative political projects." It establishes the structure of the past and future by way of the material remnant, which links the two, and it does so precisely by linking the past and future *with us*.

But it is not *all of us*. What is most important about the ghost, like cultural memory in general, is that its political impetus is determined, as David Berliner notes, by "lasting traces of the past [that] persist within us" (200–201). In his essay on the memory boom, Berliner avers, for example, that the cultural transmission of memory, much like Rosencof's idea of blood language, functions *not* as a "set of representations of events and experiences that are shared but as the way lasting traces of the past persist within us, as the transmission and persistence of cultural elements through the generations" (200–201). Following this culturalist argument, memory as a trace is not something that we directly have to experience, but it is nevertheless transmitted from the past and lives within *us*. Furthermore, since it is neither representation nor exactly history, it cannot, by definition, be shared by all; it is defined, in short, by its exclusion, and thus by who we are, whether that is individual or collective. Pierre Nora puts it this way: "Memory is blind to all but the group it binds" (9). As a political act, it "binds" or resists precisely because it is transformed into a genealogy or an inheritance carried within culture from one generation to the next, safeguarding itself not only from the totality of history but also from those, like the SS or Junta, who wish to erase it.

In this way, the ghost as a transmitter of memory looks strikingly similar to Rosencof's commitment to blood language between father and son. The ghost as a trace haunts only the familiar—why would it do otherwise?—whether it be locational, or an individual, communal, cultural, national, or even generational grouping. Unlike a "set of representations of events and experiences that are shared" (i.e., history), the ghost insists on its exclusion and affirms that "memory is blind to all but the group it binds" (Berliner 200–201; Nora 9). Or as Derrida argues, "this being-with specters would also be, not only but also, a *politics* of memory, of inheritance, and of generations" (*Specters* xviii).[16] The ghost may not be blood, but it is deeply committed to imagining politics as if it were. To be sure, the ghost is not a subject, but, unlike beliefs, it returns to insist on the subject and the world of positions (since memories cannot be shared by all but only inherited by some).[17] So even despite the desire for a radical politics, the specter still insists on who we are.

Of course, Martín-Cabrera's approach is perhaps the most explicit in the rejection of neoliberalism (and also human rights); nevertheless, this rejection, and the project that is meant to emerge from it, rests on a more just form of memory, or what he calls a "spectral approach to memory" that is outside both the state and the free market (9). Yet, if the desire of the ghost is to be outside the state and the market, the very conceptual apparatus of the ghost brings us right back to the state and to the market. That is, if, on the one hand, the desire of the specter is to leave open a future political project, on the other, the insistence on who we are returns us again to a posthistorical world where neoliberalism now goes uncontested. The demand of the ghost, in other words, asserts that our subject positions are the point of departure from which all politics emerge. That is, the so-called justice-to-come must always be envisioned through the lens of who we are. Or, said differently, the memory trace—even when attempting to move beyond liberal pluralism—insists on the absence of beliefs as the only way of approaching politics, which, in turn, is not a rejection of or resistance against, but rather, as already noted with Huntington, the epitome of neoliberal logic.

The ghost, then, functions as a technology through which our beliefs about politics are eliminated, since it demands that we perceive (and conceive) politics—even radical politics—as something that is passed on rather than learned. Indeed, it is something that visits us without our consent or effort, without our ability to decide whether it is right or wrong. As Berliner suggests, the trace is an "accumulated past which acts on us and makes us act" (201). Unlike history, and much like our genetic makeup, memory traces determine our actions and demand something from us; usually they "demand restitution for what has been lost and forgotten" (Avelar, *Untimely* 1). The cultural trace comes to us, much like blood, regardless of whether we conjure it up or of what we believe. It comes to us despite our beliefs. From this position, the ghost, like blood, does not mean, it just is. The ghost is not the rejection of blood, but rather something like the postmodern reincarnation of blood, since its primary function is to ontologize beliefs (without blood). As such, if the fantasy of the ghost is to accept the rules as they have been defined by the likes of Huntington and Fukuyama, it is no surprise to also note that, like the disabled figures of the transition, the ghost does not present a contradiction, or even an alternative to the politics of neoliberalism, but functions as the affirmation that the end of history is the only politics possible. In short, ghost memory, like blood memory, is still neoliberal memory.

History and Memory in Neoliberal Times

Jean Franco has suggested that memory must be understood in relation to history. History is teleological, totalitarian, and closely connected to power and official history; it is connected, that is, to the type of history that the authoritarian regimes wish to impose on their citizenry.[18] Memory, on the contrary, is fragmented and faltering, but also intimate, personal, and plural, and for these reasons, in part, "memory work" is crucially framed as resisting official history.[19] I would like to conclude this chapter by historicizing this conceptual difference between memory and history a bit more. The question of memory undoubtedly served an important purpose in the 1980s as it shed light on the abuses that were taking place and counteracted these regimes' imposed silence. Memory in that period was a necessity.[20] Yet, as Charles Hatfield has pointed out in his insightful book *The Limits of Identity*, the discourse of memory, prior to the 1990s, always "entailed turning memory into history" (84). Pointing to Elena Poniatowska's *La noche de Tlatelolco* (*Massacre in Mexico*) or the CONADEP report, Hatfield argues that memory served on behalf of history; that is, memory was the attempt to establish historical facts and truth, to account for the past. As discussed above, history, like representation and language—and unlike the memory trace—entails that the past is something that could be learned by all regardless of who you were. Nora puts it this way: "History [. . .] belongs to everyone and to no one, whence its claim to universal authority" (9). History has neither a subject position nor a perspective; instead, it insists that all have access to its knowledge and truth. What is important about history is that it doesn't belong to any one individual, culture, generation, or group but transcends them all.

Increasingly in the last two decades, memory has turned into a mechanism to reaffirm one's subject position by replacing the question of truth with a multiplicity of perspectives, a shifting ground where truth is relegated to one's experience. For this reason, Hatfield suggests that "if we give up on the notion that there is a truth about the past and replace it with the notion that there are multiple truths about the past, then the past that is individually or communally ours becomes a marker of our difference" (85–86). Memory today functions to construct a narrative of who we are rather than to form a universal claim. To put this differently, memory exists not to *become* history but to undermine it. From this standpoint, the force of narratives like Rosencof's or Carri's, much like *Death and the Maiden,* is to imagine a world that revolves around subject positions. But where *Death and the Maiden* embodies a tension of transition, the ontologizing logic of memory in the 1990s reflects a moment in which the hegemony of neoliberalism has been fully consolidated into the state. The posthistorical discourse of memory, in other words, solidifies Huntington's neoliberal conception of the world by redescribing the past as a "marker of our difference" rather than as a (political, ideological, critical, etc.) history that we can disagree on.

Memory thus eliminates history by turning the past into a mechanism to inform our subject positions; it also eliminates our ability to disagree with knowledge and truth, since the trace is not something one can disagree (or agree) with. As stated above, much like the blood that streams through our veins, memory does not mean, it just is. Yet once the past becomes something that is transmitted to us because of who we are, it both replicates the posthistorical world of the present and redescribes the ideological disagreement between socialism and liberalism that was at the center of the dictatorship in a world in which people were killed because of who they were.

This redescription is undoubtedly historically inaccurate and politically detrimental, especially if we care about the growing economic divide in our neoliberal period. For this reason, the final point of this chapter is to suggest that a cultural critique of neoliberalism today must begin not simply with a radical rejection of neoliberalism, but also with a radical rejection of the discourse of memory, whether its transmission arrives through blood or through the specter, as Nouzeilles and Martín-Cabrera imagine it. Indeed, it is only in relation to history that a transformative politics can take place, since only history transcends blood, family, the community, and the nation itself. The second part of this book attempts to reestablish (and redefine) Latin American aesthetics within this transformative project, an attempt that gestures toward universality and the negation of subject positions and insists on representation, intention, beliefs, and meaning. This attempt begins in the next chapter by dismantling the moral aesthetics of neoliberalism.

PART 2

TOWARD A POLITICS OF THE FRAME

CHAPTER 4

The Reappearance of the Frame

In this chapter, I discuss the aesthetic and political value of a 2005 collection of more than fifty paintings by the Colombian artist Fernando Botero depicting the abuses at Abu Ghraib prison. Introducing the book *Botero: Abu Ghraib* (2006), David Ebony writes, "Certainly, Botero, in his Abu Ghraib series, suggests that anyone with a sense of humanity must realize that fighting terrorist attacks with further acts of cruelty and terror is not the right solution" (18). Like other critics who have discussed the images, Ebony understands these paintings as strategically situated within a human rights discourse about the incriminating Abu Ghraib photos, which Susan Sontag had announced as "a pattern of criminal behavior in open defiance and contempt of international humanitarian conventions" ("Regarding"). Similar to Sontag's comments on the photos, Ebony imagines a sort of unmediated demand ("must realize") in the paintings that prompt this moral response ("fighting terrorist attacks with further acts of cruelty and terror is not the right solution").[1]

Yet, while it is undoubtedly true that Botero's series portrays the torture that occurred in this Iraqi prison, the question that I would like to pose is whether the paintings are reaffirming an aesthetics of human rights or rather pointing to another project that goes beyond it. In the aftermath of what Arthur C. Danto calls the "world event" of Abu Ghraib, the appearance of Botero's *Abu Ghraib* series raises several important ideas not only about human rights but also about the photographs ("Body"): Is there something that Botero's paintings capture that is absent in the photos? What else could these aesthetic depictions say about human rights violations at Abu Ghraib that the photos had not already stated? Does this collection—and its commitment to aesthetic form—suggest perhaps another interpretation that does not fit within the "moral utopia" of human rights (Moyn 214)?

In this chapter I consider these questions from within the field of Latin American cultural studies and in dialogue with a human rights discourse that has been developed in the preceding chapters; more precisely, I argue here that Botero's collection represents a break with the logic of human rights that dominates contemporary Latin Americanist criticism and theory. As we have seen in previous chapters, since the 1970s Latin Americanists have sought to denounce abuses that occurred, especially in the Southern Cone. At the same time, and as I explore in more detail in this chapter, they have also insisted on a type of aesthetic project that seeks to eliminate the division between art and life on behalf of human rights. This desire is perhaps most visible in the emergence of, and the theoretical responses to, the Latin American *testimonio*. Scholarship has treated works such as Elizabeth Burgos's *Me llamo Rigoberta Menchú y así me nació la conciencia* (*I, Rigoberta Menchú: An Indian Woman in Guatemala*; 1983) or Domitila Barrios de Chungara's *Si me permiten hablar . . .* (*Let Me Speak!*; 1977) not only as a means to draw attention to state-sponsored abuses, but also, and more importantly for the argument of this chapter, as a type of indexical "emanation" through which we as readers or viewers come to share the experience—the experience of pain in particular—of those who have suffered these abuses (Barthes, *Camera* 75). By applying Michael Fried's conception of absorption, I suggest, however, that in the aftermath of the "world event" of Abu Ghraib, the commitment to the aesthetic frame in Botero's *Abu Ghraib* paintings signifies a fissure rather than a continuation of this emphasis on human rights in discourses about art in Latin America (Danto). I assert that Botero's series shifts viewers away from the demand of the contemporary postdictatorial narrative, and in so doing, the collection makes available another reading of utopia that moves beyond the discourse of human rights.[2]

Botero's *Abu Ghraib* in Context

From the position of art history, and pictorial depictions of violence in particular, Botero's paintings of the Abu Ghraib prisoners as they are beaten, sexually abused, blindfolded, hooded, bound with ropes, and attacked by dogs do not present a radical break with a school or style. Even within a Hispanic tradition, the collection clearly follows a long genealogy of works representing real-life atrocities, ranging from Francisco Goya's *The Third of May 1808* (1814) and Pablo Picasso's *Guernica* (1937) to José Clemente Orozco's *Man of Fire* (1939) and David Alfaro Siqueiros's *The Torment* of *Cuauhtémoc* (1950). Nor does *Abu Ghraib* represent a departure from Botero's own oeuvre, which includes one series on the Israeli-Palestinian conflict as well as another that examines the violence in Colombia during the 1980s, including depictions of the cocaine kingpin Pablo Escobar. Documenting violence and human rights violations, then, has been as present in Botero's work as his boteromorphs, his puffed-up, exaggerated figures.[3] In this way, if Botero's *Abu Ghraib* is regarded as significant, this is not because it symbolizes a thematic break with either a universal or Latin American pictorial tradition; nor does it represent a rupture in his own career of depicting atrocities.

To frame Botero's *Abu Ghraib* series as simply a question of subject matter, or even within the trajectory of an individual artist, is to miss a striking difference between the pictorial tradition of violence and Botero's collection. This difference has less to do with Botero's own wish to represent Abu Ghraib than with living in a world where technological advances in other media render painting increasingly less relevant as a form for depicting these events. Undeniably, this phenomenon is not new. The emergence of photography in the nineteenth and twentieth centuries has revealed, among other things, that painting as a medium to record events becomes less reliable than photography's indexicality.[4] In contrast to, for example, an eighteenth-century landscape painting depicting unexplored lands, painting today is no longer conceived as a primary form to document, much less to make truth claims beyond the subjective realm.[5]

This irrelevance of painting in relation to documentation has only grown in recent years with the advent of digital cameras and the Internet.[6] And the photos of Abu Ghraib—and the event that it becomes—could not have existed without either the Internet or digital cameras. As Arthur C. Danto keenly notes, these photos constitute a "world event," given the speed with which the images traveled around the globe, creating strong affective responses for many who saw them—a speed and immediacy that no painting could ever achieve. A return to Picasso's *Guernica* serves to highlight the radical shift from painting to photography in recent years. Despite the existence of photos of the Spanish Civil War, few knew of the atrocities that had occurred in this small town in northern Spain until Picasso's painting appeared; the horrors depicted by the photos of Abu Ghraib, on the other hand, have achieved almost immediate universal recognition (and condemnation). In other words, while *Guernica* as an event emerged in spite of photography, Abu Ghraib was born because of it.[7]

But this "world event" is as much about technology as it is about a human rights ideology that has spread across the globe. As we already saw in chapter 1, since the 1970s, human rights have become the primary lens through which we see abuses and understand violence. In comparison to how the photos have been received, Botero's paintings of Abu Ghraib, at best, can be understood as providing a gentle reminder of these human rights abuses. More likely, and again in comparison to the photos, Botero's collection speaks to the growing irrelevance of painting as a medium to inform, much less to impact, our relationship to human rights in any substantive way. Insofar as there is a difference between the photos and the paintings, that difference cannot be reduced to a question of medium alone, just as the similarities between them cannot be reduced to a question of morality alone. Indeed, the force of Botero's *Abu Ghraib* is found not in its repetition but rather in a certain rejection of what the photos already allow.

The Vanishing Frame in the Human Rights World

One can begin to see something like this refusal in Botero's own account of how he first conceptualized the *Abu Ghraib* series. In this narrative, Botero stresses that he was inspired not by the photos but by reading several articles, including Seymour Hersh's *New Yorker* essay, the first major essay that reported on the violations (Juan Carlos Botero 16). Botero's mention of Hersh's essay highlights an idea or fantasy not only to create an image from one that was not there but also to produce a distance from the photos that could be found everywhere. One also sees this distancing in the *Abu Ghraib* collection's complete absence of references to iconic photos such as the hooded man, Sabrina Harman's smile, or even Lynndie England holding a leash.[8] In fact, the perpetrators, who are present in most of the iconic photos, smiling and posing, are almost nonexistent in the paintings. Instead, the paintings illustrate prisoners who are agonizingly by themselves, suffering in dark corridors, confined to their cells and to their own immediate pain. Moreover, the representational figures are painted in rich tones, saturated yellows and reds that intensify the mass presence of these rotund bodies in pain. As several critics have suggested, Botero's *Abu Ghraib* brings to mind Baroque representations of Christian martyrdom.[9] Yet this gesture toward the Baroque in Botero's series has less to do with a theme or style than with a certain exaggeration of aesthetic form that was vital to the Baroque; that is, the commitment to the amplified figurative representation registers an important aesthetic difference from the grainy realism of the photos. The idea here is that Botero's series attempts neither to create another version of the photos nor to reproduce the pain that the photos make evident. Instead, the idea is that *Abu Ghraib* sets out to create a space in which Abu Ghraib can exist without the photos. That is, the distance between the photos and these representations functions to assert a space for aesthetic form.

A closer look at the composition of these paintings reaffirms this investment in aesthetic form in relation to the photos. In Botero's *Abu Ghraib*, one is immediately struck by the absence of perpetrators as well as by the prisoners who never look outward toward the beholder. Unlike, for example, the iconic photo of Harman's smile, Botero's figures either are looking off to the side, are blindfolded, or have their bare backs facing the viewer. These figures deliberately turn away from the beholder, denying not only the beholder's presence, but also whatever reaction he or she may be experiencing. This disregard for the beholder is doubled by other techniques that are internal to the paintings, techniques that not only point inward toward the lives of these representational subjects but also produce a sort of spatial fissure between these figures and the beholder. For instance, in *Abu Ghraib 56*, one sees two prisoners who are blindfolded and turned away from the beholder, facing each other, one looking upward toward the sky, perhaps praying, while the other prisoner is forced to look downward as a blue-gloved hand of a military policeman pushes him forward. Prison bars, noticeably, are placed between the prisoners and the beholder, which, as the critic and artist Juan Carlos Botero notes, creates "a sort of distance, a visual barrier between the viewer and the brutality of the scene" (20). *Abu Ghraib 65* presents another version of this distance between the beholder and the figures in the paintings by adding a perspectival movement toward a vanishing point. Here, a hooded prisoner stands in a long corridor, hands tied behind his back and ankles shackled; his naked body is turned away from the viewer and toward the end of the corridor, where a barred window lets in some light. The painting directs the beholder first to his body and then farther toward the end of the corridor, away from the beholder's position as viewer, away from whatever experience he or she may feel.

What these prisoners—who are utterly absorbed in their own pain—reveal, and what these visual barriers reconfirm, is less a physical or emotional distance than a conceptual distance that reinforces a space for the work of art. Indeed, these figures, who turn figuratively from the photos and literally from the beholders, serve to better delineate and define the aesthetic proper. We might say, therefore, that Botero's *Abu Ghraib* finds its theoretical equivalent in what Michael Fried has called absorption. In his 1980 book *Absorption and Theatricality*, Fried examines a period of French painting and criticism that centers on the work of Denis Diderot and how this shift away from the beholder came to be a primary concern for painters. Fried describes absorption as paintings that "treated the beholder as if he were not there" (5). For Fried, absorption, of course, does not signify that the artist does not paint with the beholder in mind, but rather, it provides the most effective account of art as a "supreme fiction," requiring an "absolutely perspicuous mode of pictorial unity" (103). Here, the "supreme fiction" and "unity" of art reflect a commitment not to a certain genre or style, but rather to marking an autonomous aesthetic space that lives outside the beholder and his experience. That is, absorption offers the clearest theoretical conception of the creation of aesthetic form. In this way, the importance of the absorbed figures in Botero's *Abu Ghraib* is found not only in the series' refusal to depict the iconic photos, which have triggered strong affective responses in beholders, but also in the reassertion of the series's status as art that renders the beholder and his experience—political or otherwise—irrelevant.[10] This leaves open the question of whether Botero's *Abu Ghraib* is less invested in presenting a political testimony that denounces "a pattern of criminal behavior in open defiance and contempt of international humanitarian conventions" than in asserting a space of aesthetic form that may in fact come at the expense of these politics (Sontag "Regarding").

As the title of Fried's book makes clear, absorption intersects with the idea of theatricality, a type of painting that openly acknowledges but also demands the absolute presence of the beholder and his lived position. Theatricality, according to Fried, becomes central to minimalist work beginning in the 1960s, but it also becomes central, as I want to suggest here, to works depicting torture in the more recent human rights era. In fact, unlike Botero's absorptive project, many recent paintings depicting torture are theatrical, including Leon Golub's *Interrogation II* (1981), which illustrates two mercenaries smiling at the beholder while they torture a person sitting in a chair. Botero's collection is also quite different from other artistic projects that relate to Abu Ghraib, such as Gerald Laing's *American Gothic* (2004), which uses the backdrop of Grant Wood's painting and replaces the farmers with the American MPs Lynndie England and Charles Graner. With their thumbs up, both look directly and triumphantly at the beholder. Graner smirks and England smiles, while right below them lies a human pyramid of naked Iraqi prisoners.

These recent theatrical works make the beholder structurally essential to the composition, for they not only look at but also attempt to interpellate the viewer. To return to the critic Juan Carlos Botero, these theatrical works demand that "there is no space between us and the victim, since we share the same visual reality. That is to say that we are not only direct witnesses to this barbarity, we are also included within it, whether we like it or not, and thus we participate in the horror" (20).[11] Juan Carlos Botero's observation is important because it highlights a crucial theoretical point, which is that the beholder is transformed into a subject that must be conceptually and morally included in the event. It is not just the connection that the beholder maintains with the "horror," but that the beholder ceases to be a beholder and instead is transformed into a "direct witness" who "participate[s]" in the event "whether we like it or not" (20).

This conceptual and moral demand marks a difference from a certain negation of the viewer in *Pedro y el Capitán* when Benedetti declares that he did not want to directly represent torture in theater because it would overwhelm the public: "[Torture's] aggression is felt too directly, and this makes it difficult for the spectator to keep a needed distance. If the torture is there only indirectly, however, as an evil yet unseen presence, then the audience is able to be more objective, and if what we are judging is the degradation of a human being, objectivity is essential" (xiii–xiv). Instead, Juan Carlos Botero's claim is more in line with the political and aesthetic objective of *Death and the Maiden*, an objective that becomes most evident in the last scene of Dorfman's play. As seen in chapter 2, Dorfman's play concludes with an open ending as to whether Dr. Roberto Miranda had tortured Paulina Escobar. But it also limits the question of justice (in my reading) to one of remembering or forgetting this disabled body. In the last scene, as indicated in the stage notes, a mirror descends on the stage and is placed right in front of the audience, thus reflecting back the presence of the people in theater. From the position of a human rights aesthetics, this metafictional device in the play is deployed not only to demand our presence but also to turn us into "direct witness[es]" of "the horror" (Juan Carlos Botero 20).

Metafiction is discussed further in chapter 6, as it also seeks to destabilize the division between what is onstage (the play) and what is offstage (the audience). For now, however, it should be noted that this new status of the beholder as a "direct witness" also alerts us to another important idea about theatricality: the desire to alter the status of the work of art. Indeed, according to Juan Carlos Botero, what the "direct witness" sees is no longer described as art but as "horror" (20). Fried, in a related context, suggests that this commitment to the primacy of the beholder's presence and experience is, at the same time, the "negation of art" ("Art" 153), since structurally there is no longer a distinction between art and the beholder. Rather than art, there is a "situation"—one that, by definition, *must include the beholder* ("Art" 153). In short, these theatrical works on torture seek to eliminate their status as art in order to immerse the witness in the politics of the event. But if these antiabsorptive works reveal that the status of art comes at the expense of the beholder's experience, Botero's *Abu Ghraib*'s investment in aesthetic form, and absorption in particular, signals the complete rejection of the idea of the beholder, who, "whether we like it or not [. . .] participate[s]" in this "horror" (Juan Carlos Botero 20). And this commitment to aesthetic form represents not only a distance from the photos and the theatrical paintings but also, and more importantly for this chapter, a break with a Latin American human rights project that has sought both to eliminate aesthetic unity and to force the beholder to "participate" (20) in the discourse of human rights. Latin American scholarship has insisted on imagining a world in which the beholder is a "direct witness" who must envision all injustices through the lens of human rights.

The Fantasy of the *Testimonio*: In Context

I started this chapter by noting that for Ebony, the significance of Botero's *Abu Ghraib* series is located in its ability to document and to make us morally aware of these human rights violations: "Botero, in his Abu Ghraib series, suggests that anyone with a sense of humanity must realize that fighting terrorist attacks with further acts of cruelty and terror is not the right solution" (18). Francine Masiello has extended this human rights project beyond the context of the United States, arguing that the paintings also draw awareness to violations in Botero's own Latin America. In particular, she contends that the collection speaks to the torture and disappearances that have taken place during the years of state-sponsored terrorism in countries such as Mexico, Argentina, and Chile. For Masiello, Botero's paintings represent a "comprehensible and earnest offshoot of [this] ethical expression" ("Art" 14), and thus work within a larger framework of Latin American cultural production that has dedicated itself to remembering the countless human rights violations that occurred during the 1970s, 1980s, and 1990s in these and other Latin American countries. Yet Botero's absorptive project, against Masiello and Ebony, problematizes this "ethical" approach to Latin American theory and criticism.

While Botero's *Abu Ghraib* insists on a distance between aesthetic form and the beholder—that is, a space between art and life—Latin American human rights scholarship has sought to eliminate this space and to imagine this elimination as crucial to critical projects mobilized on behalf of human rights. As explored in previous chapters, these projects take on various genres and forms, including documentaries, fiction films, plays, and novels that raise awareness and denounce the state's inability to protect its citizens from these violations.[12] Perhaps the genre that has framed itself as the most politically adept in carrying out this objective is the Latin American *testimonio*. The *testimonio* has been described as the Latin American form par excellence and was considered by the academic Left in the 1980s and 1990s as exemplary of a "poetics of solidarity," as "resistance literature," and as a project that promoted "international human rights and solidarity" (Moreiras, *Exhaustion* 217; Harlow 28; Beverley, "Margin" 37).

The force and the fantasy of the *testimonio* is that it is imagined as a type of writing that not only reports but also bears witness, much like (the fantasy of) the photos of Abu Ghraib, to these abuses that are taking place throughout Latin America. This is why George Yúdice defines the *testimonio* as "an authentic narrative, told by a witness who is moved to narrate by the urgency of a situation (e.g., war, oppression, revolution, etc.). Emphasizing popular, oral discourse, the witness portrays his or her own experience as an agent (rather than a representative) of a collective memory and identity" (44). The question of authenticity is linked to identitarian claims, and as was explored in the last chapter, identity becomes particularly relevant during the 1980s and 1990s in Latin American cultural production. This point no doubt is visible in Gareth Williams's work on the *testimonio* when he correctly notes that in this genre "the discursive reconfiguration of personal and collective experience" becomes "the very basis of cultural resistance and survival" ("Translation" 97).[13] Building on Williams's work, Moreiras has argued that the "identity-politics dimension of testimonio grows immensely during the 1980s and 1990s, and that such an identitarian dimension is dominant today in testimonio's cultural capital" (*Exhaustion* 317). These identitarian claims are partially sustained by the idea that the *testimonio* is written by (or in collaboration with) an "authentic" subaltern. At the same time, this claim that the *testimonio* is an authentic narrative is meant to safeguard the genre from a possible accusation of manipulation or embellishment that is leveled at a professional author. In short, unlike a writer or a journalist, a subaltern does not represent but rather authentically relays his or her experience.

Indeed, for many critics, the fantasy is that the *testimonio* does not actually represent. According to Beverley, conventional literary form—and representation more generally—is linked not only to "bourgeois writing since the Renaissance" but also to authoritarianism in the dictatorship and neoliberal consensus in postdictatorship ("Margin" 35).[14] Or as per Richard's critique of representation in chapter 2, what is wrong with representation is that it is symptomatic of an epistemic mode that endorses a logic in which truth, belief, meaning, intention, and interpretation are intimately connected to modernization and capitalist production. Importantly, then, the *testimonio* is understood in opposition to representation. For Beverley, the *testimonio* "constitutes itself as a new form" and "implies a radical break" with literature and the literary ("Margin" 40, 42). Or, to return to Yúdice: "The [*testimonio*] speaker does not speak for or represent a community but rather performs an act of identity-formation" (42). The performative aspect of the *testimonio* marks a difference from documentaries, novels, or plays that can only represent (and denounce) but can never demand or produce the *testimonio*'s "truth effect" (Beverley, "Margin" 33). Even though, for example, a play and a *testimonio* may share the same objective, they will nevertheless produce different political responses. That is, a play that condemns human rights violations is imagined more as representing human rights violations and thus draws us away from the reality that produces these violations. The *testimonio*, on the contrary, is less a representation, so it brings us into the world of these violations, closer to witnessing them, closer to the victim's pain.[15]

What this "authentic narrative" is, or what Yúdice (and Beverley) want to imagine, is that the *testimonio* is something like a window into the events that are taking place, something like a camera, whose indexicality disallows the photo to be manipulated, doctored, or staged. It is worth recalling that indexicality, as Charles Sanders Peirce suggested in the *Collected Papers*, concerns photography insofar as photos do not simply represent the object but also maintain a direct causal link to the object. The photos—unlike, say, a painting—are physically or causally linked to their referents in the same way that smoke from a roof is an indexical sign of a fire. And like the insistence on indexicality in photos, the *testimonio* is meant to function as a repudiation of the author's intent, since it, like the camera, captures something despite what either the photographer or the *testimonio* writer intends. This is part of the reason why Beverley believes that the *testimonio* evacuates the "author" and "authorial intention" that has been "bound up" in the literary ("Margin" 35).

This point might seem paradoxical, especially when considering how important the subaltern speaker is to the *testimonio*. Consider, for example, *Me llamo Rigoberta Menchú y así me nació la conciencia*, which puts the subaltern figure Rigoberta Menchú at its center as it communicates the events that were taking place in Guatemala in the late 1970s and early 1980s. What *testimonio* criticism wants to imagine, however, is Menchú less as an agent who intends to represent these abuses than as a witness whose *testimonio* captures these events (regardless of her intention). That is, the *testimonio*, like the camera, testifies to her presence, to her pain, to "the urgency of a situation" that crafting a poem, article, or novel would delay, if not impede (Yúdice 44). I return to intentionality in chapter 5, but here it should be recognized that the indexical nature gives rise to a critique of intentionality and allows for the fantasy that the *testimonio* does not represent but is an unmediated opening into an event. The immediacy that *testimonio* critics wish to imagine is constitutive of indexicality, since the reader no longer has to be bothered by questions of interpretation (or doctoring, manipulation, etc.). From this perspective, the photos of Abu Ghraib that emerged in 2004 and quickly spread across the globe become something like the theoretical realization of the political and aesthetic fantasy of what the Latin American *testimonio* always wanted to be, just as Botero's *Abu Ghraib*, as I argue below, becomes a kind of repudiation of this fantasy.[16]

After Interpretation; or, "People feel it [. . .] they feel it"

As I stated previously, Botero's *Abu Ghraib*, particularly the absorbed figures, reveals a commitment to the aesthetic proper and to the irrelevance of the beholder and his or her experience. One can see that absorption within painting (at least since Diderot) allegorizes a certain relationship between art and the beholder. On the one hand, against Juan Carlos Botero's claim that "whether we like it or not [. . .] we participate in the horror" (20), absorption insists on a space for the beholder to interpret the object as artwork—that is, insists on a space from which interpretation can take place—rather than as a sense of "horror" that one must experience. On the other, absorption turns away from the beholder, since, unlike the *testimonio*, the meaning of the object is not constitutive of the beholder's presence or experience. That is, the meaning of the painting is found within the frame, and not within the beholder or a "situation—one that by definition *includes the beholder*" (Fried, "Art" 153). This "negation of art" thus underscores that the beholder is experiencing rather than interpreting an aesthetic object (Fried, "Art" 153). In this way, if the commitment to absorption is a commitment to aesthetic interpretation, the gesture of turning art into "horror" is also a gesture of eliminating a space of interpretation and replacing it with a sense of one's experience. In other words, and returning to the Latin American context, the *testimonio* attacks aesthetic unity as well as imagines that politics begin once the divide between art and life is overcome. *Testimonio* critics thus insist that art be reinscribed as a situation—as a situation of pain in particular—that is witnessed and felt rather than communicated or understood.

From the vantage point of testimonial writing, experience becomes a way of resisting and contesting power that attempts to impose a "truth," representation, and official history on its citizenry. As such, the political relevance of the *testimonio* is located not in producing truth or representation, but rather in transmitting a "truth effect" (Beverley, "Margin" 33) or "an encounter with the Real" (Lacan, qtd. in Beverley, "Real" 70). As posed above, it is the indexical nature—rather than the representation—of the "authentic" subaltern's experience that brings the *testimonio* one step closer to triggering what Beverley calls an "ethical and political response" in the beholder ("Margin" 31). The *testimonio*, accordingly, is concerned more with making the beholder experience the pain of the subaltern than with providing a space for the beholder to interpret a representation of that pain.

Interpretation, of course, is constitutive of beliefs that the beholder has about the meaning of text (whether the meaning is right or wrong). The importance of the *testimonio*, however, is not found in the beholder's beliefs about the meaning of the text, since beliefs, for these critics, are intrinsic to an epistemic mode connected to the market. Instead, beliefs—about what the text means—stand in the way of how the text makes us feel. That is, the ethical importance of this "new form" is related not to the beholder's interpretation and understanding of the literary work but rather to his or her response or a demand as such. What makes this form politically significant is a theoretical turn away from the meaning of the text and a turn toward how the "horror" (Juan Carlos Botero 20) affects the viewer. Or, like the recent paintings of torture and the Abu Ghraib photos, the *testimonio*, according to this theatrical account, insists on the presence of the beholder and on the elimination of a space of representation.

To the extent that theatricality has become integral to the way *testimonio* critics—and Latin Americanists more generally—approach politics and ethical responses to atrocities, it should come as no surprise that it is also essential to a host of critics who have written about Botero's collection as part of a human rights project. One can return, for example, to Masiello, who declares that the political power of Botero's *Abu Ghraib* lies in the fact that "we feel the substance. We are here in a sensate world that demands us to be awakened. [The paintings] work with the senses, then, as a way toward political awakening" ("Art" 17). In much the same way as Masiello, Thomas Laqueur articulates this "political awakening" vis-à-vis affect: "Images of suffering and violence constitute a claim [. . .] to be regarded, to be noticed, to be seen as images of someone to whom one has ethical obligations" ("Botero" 8). And Botero himself has argued that what distinguishes his paintings from the photos is the "concentration of energy, of emotion that goes into a painting [. . .] people feel it [. . .] they feel it" (qtd. in Laqueur, "Botero" 8). What all these claims insist on is not representation per se, but rather the materiality of objects (e.g., "feel the substance," "concentration of energy") as a way of "demand[ing]" or "constitut[ing] a claim" on the beholder. More specifically, these accounts highlight that an "ethical obligation" is triggered more by what the materiality makes the viewer feel than by the aesthetic world that Botero's *Abu Ghraib* portrays ("Botero" 8). In brief, the aesthetic frame, according to this logic, must be overcome in order to feel the real political force of Botero's series.[17]

But where the logic of human rights wants to negate art and representation, Botero's *Abu Ghraib* insists that it can only be art and representation. Indeed, in the face of contemporary Latin American human rights projects, Botero's collection rests on its clear absorptive commitment to aesthetic form and interpretation. That is, absorption represents a break from a type of theatrical project found not only in more recent paintings on torture but also, and more importantly for this chapter, in the *testimonio* that radically invokes the beholder, demanding an "ethical obligation" (Laqueur, "Botero" 8) or an "ethical response" (Beverley, "Margin" 31) from him or her. Thus, Botero's *Abu Ghraib* is significant not because it "constitutes a claim" ("Botero" 8) but because, in an important way, it demands nothing from us. And it is precisely here that Botero's paintings present the most dramatic departure from recent Latin American human rights art and criticism. While Botero's paintings attempt to treat the viewers' reaction—and even the viewers themselves—as a matter of indifference, Latin American theory and criticism has set out both to invoke and to make viewers complicit with this human rights world, a world in which, as Juan Carlos Botero reminds us, we must "participate" (20).

In this sense, Botero's paintings are breaking with the theatricality that a human rights orientation demands of art. If what counts for Latin American critics is "how things present themselves to us" (Beasley-Murray, *Post-hegemony* 205), the collection instead signals a project that rejects our presence; that is, for the series to do its political work, we and our experience must be considered irrelevant. I want to be clear that the idea here is not to negate the subject matter: Botero's paintings clearly depict torture and abuses. Nevertheless, what I want to highlight in this chapter is how the integrity of "pictorial unity" and the irrelevance of the beholder signal an important break with a tendency that has dominated human rights aesthetic projects: namely, the primacy of the beholder and his experience (Fried, *Absorption* 103). In the next section I argue that Botero's insistence on the aesthetic—vis-à-vis contemporary Latin American cultural output—not only represents a certain move away from predominant human rights theoretical work in Latin America but also points to a political project that goes beyond this human rights world—a project that shifts from the complicity of human rights to interpretation, beliefs, and an anticapitalist reading of Botero's *Abu Ghraib*.

The "Last Utopia" of Human Rights

Insofar as the Abu Ghraib photos as a "world event" draw awareness to human rights violations, the ideology of human rights is the primary lens through which we see not only the photos but also the world. In short, we now live in a world where the "moral utopia" of human rights has transformed itself into the primary ideology through which we articulate our politics (Moyn 214). Samuel Moyn argues that human rights are the "last utopia" (4), since they have outlasted all other political ideologies, including communism. For Moyn, the aim of human rights is to protect the rights of the individual against the state. Undoubtedly, this objective departs from Cold War politics, which centers on an ideological disagreement between communism and liberalism. In this sense, the 1970s mark a watershed moment for human rights, since this Cold War disagreement begins to come apart, and what counts is no longer whether we believe socialism or liberalism is right or wrong but whether our beliefs are respected or not, regardless of what they are; beliefs are treated as a function of who we are and what we feel. What becomes central in this "moral utopia" is not the meaning of our beliefs but rather that these beliefs are innately ours. In this way, bereft of their political antagonism, beliefs are now conceived primarily as affective signs of human life that, like speech, race, and language, should be valued and respected.

As I have shown, the best example of this disarticulation of beliefs in Latin America is established in the very exercise of recuperating the memories of human rights abuses in *testimonios*, novels, and films, rather than in understanding the geopolitical events that brought about the events. From the perspective of a progressive politics, when remembering the period of the 1970s and 1980s, as Masiello clearly attempts to do with her reading of Botero's *Abu Ghraib*, what becomes paramount are questions about the abuses and violations brought about by the state and not the political beliefs that create the conflicts in the first place, namely, the ideological disagreement between liberalism and communism. As we saw in chapter 1, during the 1960s and early 1970s, communism was envisioned chiefly as a project to eradicate class inequality and the system that sustained it. But where the Left in the 1960s and 1970s wanted to eliminate the capitalist state that produced inequality, the Left in power today wants to remember the past as a moment in which life, citizenship, and human rights were violated. And as noted in the last chapter, this point reveals that the investment in memory today revolves around remembering these human rights abuses and not an anticapitalist project that had little to do with protecting individuals from state abuses.

The absence of an anticapitalist Left and its replacement with a human rights Left is felt everywhere, as the neoliberal policies of the last thirty years have only increased the level of economic inequality throughout Latin America. Although it is significant that the rise of the Left was partly a response to the 2000 debt crisis (and the devastating neoliberal policies that led up to it), since coming to power, the Left has done very little to alter the neoliberal policies that were first put in place by the Right, policies that have produced the highest levels of inequality anywhere in the world. To be sure, while it is true that in the last two decades human rights justice regarding punishing perpetrators has improved, and while it is also true that the Left does a better job of treating the poor as fellow citizens and representing them within the national imaginary, the objective of the Left in the 1960s and 1970s was not to respect or even do a better job of representing the poor but rather to eliminate the conditions that created the poor in the first place, that is, to eliminate the system that produced poverty. Today, the Left's commitment to the poor under a human rights umbrella involves not eradicating poverty but treating it primarily as part of a discriminatory practice that limits democracy. The problem with poverty, according to this logic, is that it unfairly prohibits full participation in the benefits of living in a liberal society (see chapter 2).[18]

At the same time, the main attack leveled at the Right by the Left today is that it continues unjust practices against not only victims of past human rights abuses but also the poor, women, indigenous peoples, and other groups. The principal accomplishment of the Left, and the success of the so-called leftist turn, is understood primarily through the lens of tolerance, respect, and the growing diversity and stability of Latin American democracy.[19] What is lost in this vision, of course, is that the Left and the Right now endorse the same system that continues to produce economic inequality. That is, while the Left seeks to unite people under the banner of human rights, it does so by ignoring the economic gap that continues to divide the rich and the poor. From this position, human rights as a dominant form of leftist politics have become the key technology through which the Left masks its complete capitulation to neoliberal orthodoxy in Latin America. Far from producing an alternative to capitalism, the Left today now endorses the capitalist system and the capitalist state that they, in their most radical form, once sought to destroy. Or to make the claim more forcefully still, the Left today—through their emphasis on human rights as the "last utopia"—has successfully, and perhaps paradoxically, concluded the emancipatory project that the military dictatorship first set out to destroy in the 1970s (Moyn 4).

Aesthetic criticism, as seen already, is also imagined as a means to emphasize the commitment to human rights; in fact, it demands it. Within the predominant form of Latin American criticism and theory today, the theoretical concern focuses not only on denouncing abuses but also on imagining that one's experience is somehow intrinsic to this project. In her seminal book *Tiempo pasado*, Beatriz Sarlo argues a similar point about the *testimonio*, a form whose first-person narrative makes it exceedingly difficult to imagine a way of critiquing the narrator's experience. While Sarlo believes that producing an experience over an interpretation is limited to the *testimonio*, it is also integral to the neo-avant-garde (see chapter 5). Indeed, the way one approaches art is centered no longer on disagreement—I believe that Botero's *Abu Ghraib* is a critique of human rights, but you disagree—but rather on a question of how viewers respond to the text through their different experiences and affective responses—I experience pain, but you do not. Here, there is no disagreement, we are just experiencing different emotions; and, of course, experiencing these different emotions is chiefly viewed through the viewers' interests and identities rather than beliefs about what the text means, which are imagined as right or wrong, regardless of who the viewer is and what he or she feels. The utopia of human rights, in other words, insists on turning antagonistic beliefs about the meaning of the text into experiences that inform the viewer's subject positions.

Insofar as human rights are the dominant discourse today—that is, that what counts is that the victim's experience is our own—they became so by imagining that beliefs about the meaning of a text are secondary to feeling the pain of the other. This evacuation of beliefs by the critics discussed in this chapter both situates Botero's paintings exclusively within the discourse of human rights and envisions past anticapitalist projects in Latin America as if they were Abu Ghraib. This ideology—the "moral utopia" of human rights—keeps us from talking about the world in different ways and keeps us thinking up new technologies to imagine human rights as the only project for the Left that counts. As a result, the mobilization of human rights is perhaps the most persuasive discursive strategy within cultural criticism through which the Left comes not only to forget its commitment to class equality, but also, and importantly, to endorse neoliberalism today.

Nevertheless, if one reads the human rights project in this way, that representations of violence in Latin America are meant to make the beholder complicit in human rights politics rather than open to interpretation, then Botero's paintings, in their insistence on absorption and aesthetic form, can be considered a crucial intervention within Latin American art and criticism. My point is not that this aesthetic world prevents us from sympathizing with the figures or even identifying with the pain of those who were tortured. Nor does it prevent us from understanding that feelings are fundamental to the paintings. Rather, the paintings' insistence on interpretation rather than experience highlights that Botero's series, as artwork, is not reducible to the beholder's experience of it. In brief, insofar as the paintings make evident that the experience of the object cannot be the experience of the subject, they assert a space for interpretation as well as a theoretical possibility of thinking outside the world of human rights.

In a contemporary moment when antagonistic political and aesthetic beliefs are seen increasingly as less relevant, Botero's *Abu Ghraib* makes visible a structural position in which beliefs are considered paramount. To be sure, the argument of this chapter has not been to suggest that Botero rejects human rights or that he intentionally rejects the market (despite the fact that he refuses to sell any of the pieces in the *Abu Ghraib* series. We are talking, after all, about an artist whose commercial fame outside of Latin America can only be matched by that of Isabel Allende). Rather, the idea is that the aesthetic (creating a space for the aesthetic proper) rather than experience (eliminating a space between the art and the beholder) provides a theoretical position from which the viewer can move away from human rights immediacy and complicity. That is, in the face of human rights theatricality—emblematic of the *testimonio*—Botero's *Abu Ghraib* series asserts a position in which beliefs, interpretation, and representation are still understood as crucial.

Thus, Botero's series, perhaps unexpectedly, reveals the importance of the aesthetic today, as a space where human rights ideology is not simply made visible but also contested as a project that endorses present-day neoliberal policies. Botero's *Abu Ghraib*, and the assertion of the frame more generally, provides an opening that allows us to think beyond the limits of the last utopia of human rights and the supremacy of neoliberalism; indeed, it allows us to understand that human rights are the morality of neoliberalism. The next two chapters move past this political morality and begin to untangle the question of art and the market. These chapters are framed around the end of the postdictatorship and the various artists who both inform and reflect this end.

CHAPTER 5

Anti-intentionalism and the Neoliberal Left

Where does the frame take place.
DERRIDA, *THE TRUTH IN PAINTING*

An Aesthetic Problem

In Roberto Bolaño's *Estrella distante* (*Distant Star*; 1996), the ex-detective Abel Romero asks Arturo B. to help him find Carlos Wieder, the fascist lieutenant, avant-garde poet, and serial killer who, having disappeared from Chile sometime during the mid-1970s, is now believed to be living in Spain. Romero's reasoning is that Arturo, who is also a poet, can guide him "by advising me on poetic matters," since, according to the detective, "to find a poet, he needed the help of another poet" (117). Although Arturo fundamentally believes that "Carlos Wieder was a criminal, not a poet" (117), he agrees to help Romero and sets out, much like an investigator, to track down Wieder by searching through literary magazines, zines, and films until he finally identifies the killer (126). Yet, if Arturo helps the detective find the criminal, one might ask what it means to read these works not simply as evidence but as poetry—to think of Wieder, in other words, as not only a criminal but also, as Romero himself insists, a poet. No doubt there is a long history of works that draw an analogy between the detective and the reader, between the text and evidence, as is the case with Edgar Allan Poe's "The Purloined Letter." Indeed, this analogy has underwritten a good deal of the genre of detective fiction since at least the late nineteenth century.[1] In fact, Bolaño's decision to turn to this genre is largely motivated by a concern with the question of what makes interpretation possible and—perhaps more importantly—with what makes a piece of writing, a film, or a photograph something more than evidence; that is, what makes each of these a work of art?

In this way, Bolaño's interest in detective fiction also takes up concerns that have proven to be central to the development of Latin American theory and criticism, in particular, to the emergence of postmodern theory in the late 1970s as the dominant form of cultural analysis. To be sure, postmodern theory assumes a more political valence in Latin America, as it develops within a context marked by the realities of state-sponsored terror, repression, and market deregulation. As Avelar notes, "Latin American postmodernity is postdictatorial—that is, the continent's transition to a postmodern horizon is carried out by the dictatorships—because the old populist or liberal states could not usher in the new phase of capital, because they were global capital's prospective victims themselves" (*Untimely* 79). More specifically, the postmodernism debate in Latin America has revolved around discourses such as uneven modernity, hybridity, center versus periphery, subalternity, and human rights as well as authoritarian rule.[2] One tendency largely ignored—because it has generally been dismissed as a fallacy—in this debate is the postmodern scrutiny of "conventional literary scaffolding such as authorship" and the autonomy of the work of art (Schwarz, "National" 269). In the last chapter I focused on the *testimonio* as one project that attempted to do away with aesthetic form, and with autonomy more specifically; in this chapter I extend the argument to talk about another project, the neo-avant-garde movement Colectivo Acciones de Arte (CADA) in Chile.[3] Although scholars have envisioned these two projects (the *testimonio* and CADA) as aesthetically and ideologically opposed to one another, I suggest here that both have been underwritten in large part by a broader attempt to destabilize aesthetic autonomy and intentionalism as a means to democratization in the dictatorships and an opposition to neoliberal policies that have flourished in the postdictatorship.[4] In other words, within the context of Latin American cultural production, dismantling aesthetic autonomy and anti-intentionalism becomes a political position, a site of mobilization and intervention directed against capitalist ideology and state-sponsored terror. Does *Estrella distante*, however, subscribe to this attack on art and autonomy as a form of resistance to capitalist ideology and authoritarian rule? What might Bolaño's text tell the reader about the status of postdictatorial critical thought in Latin America today?

I make the case that *Estrella distante* marks a break with postdictatorial critical thought's commitment to heteronomy and insists instead on a reconsideration of intentionalism and aesthetic autonomy as a leftist project. *Estrella distante* is a detective story about finding a killer, but it is also a story that makes aesthetic autonomy intrinsic to finding this killer; that is, by allowing Romero to catch Wieder, the narrative requires identifying a space for the aesthetic proper. In so doing, the detective story contests a tendency in Latin American criticism and theory located in theorists such as Nelly Richard and Néstor García Canclini, who are deeply suspicious both of aesthetic autonomy and of interpretation. Their endorsement of heteronomous forms entails a new kind of critical reading that has less to do with interpreting what the text means than feeling the effects of what Alberto Moreiras calls the "singularity of a pain," and Idelber Avelar identifies as "luto," or mourning (*Exhaustion* 237; "Alegoría" 25). Accordingly, in this chapter I take up the ways in which Wieder's "art of the future" challenges postmodernism's critique of aesthetic autonomy and its investment in anti-intentionalism, which increasingly have been imagined as the foundation for a leftist project in Latin America (Bolaño, *Estrella* 84). In brief, I contend that *Estrella distante* considers a return to aesthetic autonomy and intentionalism not simply as a break with postdictatorial logic but also and more importantly as a larger critique of neoliberal politics that reinforces this logic.

The Idea of Aesthetic Form

Estrella distante's interest in aesthetic form becomes apparent when Abel Romero approaches Arturo B. and asks for help locating Wieder, who may be living in Europe and writing under various pseudonyms. Arturo, who now lives in Spain as an unsuccessful poet, had met the killer in Chile in the early 1970s, when Wieder went by the name of Alberto Ruiz-Tagle. Both were students in poetry workshops in Concepción, where, as Arturo points out, Ruiz-Tagle was known less for his poetry than for having "conquered" the women poets in these classes (Bolaño, *Estrella* 12). He also notes that an aura of mystery hovers over Ruiz-Tagle, who seems to be hiding a secret about his identity and his art. After the 1973 coup, his identity and his aesthetic project are revealed, as Arturo witnesses Wieder's first skywriting poem across the skies of Concepción. Wieder soon becomes known as the "aviator poet" throughout Chile and is even celebrated by Pinochet's regime (109).[5] The poet's success, however, comes to an abrupt end following his photography exhibition, where he showcases photos of women he has murdered, including the Garmendia twins, who were members of the same poetry workshops that both Arturo and Wieder attended.

While it is true that Wieder and Arturo share a common history, it is not necessarily his familiarity with Wieder as a man, a fellow Chilean, or a killer that prompts Romero to look for Arturo in the first place. Instead, Romero needs his assistance precisely because Arturo is a poet who can advise him "on poetic matters" (117). Arturo, the first-person narrator of the novel, describes his conversation with Romero in this way:

> But how can I help you? By advising me on poetic matters, he said. This was his reasoning: Wieder was a poet, I was a poet, he was not. To find a poet, he needed the help of another poet. I told him that in my opinion Carlos Wieder was a criminal, not a poet. All right, all right, let's not be intolerant, said Romero. Maybe in Wieder's opinion, or anyone else's you're not a poet, or you're a bad one, and he's the real thing. It all depends on the glass we see through . . . (117)

Romero's reasoning that "Wieder was a poet, I was a poet, he was not. To find a poet, he needed the help of another poet," underscores that the detective approaches him because Arturo and Wieder have something in common (117). What brings Wieder and Arturo together is that they are, first and foremost, poets.

But to the extent that the detective story is about finding a poet, knowing what a poet is seems also central to Romero's attempt to solve this mystery. The amusing exchange between Romero and Arturo shows that for the detective, what makes a poet a poet has little to do with a critique of a "good" or "bad" poet and even less with a rigorous analysis of formal stylistics or of genre (117). Furthermore, even though a good or bad poet "depends on the glass we see through," where one stands does not determine the status of whether Arturo and Wieder are poets and Romero is not (126). What this means, following Romero's reasoning, is that to be a poet has nothing to do with one's subject position (where one stands), much less the value the work takes on because of this position. That is, this reasoning represents a conceptual distance from positionality that has informed postdictatorial projects already discussed. Instead, a poet is someone who writes poetry, a minimum requirement that, despite Arturo's opinion, both Arturo and Wieder fulfill. For Romero, to be a poet entails the structural presence of the poem, and, of course, the inverse is true that without the poem, there is no poet. The primacy of the poem, in this way, is integral to Romero's reasoning of what defines a poet, which is his intention to write poetry.[6] In other words, if a poet is defined by his intention to create poetry, locating the aesthetic object in *Estrella distante* becomes equally important to Romero's efforts to find Wieder and to the development of the detective story more broadly.

If, in this sense, the detective story in Bolaño's novel is inextricable from the effort to locate the aesthetic object, this stems largely from the novel's concern with distinguishing aesthetic and nonaesthetic objects. This is why Arturo repudiates Romero's claim that Wieder is a poet. After Arturo accepts the offer and the detective leaves him a suitcase filled with literary magazines, Arturo sets out to investigate the material until he finally locates "Wieder's presence" (124) in the work of the avant-garde artist Jules Defoe (124). By systematically working through these materials, what becomes clear about Arturo's investigation is how committed he is to approaching this evidence as if it were not a poetic matter but rather something closer to a footprint or a gun left at a crime scene; that is, the close scrutiny paid to the material reveals Arturo's desire to treat Wieder's artwork as if it were *not* an aesthetic object. Thus, by identifying Wieder primarily as a criminal, Arturo seeks to reject Romero's logic and to imagine Wieder's artwork as nonart.

Yet, the fact that Wieder is found and killed serves to show that ultimately Romero is right not only about his hunch ("To find a poet, he needed the help of another poet") but also about his theory of aesthetic form (i.e., the poem is constitutive of the poet's intention; 117). Moreover, against Arturo's notion of nonart, the insistence on aesthetic autonomy gives rise to the entire structure of the novel. Without Romero's commitment to the primacy of the poem, there would be no link between the two poets, and thus the novel would not end with Romero killing Wieder; that is, if these objects were nonart (as Arturo believes), then there would be no reason for Romero to search out Arturo in the first place, nor would Arturo, who is the narrator, be able to tell this particular story of Carlos Wieder. Thus Romero's logic insists on a space for the aesthetic proper. As such, Bolaño's novel is invested not in blurring the lines between art and nonart but rather in marking a difference between the two. In short, in *Estrella distante* one cannot find Wieder without first finding aesthetic form. One cannot find the killer without asserting the author's intent.[7]

This significance of intentionality is on the first page of the novel when Arturo B. and the fictional author discuss the "ghost" of Pierre Menard (1). What the two characters are referring to is Jorge Luis Borges's "Pierre Menard, autor del Quijote" (1939), a short story in which a modernist writer wishes to reproduce several chapters of *Don Quixote* word for word but not by copying it or even composing a different version of the text; rather, he would prefer to "continue being Pierre Menard and arrive at *Don Qui-*

xote through the experiences of Pierre Menard" ("Pierre" 49). At the center of Borges's story, as Jean Franco has suggested, is a reflection on authorial intention, an exploration of whether authorial intention is possible (Franco, *Introduction* 315). Although the story has produced innumerable critical responses, almost all critics today see it precisely as an indictment against intentionalism. For example, Román de la Campa has noted that Borges's story anticipates the postmodern commitment to aesthetic reception and the irrelevancy of the author (88). Yet, as Charles Hatfield has argued, far from an indictment against intentionalism, Pierre Menard presents a clear commitment to the idea that the meaning of the text must be the author's intended meaning:

> The two texts in question in Borges's story are identical, and yet the narrator sees two different texts that mean two different things. This is possible only because the narrator posits two different authors: since the texts are identical, only something external to both the words on the page and the reader's experience could justify thinking that there is a difference between them. This is in part what Borges means when he qualifies a list of Pierre Menard's work that does not include *Don Quixote* as merely a list of his "visible work" [. . .]. In the case of Menard's *Don Quixote*, the work is *invisible*: it cannot be seen when the two texts are put side to side, and it is only because the narrator sees the text and then appeals to something that cannot be seen (in other words, Menard's authorship) that Menard's work can then be recognized and evaluated. If meaning were located in the words themselves, there would be no way to distinguish between Cervantes's "mere rhetorical praise of history" and Menard's "brazenly pragmatic" lines. (58–59)

To be sure, Borges's comparison of these two texts is meant to be ironic, yet the only way theoretically to read this irony is by positing two different authors. It's the assertion of the authors that allows us to understand not only the meaning of this text, but also that these two texts are different despite their similarities. As I discuss below, this commitment to intentionalism will make Bolaño's critique of postdictatorial theories of art visible. For now, however, it is important to recognize that just as Menard's *Don Quixote* looks like Cervantes's *Don Quijote*, the same can also be said about Wieder's art looking strikingly similar to the work of the avant-garde and the neo-avant-garde.

For this reason, critics have tended to approach Bolaño's text as a response to the various avant-garde movements. The reader is alerted to this interest in the avant-garde through Wieder's photography and especially his aerial poetry. Ina Jennerjahn, for example, has noted that Bolaño's text is in dialogue with the historical avant-garde, for aeropainting, or "aeropittura," is a major feature of Italian Futurism during the 1930s and early 1940s.[8] Gareth Williams has instead suggested that the novel is a response to and a critique of the Chilean neo-avant-garde, in particular, to the CADA artist Raúl Zurita's messianic skywriting performance over New York City in 1982.[9] While it is no doubt true that Wieder's aesthetic draws from the avant-garde, the emphasis on the avant-garde tends to overlook the primacy of the aesthetic object that is key to the logic of the detective story. Indeed, the detective story in Bolaño's text is committed to upholding Romero's reasoning that regarding the work of art, what counts is neither the movement nor the genre of Wieder's artwork, but rather that whatever the movement or genre is, it is ultimately determined by the author's intention to create art. To return to Hatfield's point, if we are meant to read Wieder's aerial poetry as a critique of Zurita's aerial poetry (and CADA more generally), this critique only becomes legible vis-à-vis intentionalism. For the detective story, what is important about Wieder's aerial poetry has less to do with reproducing the work of Zurita or critiquing the various avant-gardes than with asserting a space that belongs to the aesthetic proper, a space that has all but vanished in the postdictatorial period.

While the detective story in *Estrella distante* insists on aesthetic autonomy, postdictatorial narratives have sought to destabilize it. This attack on autonomy is at the heart of Nelly Richard's description of Zurita's own aerial poetry, and CADA's work more generally, which, borrowing from Germán Bravo, is "neither poetry, sculpture, painting, architecture, a monument, 'public work,' publicity, nor popular maxim" (Bravo, qtd. in Richard, *Insubordination* 35).[10] Unlike Romero's insistence on aesthetic autonomy, what makes CADA's work valuable, according to Richard, is precisely its inability to be strictly art; that is, its value is found in the attempt to dismantle or blur the lines between art and nonart. More to the point, CADA, and postmodernism more generally, as a critical intervention sees itself as deconstructing essentialist binaries (art versus nonart, truth versus fiction, writing versus speech), including but not limited to the binary between art and life.[11] By identifying language as the epistemological foundation that governs reality, postmodernism eliminates these binaries by transforming them into signifiers, texts, and discourses. In this way, by asserting that everything is a text, not only does the distinction between art and nonart vanish, but the political readings that were once grounded in the aesthetic now move beyond the aesthetic proper. In other words, and as explored in previous chapters, to the extent that the difference between art and nonart disappears, postdictatorial theory locates the political in the tendency to destabilize the literary.

Thus, if postdictatorial criticism is defined by the effort to undermine aesthetic autonomy and to detect the political beyond the literary, it becomes clear that *Estrella distante*'s critique is aimed at something other than the neo-avant-garde or historical avant-garde alone. One can also witness this tendency in forms that have traditionally been considered opposed to the avant-garde, including, or especially, the social realism of the *testimonio*. In *Estrella distante*, the idea of the Latin American *testimonio* emerges most emblematically in the figure of Amalia Maluenda, the Garmendia twins' Mapuche servant who narrowly escapes being killed by Wieder, and who will later testify against him in court. Recalling significant *testimonios*, such as Elizabeth Burgos's *Me llamo Rigoberta Menchú y así me nació la conciencia* (1983), Maluenda's testimony in court is complicated not only by the challenge that speaking Spanish poses but also by the collective trauma she traces back, in part, to the history of a nation and its exploited people. Nevertheless, in *Estrella distante* the *testimonio* is conjured up only to signal its complete exhaustion, entirely devoid of the political euphoria that was once attached to the form. In fact, this novel has little interest in imagining the *testimonio* form, or in realism more broadly, as committed to a leftist project.[12] Romero's insistence on the primacy of aesthetic form challenges the indexical project that informs *testimonio* scholarship as much as it challenges the heteronomous project that informs the neo-avant-garde.

As discussed in the last chapter, the *testimonio* "constitutes itself as a new form" and "implies a radical break" with literature and the literary (Beverley, "Margin" 40, 42). More specifically, the *testimonio* signals the end of literature by overcoming the limits of "bourgeois writing since the Renaissance," as it evacuates the "author" and "authorial intention" that has been "bound up" in the literary ("Margin" 35). In contrast to Romero's insistence on the poet and the poem, the *testimonio* imagines itself as breaking with both the author's intention and aesthetic autonomy precisely by insisting on its indexicality. Indexicality, of course, is as much a claim to reality as it is a rejection of representation. And the commitment to intentionality denies (or at least complicates) the question of reality, since it insists on something outside the direct and immediate link between the object and what Barthes calls its "emanation" (*Camera* 88). Or, stated differently, if the subaltern is central to the *testimonio*, its centrality is connected to his or her authenticity and not to his or her intention to create the *testimonio*.

To link the subaltern to the question of intention is also to imagine the *testimonio* a bit more like Botero's painting and less like an "an authentic narrative, told by a witness" (Yúdice 44). For this reason, Beverley suggests that the author be understood as a subaltern and that the subaltern be understood as breaking with intention. Furthermore, and for this same reason, the *testimonio* is regarded as an "extraliterary or even antiliterary form of discourse" (Beverley, "Margin" 42). What is paramount about this "antiliterary form of discourse" is that it is envisioned as a new object that "functions in a zone of indeterminacy" between antiliterature and a "new, postfictional form of literature" ("Margin" 42; Beverley and Zimmerman 178–179). Like Zurita's aerial poetry, the political value of the *testimonio* appears once autonomy disappears into a postautonomous state.[13] As I show below, as the author and the autonomous object vanish, the relationships between text and reader, between meaning and interpretation, also undergo a radical change. The attack on autonomy in the postmodern period announces a new process of reading that has less to do with attaining a better interpretation of what the text means than with imagining the text as a mechanism through which the pain of the other can now become our own.

From Interpretation to Anti-interpretation

Asserting the primacy of the poet and the poem is crucial not only for Romero and for the detective story but also for Wieder and the creation of his "art of the future" (Bolaño, *Estrella* 84). This becomes clear when, sometime soon after the coup in Chile, Arturo finds himself in jail for what he describes as a trivial reason. While looking at the sky in the prison yard with other inmates, Arturo spots an airplane that looks like a "Rorschach" (29). As the plane sweeps across the clouds, smoke begins to billow out, slowly producing a series of letters in the air. Almost no one in the prison yard recognizes that the smoked-filled words are written in Latin, much less that they inaugurate what Wieder had declared months earlier as a new type of poem that would "revolutionize Chilean poetry" (15). Rather than a poem, Arturo thinks he is observing an "optical illusion" produced by some natural occurrence in which "the letters" are "secreted" by the sky (35). Other inmates have different responses to what they see: one prisoner believes that the "Second World War is returning to Earth," and even Arturo himself considers for a moment that the pilot has gone "mad" and in a "fit of desperation" will "crash into a building or a square in the city" (25, 28). As the plane disappears, leaving hazy traces of what were once "perfectly formed letters of grey-black smoke," Arturo hears someone weeping in the distance (25). What Wieder's first poetic act reveals is that despite the viewers' inability to understand the poem, the poem nevertheless produces a series of responses for those who witness it (28).

Emilio Sauri has suggested that Wieder's first poetic act alerts the reader to the novel's distinction between a poem being "understood" and it being used "to provoke responses (create an effect)" ("A la pinche" 411). More specifically, Wieder's first poetic act announces a difference between interpretation (what the text means) and affective responses (how it makes us feel). Nevertheless, if Wieder's first poetic act provokes a response in the beholder, it does so in part because Wieder's intention is to create an aesthetic object that produces that intended effect, which, undoubtedly, is part of its aesthetic meaning. Said differently, unlike a natural occurrence (e.g., a cloud), the aesthetic object gives rise to an act of interpretation.

A more forceful version of this commitment to creating artwork and interpretation appears in Wieder's photography exhibit. Wieder invites a small group of Chile's elite to the house of one of his acquaintances, explaining that what they will see is "something spectacular" that will "show the world that the new regime and avant-garde art were not at odds" (Bolaño, *Estrella* 77). Little is known about these photos except that Wieder "wanted to surprise the guest" and that "it was visual poetry, experimental, quintessential, art for art's sake—and that everyone would find [it] amusing" (78). At midnight, Wieder announces that it "is time to plunge into the art of the future" (84). The first person to enter the room is Tatiana Von Beck Iraola, who, soon after, exits "pale and shaken" (86). Others also enter the room and are equally disturbed and traumatized by Wieder's photos of the mangled corpses of those he has tortured and killed. As one guest explains, there were "hundreds of photos" that followed "a progression, an argument, a story (literal and allegorical), a plan" (88). The photos produce a type of visceral, collective realization, a rare moment of lucidity, where "our faces were [. . .] like the faces of sleepwalkers or idiots" (89). Wieder's intention to create a type of art that will be a "surprise" for his guests speaks directly to the avant-garde's—and more generally modernism's—aesthetics of defamiliarization (77).[14] Nevertheless, the idea of Wieder's "art of the future"—like the idea of *Estrella distante* more broadly—is not to gesture toward the avant-garde, but rather to insist on the autonomy of the aesthetic object and interpretation (84). More to the point, what is important for the detective story is that Wieder's photos are understood less as evidence, or an event such as a natural occurrence (clouds), than as a poem that is open to aesthetic consideration.

But where Wieder's "art of the future" insists on the poem and its autonomy as something that needs to be interpreted as artwork, postdictatorial criticism wants to erase the lines between art and nonart and to imagine this erasure as an opening into a proliferation of responses— responses that included, of course, the idea that what Wieder produces is not art. Once what counts is one's response (rather than one's interpretation), then the ontological question of the object also becomes irrelevant. Like Arturo, scholars and artists have suggested that the meaning of the work of art lies with its readers or viewers rather than with its author and his intentions, that is, that the meaning is determined by whatever the reader determines the object to be.

This is precisely what Roland Barthes means in his seminal work "The Death of the Author" (1967) when he claims that "it is language which speaks, not the author" ("Death" 143). As we saw above, language here is meant not to stand in for literature but to encompass it, extending to all forms of expression regardless of medium. Barthes's essay, of course, is not simply about the death of the author, since his or her death also gives rise to "the birth of the reader" and its political offspring, the birth of identities in the 1980s and 1990s and, as discussed in the next chapter, the birth of affective bodies in the new millennium ("Death" 143). For the postdictatorship, "the birth of the reader" is imagined as a political project that produces a plurality of subject positions that resist what Derrida called "force" (*Limited* 102) and Barthes calls "capitalist ideology" ("Death" 143).[15] And, at the same time, with his "birth of the reader," Barthes, much like Sontag before him, considers aesthetic autonomy, intentionalism, and "the project of interpretation" to be "largely reactionary" (Sontag, *Against* 4).[16]

In Latin America, "the birth of the reader" has been crucially tied to the *testimonio* and the Chilean neo-avant-garde as forms that highlight the readers' experiences—the experience of pain in particular—that are absent in more conventional forms. Latin American postmodernity, as such, is underwritten by the idea that the pain of others is not represented but felt. From this postmodern position, aesthetic autonomy is seen less as a potential tool in understanding political injustices than as a real obstacle that must be overcome in order to feel these injustices. Or, more simply, what defines this moment is not the importance of the reader as someone who interprets what the text means, but rather imagining textual pain as a mechanism through which we come to construct who we are and what we feel. In other words, the postdictatorial moment is committed to experience. From this postmodern standpoint (a standpoint that I am against in this chapter), Wieder's aerial poetry is important not because Arturo and his fellow inmates understand the meaning of Wieder's artwork; nor is it important because they even consider it art. Rather, it is significant because of the responses that the event provokes regardless of whether it is art. That is, considering the premises of the reader's experience, what is fundamental here has less to do with Wieder's aim to create artwork than with imagining the primacy of the beholder's experience as rendering the distinction between art and nonart irrelevant.

Above, I argued that the political value of CADA is constitutive of its attempt to destabilize aesthetic autonomy, but this political project is also constitutive of the response that this rejection of autonomy produces. This assault, not only on autonomy but also on intention, meanings, reasons, and beliefs, as noted in chapter 2, is clearly evident in Richard's reading of Diamela Eltit's anti-*testimonio* *El padre mío* (1989), a narrative that consists of an incoherent conversation that Eltit—who, like Zurita, was a member of CADA—has with a schizophrenic man. Most of what is found in *El padre mío* makes little sense, which signals, for Richard, a radical break with realism, whose "individual 'I'" and "socialpolitical referent of action" impose their monolithic sense of "social truth" on the reader (*Cultural* 53, 54). In opposition to realism, what gives *El padre mío* its political value, according to Richard, is precisely the heteronomous nature of the schizophrenic man's utterances, which are described as a "hyperbolic parade of false identifications, disconnected references, disintegrating phrases, erratic pronouncements, and crazy interpellations," all of which, in turn, give rise to a "maniacal and obsessive delirium" (*Cultural* 53, 54).

More to the point, *El padre mío* is considered political not because it implies arriving at a better interpretation of what the text means, but rather because it follows a logic that produces "convulsions of sense" that are absent in realism (*Cultural* 17). Richard's reading of Eltit's text points to the primary role experience plays in determining the relationship between the object and the reader or beholder. To be sure, the schizophrenic man's condition ought to be read symptomatically as evidence of the brutality of Pinochet's regime. But the more important point here is not what the readers interpret or what the schizophrenic man's intentions are, but rather that his disability renders illegible any form of intention that might suggest a distinction between art and nonart.[17] Once the difference between art and nonart vanishes, the affective impetus behind *El padre mío* becomes apparent. [18] As Moreiras points out, and recalling the *testimonio*,

Richard's reading emphasizes the "indexical reference to the singularity of a pain beyond any possibility of representation" (*Exhaustion* 237). Indeed, for Moreiras, *El padre mío* finds its political force not in the process of being read, but in its "extraliterary dimension" of making felt the unrepresentable "singularity of a pain" (232, 237).[19]

What is significant about this "extraliterary dimension" is not only that it produces a kind of experiential fantasy (i.e., "convulsions") in readers, but also that it creates an opposition to political consensus and capitalism (Moreiras, *Exhaustion* 232; Richard, *Cultural* 17). More specifically, Richard imagines that an effect, such as pain or grief, presents itself as the most radical form of antagonism toward the market, since it is deemed useless vis-à-vis the market. And this is why she argues that the object of grief is a ruin or a leftover, which is, at the same time, "contrary to neoliberal realities that are technically oriented toward a sole economic capitalization of that which is 'useful'" (*Cultural* 58). Richard, of course, is not the only critic who believes in the incompatibility of emotions and the market. Idelber Avelar, for example, contends that "the value of pure emotion [. . . is] without a doubt an antivalue, since what would define grief is its being withdrawn from any circuit of exchange" (qtd. in *Cultural* 180).[20] According to these theorists, it is only when art starts to be envisioned less as something that one understands and more as "pure emotion" that one feels that a resistance to capitalism becomes possible (25).

As I suggested before, this experiential antagonism to the market is also paramount for the *testimonio*. Since any progressive newspaper, novel, or essay can speak to the relevant social injustices, content contributes little to the political value of the *testimonio*. Most scholars thus see the emphasis placed on this antiliterary text's effects, not its content, as bringing the genre closer to a politics of "international human rights and solidarity movements" (Beverley, "Margin" 37). To be sure, unlike Richard's theory, which values the proliferation of responses, and is clearly a critique of human rights politics, *testimonio* scholarship imagines that the *testimonio* triggers a univocal affective political reaction, or what Beverley himself calls an "ethical and political response" (36).[21] Nevertheless, insofar as this object is defined by the effect it has on readers rather than by the attempt to interpret its meaning, it is the readers' experience—and, more precisely, the pain they feel—that makes Beverley's underlying logic quite similar to Richard's. To put this within the context of *Estrella distante*, the logic of experience imagines the photo exhibit less as art than as an indexical marker to turn the reader into a traumatized witness who cannot help but be pale and shaken by the horrific scenes he or she sees. Experience, in other words, reinscribes Wieder's intention to create a poem that may surprise the reader into an experiential position that renders this intention, and the poem or photo more generally, irrelevant.

But if the experiential position is committed to neither Wieder's intention to create a type of art that shocks its reader nor Romero's insistence on the author's intention to create a poem, it also cannot be committed to Wieder's intention to create an aesthetic object that endorses Pinochet's regime or may even be aligned with Pinochet. Indeed, as signaled above with Hatfield's intentionalist reading of "Pierre Menard," if the meaning of the text is not determined by the author's intended meaning, then, like the schizophrenic man above, the political project that is central to Wieder's work is also rendered invisible. Following this anti-intentionalist logic, what becomes important about Wieder's artwork is not that it represents the symbolic or political consequences of fascism in Chile, but rather that it highlights the various responses one might have (regardless of the object). What this implies for postmodernism, however, is that experience cannot draw a distinction between different types of political or aesthetic texts, since the theoretical impetus of response antedates any question of aesthetics or politics proper. This commitment to the birth of the reader, in other words, eliminates the political difference between Wieder's intention to create a fascist project and Zurita's to create a leftist one, since what divides them is not, like Cervantes's and Menard's *Don Quijote*, the form that looks exactly the same. Once the intended meaning is eliminated, it also renders irrelevant the political meaning that separates them. Or, once the authorial intent vanishes, so does history, even a history, like Zurita's, that seeks to critique capitalism.

But where postmodern theory negates intention and meaning, *Estrella distante* insists on not only Wieder's intention to create artwork but also his intention to create artwork that endorses Pinochet's politics, a politics that can only be accessed by interpreting his artwork rather than feeling the "convulsion" of the event (Richard, *Cultural* 17). At the same time, by asserting the autonomy of Wieder's art, *Estrella distante* challenges postdictatorial theory that imagines experience as oppositional to the supremacy of the market, since it contests the notion that experience could directly lead the beholder to claim a political commitment as his or her own (a political commitment like socialism). In putting the claims of postmodern theory in the hands of a fascist, *Estrella distante* illustrates that the aesthetic and political difference between Wieder's and Zurita's artwork cannot be had without recourse to intentionalism, aesthetic form, and interpretation. In short, Wieder's artwork effectively debunks the theoretical foundation from which much of the postdictatorial aesthetic project has been built. Nevertheless, as I argue below, by insisting on the autonomy of the work of art and the irrelevance of one's experiential position, *Estrella distante* not only distances itself from the human rights projects discussed in the previous chapters, but also begins to make available an aesthetic critique of neoliberal politics.

Reconsidering Autonomy and Interpretation

Estrella distante is a detective story that roughly spans the rise and fall of Pinochet's dictatorship in Chile. But unlike the texts discussed in chapters 2 and 3, *Estrella distante* has less interest in denouncing the authoritarian state than in relocating an aesthetic world in the intersection of Chile's transitional government's "democracy of agreements" and what Moreiras describes as the "planetary dominance of transnational capitalism" (qtd. in Richard, *Cultural* 15; "Afterword" 210). As noted in chapter 3, this dominance is the result of a radical shift in global politics that concludes with the fall of the USSR in 1991. Francis Fukuyama has famously termed this moment as the "end of history," a moment in which democratic liberalism wins and the *conflict* between two antagonistic ideologies—namely, socialism and liberalism—concludes (114). Building on Fukuyama's claims, as also noted, Huntington argues that the "end of history" means that "the fundamental source of conflict in this new world will not be primarily ideological" (Fukuyama 114; Huntington 67). Instead, for Huntington, "The great divisions among humankind and the dominating source of conflict will be cultural" (67). In this new world order, or what Huntington calls the "clash of civilizations," disagreements between ideologies (socialism and liberalism) are now redescribed as differences between nations, ethnicities, groups, interests, and identities (67). Moreover, in this new world, the central question shifts from "'Which side are you on?' and people [can] and [do] choose sides and change sides" to "'What are you?' That is a given that cannot be changed" (Huntington 71). The point here is not necessarily to suggest a change of political actors, but to recognize an epistemological shift in how subjects now approach politics; at the end of history, disagreements about beliefs (socialism and liberalism) are rendered irrelevant and replaced by a question of who we are and what we feel. What counts, in short, is our experiential position. It should, of course, come as no surprise that conservatives like Huntington and Fukuyama see this waning of ideological conflict and the primacy of experience in a positive light, for it entails liberal capitalism's ultimate victory. It should be a bit more puzzling, however, that critics on the Left have also come to celebrate the primacy of experience, since, as Huntington's endorsement makes clear, the commitment to the experience of individuals and groups in no way stands in opposition to the commitment to capitalism; it is, in this sense, a commitment that need not be anticapitalist.

Although Huntington and Fukuyama are primarily concerned with North America in the aftermath of the Cold War, one can observe the inauguration of this process in Chile and in Latin America more broadly beginning in the mid-1970s. Indeed, this neoliberal political project, which redescribes disagreements as differences of experience, has been rendered digestible in part because postdictatorial cultural production both inside and outside of Latin America has been supporting this project for some time now. What I have been mapping out above with the *testimonio* and the neo-avant-garde is crucially concerned with imagining a world in which beliefs about what the text means are turned into differences of experiential positions (who we are and what we feel). Interpretation, of course, implies a disagreement of beliefs about the meanings of the text— one reader may believe that *Estrella distante* is a critique of postdictatorial criticism, and another reader may dispute this reading; there is a disagreement about the meaning of the text; there is a disagreement about the author's intended meaning. In opposition to interpretation, the position one occupies vis-à-vis experience is a certain irrelevance of disagreement about the object. Two people who have two different experiences in relation to the text do not disagree, they just differ—he feels pain, and she does not; there is nothing for them to disagree about. Or, transposing Huntington's idea of contemporary politics onto the aesthetic, one can say that if, for interpretation, the central question is "'Which side are you on?' and people [can] and [do] choose sides and change sides," then, for experience, "the question is 'What are you?' That is a given that cannot be changed" (71). Postmodern/postdictatorial ideology, in other words, primarily imagines aesthetico-political discrepancies as differences of experience rather than as disagreements about what the text means.[22]

What is central about Bolaño's text—the whole point of insisting on aesthetic form—is that aesthetic form is not a function of (i.e., not reducible to) one's experience of it. That is, the political impetus behind the novel is located not in the erasure between art and life or between art and nonart, or the pain of the other and the reader, but rather in the assertion that the separation between art and nonart should be maintained. In this way, and in opposition to critics like Beverley and Richard, who see subjective positions as somehow standing in the way of capital, and, in turn, imagining interpretation as somehow standing in the way of feeling the pain of others, the detective story at the center of *Estrella distante* requires an aesthetic space where interpretation can take place and disagreements (aesthetic or otherwise) are considered intrinsic to this aesthetic encounter.[23]

My point is not that Bolaño's novel does, in fact, produce some sort of prescriptive utopian vision for the Left, much less that there is a form (aesthetic or otherwise) that can catapult the reader toward utopia. Nor is the point that the assertion of form is inherently a leftist project. The idea is not that insisting on aesthetic autonomy will produce economic equality. Rather, the idea is that the assertion of aesthetic form in *Estrella distante* critiques a type of contemporary thought that seeks to eliminate the aesthetic object and interpretation. In this sense, *Estrella distante* is also an indictment against the fantasy that experience is a critique of capitalism. The novel thus reminds us that the question of the aesthetic today is essential, not simply because it is a motor of dominant ideologies, but also and more importantly, because it provides a space where dominant forms of thought can be contested. What Bolaño's novel asks its readers to consider is precisely whether the Left's commitment to postmodern/post-dictatorial politics has served not to produce a more just world but rather to endorse contemporary neoliberal politics today.

CHAPTER 6

Literary Form Now

Newton did not see gravity. He felt its effect: a pain in the head.
BRIAN MASSUMI, *PARABLES FOR THE VIRTUAL*

The constant sharpening of knives is boring if one never gets around to cutting.
EUGENIE BRINKEMA, TRANSLATING HERMANN LOTZE IN *THE FORMS OF THE AFFECTS*

At the locus of the secret: where however everything is said and where the remainder is nothing—but the remainder, not even literature.
JACQUELINE HAMRIT, TRANSLATING JACQUES DERRIDA IN *AUTHORSHIP IN NABOKOV'S PREFACES*

Alejandro Zambra's novel *Bonsái* (Bonsai) has received much attention since its publication in 2006, including the Chilean Critics' Award Best Novel of the Year, translations into numerous languages, and a film adaptation. In many ways, the success of this short novel is quite extraordinary, as there is nothing particularly groundbreaking about it. There is no radical experimentation in style such as we saw with the neo-avant-garde texts. Nor does it have an explicit political message that was evident in the discussion of the *testimonio*; there is no mention whatsoever of Salvador Allende, human rights violations, or even the Chilean dictatorship. Indeed, it would appear to have little to do with the texts that I have been examining in this book; it neither imagines literature as a mechanism to transmit the pain of abused victims to the reader nor mourns the lives that were lost because of the dictatorship. There is no sense that *Bonsái* wants to disavow its literary status. In short, *Bonsái* is not a postdictatorial novel.

But if, on the one hand, *Bonsái* is not a postdictatorial novel, on the other, its aesthetic and political importance cannot be fully understood without considering its relationship to postdictatorial literature.[1] One can see how this functions when addressing the love story at the novel's center, a story about two characters, Julio and Emilia, that begins at the university and ends with Emilia's death several years later. Yet, to describe *Bonsái* simply as a love story is to miss the force of the text, since it is less the love story than the *literary creation* of a love story that signals *Bonsái*'s significance in relation to the dictatorship or to postdictatorial texts. This commitment to marking a space for the literary object is most visible in *Bonsái*'s usage of metafiction as the narrator incessantly draws attention to the narrative structure, its artifice, its status as a fiction. Beginning on the first page of the text, the narrator declares: "In the end she dies and he remains alone, although in reality he was alone some years before the death of her, of Emilia. Let's say that she is called or was called Emilia and that he is called, was called and continues to be called Julio. Julio and Emilia. In the end Emilia dies and Julio does not die. The rest is literature" (1). *Bonsái* is a story about a love that dies; but if love dies, literature does not die with it—a point that is already revealed in the epigraph of the novel: "Years passed, and the only person who didn't change was the young woman in the book."[2] Rather than its being a book that changes with or even mirrors reality, *Bonsái*'s force is the presence of literary space that stands outside of this reality, especially a postdictatorial reality. Indeed, it is the assertion of its irreducibility to reality that not only presents a departure from the postdictatorial texts of an earlier generation but also gives *Bonsái* a political potential that those texts do not have.

But to say that metafiction in *Bonsái* is politically significant today is not to suggest that metafiction did not have a politics before this contemporary moment. In the first part of the chapter, I briefly examine two texts, published during the dictatorial and postdictatorial periods respectively, that use metafiction for very different political aims. By first turning to perhaps the most important novel of the dictatorship, Manuel Puig's *El beso de la mujer araña* (*Kiss of the Spider Woman*; 1976), I show how metafiction during the period of authoritarian rule challenges the rigid Cold War ideological division between communism and liberalism. As indicated in chapter 3, metanarrative is also deployed in Albertina Carri's *Los rubios* (2003), and I return to the film to show how the device during the postdictatorship is used less to challenge the division between communism and liberalism than to deconstruct the oppositional division between reality and fiction. Undoubtedly, the aesthetic politics of Zambra's text must be understood in relation to these two periods. *Bonsái* also registers the moment in which it was written, and in so doing, it will dialogue with a posthegemonic, postdictatorial, postaesthetic world endorsed by a number of affect theorists. The second part of the chapter examines the intersection between metafiction and affect theory, which subscribes to many of the same aesthetic tendencies discussed in this book, including the vanishing frame. Against this turn to affect, I argue here that the assertion of the frame—via metafiction—provides an opportunity to think beyond the critical relationship between affect theory and neoliberalism that reigns in the aftermath of the postdictatorial era.

The Flowerpot

To be sure, *Bonsái* is a love story, but it's also a story about a love for literature. Julio and Emilia are two philology students who become a couple after meeting in a study group while preparing for their university exams. They spend most nights during their one-year relationship reading and discussing authors such as Rubén Darío, Juan Carlos Onetti, and Raymond Carver.[3] Literature is not just something the two lovers read; it also holds a quasi-fantastical power over them, directly changing their lives. For example, their final breakup seems to stem from having read Macedonio Fernández's short narrative "Tantalia," a story about a couple who buy a plant to symbolize their love, only to realize that its death will also mean their love's withering. After their breakup, literature will continue to be a primary concern in Julio's life, as he tries to find a job transcribing a novel for the famous writer Gazmuri, before ultimately writing his own novel, perhaps the novel that we are reading, *Bonsái*. This last point—Julio's search for a job—is significant here, since it textually registers an economic situation in Chile, where work has become unstable. The loss of work in a certain sense gives rise not just to the creation of the novel but also to the possibility of thinking of this creation in relation to the economic situation in Chile.[4]

I will return to this point; for now, however, it should be suggested that more than a love for literature, *Bonsái* is about asserting an aesthetic frame via metafiction. William H. Gass, who coined the term in the 1960s, defines metafiction as a type of fiction "somehow about fiction itself" (qtd. in Currie 1). This same concern with "fiction itself," as already noted, is evident in the first page of the novel, which announces that "in the end Emilia dies and Julio does not die," as well as laying bare *Bonsái*'s status as fiction. This metafictional device can be seen in the construction of the characters, as their existence has less to do with telling a story than with signaling their own status as characters within this story: "But in this account Anita's mother and Anita don't matter, they are secondary characters. The one that matters is Emilia" (40). Indeed, throughout the text, the narrator of *Bonsái* points to the formation of the story, "I want to end Julio's story, but Julio's story doesn't end [. . .] or rather it ends like this" (81). Metafiction in *Bonsái* reveals a concern with not just fiction but a type of fiction that turns away from the real world.

This turn away from the outside world and the turn toward "fiction itself" become most explicit when several years after their breakup, Julio buys a bonsai and sets out to take care of it. This project requires him to read specialized manuals about the plant, but through this investigation he begins to form a theory of artistic form. In one book, for example, he reads that "the bonsai is an aesthetic replica of a tree," but the point of the bonsai is that it can only become such a replica when it is placed in its "container" (75). For this reason, he continues, "Once outside its flowerpot, the tree ceases to be a bonsai" (75). Zambra's text is essentially about the flowerpot: it's about what makes a bonsai different from a tree. *Bonsái*, in other words, seeks to render the aesthetic frame visible, as it divides the aesthetic object from nonaesthetic objects. Others have also pointed out this concern with finding an aesthetic space in the text. For instance, Monserrat Asecio Gómez calls *Bonsái* "ficción pura" (pure fiction; "Similitudes"). Zambra himself has suggested elsewhere, "Writing is pruning the leaves until making visible a form that was already there, hidden" (*No leer* 143). The metafictional device in *Bonsái* represents a shift toward literature and, as explained below, a rejection of the aesthetic-political aims of the dictatorial and the postdictatorial eras. As I discuss below, this assertion of fiction will signal a difference between *Bonsái* and *El beso de la mujer araña* and *Los rubios*, as they deploy metafiction not to insist but rather to problematize conceptual divisions.

Metafiction and the Dictatorship

Insofar as *Bonsái* turns away from the real world, it marks a break with a type of dictatorial narrative that attempts to eliminate the divide between fiction and reality. This break can be clearly seen in perhaps the most influential text of that period, Manuel Puig's *El beso de la mujer araña* (1976). Where *Bonsái* seeks to create a literary space, *El beso de la mujer araña* sees this space, and aesthetic autonomy more specifically, as indicative of a political problem, one that leads to the dictatorship. Santiago Colás suggests as much in his masterful reading of Puig's novel when he argues that metafiction undermines aesthetic and ideological "purity" that was dominant in the 1960s and 1970s, a "purity" that ultimately and tragically leads to the Proceso de Reorganización Nacional (94). The novel centers on two cellmates who seem to be diametrically opposed to each other, the politically indifferent Molina, who is in prison for corruption of a minor, and the urban revolutionary Valentín, who is in prison for his political activities. Despite these apparent differences, they do share some interests, especially in movies, as Molina spends most of his time narrating them, while Valentín listens, comments, and critiques them.

And it is in these conversations about film that the novel's investment in metafiction appears clearest. For example, the novel begins not with an introduction of these two characters but rather in medias res with a melodramatic story of the panther woman. The fictionality of the panther woman narrative is suddenly revealed when Valentín's voice appears, interrupting what now turns out to be Molina's story of the panther woman. The effect is rather dramatic, as the reader must now decide which reality (within the novel) is real, the panther story or the conversation between Molina and Valentín. That is, the reader is left to question whether the panther woman belongs to the two prisoners' world or to a fictional one of the movies that lives outside it. For Colás, this metafictional element of the text produces a formal ambiguity between the reality of the cell and the fictional world of the panther woman, as well as stresses that these two worlds "are literally inseparable" (79). Unlike *Bonsái*, then, metafiction in *El beso de la mujer araña* becomes a means to bridge the gap between reality and fiction (169).

Bridging this gap, for Colás, functions as a critique of "purity" that had dominated the Argentine political landscape beginning in the 1960s, one that posited an ideological and utopian solution in the radical politics of the Montoneros on the Left and the Triple A on the Right (94). However, what the Left (and the Right) did not recognize, according to Colás, is that there are no pure politics: "This teleological image of development toward a utopian (pure and contradicted) truth is an illusion" (95). In the novel, Valentín is meant to embody this utopian political project and its failure. But there is also an aesthetic version of this failure, which is found in Molina and his relationship to film. Molina's idea of movies is completely divorced from politics and can be witnessed in his admiration for a Nazi propaganda film. When Valentín criticizes him for it, Molina defends himself and the film by saying that "it's well made, and besides it's a work of art, you don't under . . . understand because you never even saw it" (63). For Colás, Molina's commitment to "the work of art" allows for the fantasy of an isolated aesthetic sphere (a fantasy that is also vital to the critique of bourgeois aesthetics at the heart of John Beverley's investment in the *testimonio* and Nelly Richard's investment in the neo-avant-garde). Colás, however, doesn't imagine the *testimonio* or the neo-avant-garde as solutions to these aesthetic problems. Instead, he notes, citing Patricia Waugh, that metafiction is a device that demands its own "social construction" and thus implies an opening to "concrete, social and historical" conditions and to the *impossibility* of the text fully closing itself from the real world (80, 81). More specifically, metafiction reveals the "myth" of ideological and aesthetic purity (94). For this reason, Colás claims that "the reader of the novel may no longer approach the text as autonomous. Instead of looking to fiction as pure escape, totally divorced from the 'real' world, the reader must wonder if that fiction somehow contains traces of that real world" (82). Thus, metafiction serves a double function in *El beso de la mujer araña* not only by critiquing the artwork's detachment from the world, but also by localizing this aesthetic project within a specific moment in Argentina's history. Metafiction in Puig's novel represents a critique of the polarized world that would soon slide toward seven years of military rule, torture, and death.

Nonetheless, although *El beso de la mujer araña* does critique this polarized world, Colás ultimately argues that the novel still endorses an aesthetics and politics of purity. Part of the reason why this is so is historical, since the text, published in 1976, was written before the coup and before the complete destruction of the Left and the vanishing of the utopian horizon that drove their actions. What came after the coup, however, would radically change the aesthetic and political landscape. The Argentine junta would soon impose a new language—what Colás calls a "myth" of purity found in "official history"—a language that would be challenged, according to Colás, by a codified language of resistance in Ricardo Piglia's *Respiración artificial* (1980).[5] I will not elaborate on Colás's reading of Piglia's text but signal it here because it marks a transition in Latin American literature and theory where an ideological conflict between socialism and liberalism would be replaced by a concern with language. That is, if *El beso de la mujer araña* critiques the polarized world before the dictatorship, and *Respiración artificial* resists the regime's "official history," *Los rubios* and *Bonsái* live in a posthistorical moment, which is defined, in part, by the absence of this ideological conflict.[6] For this reason, metafiction in *Los rubios* and *Bonsái* will become a response not to "official history" but to its very absence.[7] This new situation raises several questions: What happens when the language of official history is replaced by a concern with a politics of language? What happens, that is, when there is no outside of language? Finally, what happens to metafiction, and literature more widely, in the transition from the dictatorship to full-blown neoliberalism?

Metafiction and the Postdictatorship

Eduardo Galeano famously declared that during the dictatorship "people were in prison so that prices could be free" (qtd. in Weschler 147). The primary objective for the dictatorships was to eliminate all resistance so the market could flourish. From this position, the military's objective was very successful, as it ushered in a new period of global capital. At the same time, this new postdictatorial moment reflects a crisis of socialism throughout the globe. Bruno Bosteels rightly notes that one of the results of this crisis has been the rise of language as a form of resistance. More specifically, Bosteels suggests that "during times of decline and reaction in which a real transformation of the prevailing political order seems ever more unlikely, language often comes to the rescue, allowing one to revitalize, think anew, or at the very least delimit the concepts of 'politics' or 'the political' with the simple yet thought-provoking addition of a prefix" ("Politics" 206). Bosteels has insightfully criticized the limits of this commitment to language, and the point in part of his essay is to historicize these very limits. Indeed, the objective of this "prefix" in the postpolitical moment is twofold: first, it draws awareness to the artifice of politics (that is, awareness of politics as a linguistic construction); second, and equally important, it seeks to dismantle language as a construct by drawing that awareness. In this way, politics no longer is determined by a type of division between different political ideals (e.g., liberalism, totalitarianism, etc.) but rather becomes metapolitical, as the prefix serves to endlessly construct and deconstruct the linguistic construct of the political (regardless of those ideas).

And this metadiscourse is significant to Latin American aesthetics in the postdictatorial period as well, as criticism seeks not only to expose a series of socially constructed and contingent qualities of certain claims (such as truth, "official history," heroic narrative, and identity), but to deconstruct their representational unity to motivate a political project.[8] That is, postdictatorial theory and criticism transform literature into a linguistic apparatus that metafiction endlessly constructs and deconstructs. Patricia Waugh makes this point clear when she notes that "the lowest common denominator of metafiction" is "simultaneously to create a fiction and to make a statement about the creation of that fiction. The two processes are held together in a formal tension which breaks down the distinctions between 'creation' and criticism' and merges them into the concepts of 'interpretation' and 'deconstruction'" (6). Unlike the dictatorial period when metafiction seeks to critique the ideological difference between communism and liberalism, the critical project of metafiction in the postdictatorial era is as much about the creation as it is about the need to deconstruct the prevailing aesthetic and political order of literature.

Such metagestures, as already seen, are visible in Dorfman's *Death and the Maiden* (i.e., when the mirror drops at the end of the play) and Rosencof's *Las cartas que no llegaron*, but perhaps they are most evident in Carri's *Los rubios*. As noted in chapter 3, *Los rubios* is an investigation into the lives of Carri's disappeared parents, but this investigation is continually interrupted with another narrative about the making of the documentary *Los rubios*. For example, Carri carries out interviews with real family members who provide information on her disappeared parents; and she films actors, including one that plays Albertina, who prepare their lines and rehearse their scenes. According to Joanna Page, this metadevice not only is jarring but also deliberately undermines the documentary format by revealing the "contamination" of documentary by fiction (30). Following this logic, we can say that within this postdictatorial mode the "meta" as a prefix of "metafiction" serves as a supplement to deconstruct the political projects that inform literature. And this concern with deconstructing the limits of all binary oppositions, of course, marks a difference from *El beso de la mujer araña*, which critiques but ultimately leaves these binaries in place.

But it also marks a difference from *Bonsái*, since a postmodern documentary like *Los rubios* attempts to eliminate the divide between fiction and reality that Zambra's text wants to insist on. And yet, despite these differences, critics continue to read *Bonsái* as a postmodern novel that blurs the lines between reality and fiction. For example, in her discussion of metafiction in Zambra's novel, Macarena Silva points to the years after Julio ends his relationship with Emilia, when he begins to write a novel that shares its title with the novel that we have in our hands: *Bonsái*. This thread in the story commences when the famous Chilean writer Gazmuri interviews Julio for a job to transcribe his most recent novel. Julio doesn't get the job, but he lies to his lover, María, telling her that he has. In order to give semblance to this lie, he writes Gazmuri's novel (as if he were Gazmuri), despite only knowing minimal information about its content, namely, that it is a story about a man who finds out on the radio that a lover of his youth dies, a lover with whom he took care of a bonsai. The question that arises, for Silva, is whether the novel that Julio writes is, in fact, the one that we are reading. For this reason, she believes *Bonsái* problematizes "the relations between fiction and reality" (10) and, following Hutcheon and García Canclini, proposes that Zambra's novel challenges the concepts of autonomy and transcendence (11). This reading is shared by other critics; for instance, Roberto Onell declares that in *Bonsái* "life and writing are distinct realities that become one" (166). And recalling Roman Jakobson's theory on metalanguage, Fernando Emilio Morales Gamboa thinks that *Bonsái* "tends to introduce ambiguity between narrative levels" (170).[9] All of these critics argue, as Fernando Montenegro suggests, not only for the muddied relationship between reality and fiction but also that *Bonsái* is a postmodern text because of it.[10]

And yet the opposite is true. Unlike both the metafictional gesture in *El beso de la mujer araña*, which problematizes the limits between reality and fiction, and the postmodern one in Carri's film, which attempts to eliminate them altogether, Zambra's text doesn't seem to care about the real world in the least. That is, insofar as there is ambiguity between fiction and reality in the text, there is no reason why that ambiguity cannot be read as strictly internal to the novel. Although ambiguity may be central to the narrative, the novel *dramatizes* but does not—in fact, it cannot—*embody* that ambiguity. Throughout the text, as I noted above, the reader of *Bonsái* is continually brought back to the novel by a narrator who points to the form of the story: "I want to end Julio's story, but Julio's story doesn't end [. . .] or rather it ends like this." (81). Characters, too, are as much a part of the plot as they are there to reveal their status as characters. This turn toward fiction is most visible in the novel's discussion of the bonsai itself as an "aesthetic replica" to think through the conceptual difference between an aesthetic object and a nonaesthetic object. From this perspective, the aesthetic force of *Bonsái* is found not in this postmodern metafictional quality that informs our reality but rather in the assertion of an aesthetic space that is entirely indifferent to our reality and whatever we feel as readers. This point is affirmed by Marcela Valdes when she declares that "Zambra seeks, from the beginning and through diverse means, always to maintain a certain distance between the reader and the narrative, a distance that stresses, precisely, that we are dealing with a literary text and not an imitation or transposition of reality"

("Seed"). Thus, unlike the dictatorial and postdictatorial texts discussed, to the extent that there is a postdictatorial reality—affective, political, or otherwise—*Bonsái* neither demands nor invokes that a reader experience that reality.

Bonsái, in other words, is interested in the creation of art and in making its status as artwork visible. Or to return to Zambra's point, "Writing is pruning the leaves until making visible a form that was already there, hidden" (*No leer* 143). *Bonsái*'s investment in aesthetic form breaks with rather than continues these past aesthetic-political tendencies, and therefore also breaks with postmodernism. But this break does not make *Bonsái* any less political, since its politics lie in its renovation of the literary in a supposedly dedifferentiated world of aesthetics and politics that the postdictatorship has brought forth. At the same time, pruning—that is, rendering the aesthetic visible—becomes all the more relevant in the face of affect theory, which, as we will see, considers art less as something "hidden" than as something that does not really exist. The next section will seek to show how *Bonsái* and metafiction in particular, which would cease to exist according to the logic of affect theory, challenge an affective understanding of aesthetics and politics.

The Aftermath of the Postdictatorship: Affect Theory and Metafiction

Metafiction in *Bonsái* is as much about distancing itself from postmodernism as it is about responding to more recent developments in late capitalism. By the end of the 1990s, the commitment to what Waugh calls "metafictional deconstruction" had ultimately failed (Waugh 6). Deregulation and the privatization of the public sector in the 1980s and 1990s had done much to globalize Latin America, as neoliberalism brought about new multinational companies, brand names, and foods. It also had a devastating impact on a large sector of the society, leading directly to the economic collapse that rocked Argentina in 2000–2001. As a result, by 2004 the political spectrum in Latin America had begun to shift leftward. Elected presidents in Uruguay, Brazil, Argentina, Chile, Peru, and Ecuador all represented a significant departure in regional politics from both the dictatorship and the postdictatorship. Especially noteworthy here was that some of those who had been elected, for example, had also been political prisoners who were tortured during the dictatorships, and thus their victories were also victories for human rights.[11] The Pink Tide, in this respect, was as much a response to human rights policies as it was meant to be a response to economic ones. But the Pink Tide was markedly more successful with the former than the latter. Indeed, while this turn leftward sought to restrict some of the more aggressive neoliberal policies, it largely maintained the same economic policies that had been put in place by the military—the same policies that continue to produce one of the most economically unequal regions in the world. Thus one way to describe the triumph of the Pink Tide is to suggest that it finally achieves the human rights governance that had been at the center of leftist politics since the late 1970s. Another, perhaps more accurate way to describe it is that it makes more visible that human rights justice does not equate to economic justice. Or, said differently, it dispels any doubt that the Left's human rights project could mitigate the growing gap between rich and poor. Or to return to the context of *Bonsái*, the absence of human rights in the texts allows one to better comprehend a period when social relations have been increasingly monetized and inequalities have intensified. As was already noted, it's Julio's unemployment (as a consequence of this neoliberal world order) rather than any appeal to human rights violations that structures the creation of Julio's novel.

In the cultural realm, affect criticism already anticipates the shortcomings of the politics of Pink Tide and politics of language. For the affect theorist Brian Massumi, for example, postmodern thought, as it aims to construct and deconstruct, provides little space to think outside of language, through capitalism, and the subject's role within it. According to Massumi, if language interpellates us, then subjects have little agency, and even less space for real change. Furthermore, language permeates our bodies and "codes" our identitarian positions, but even registering how these identities are positions, and how these positions can be produced and shifted like pieces on a chessboard, doesn't get us off the board (Massumi 2). That is, although these (identitarian) positions are flexible, the emphasis on language still leaves the "oppositional framework" in place (2). Massumi explains it this way:

> Signifying subject formation according to the dominant structure was often thought of in terms of "coding." Coding in turn came to be thought of in terms of positioning on a grid. The grid was conceived as an oppositional framework of culturally constructed significations: male versus female, black versus white, gay versus straight, and so on. A body corresponded to a "site" on the grid defined by an overlapping of one term from each pair. The body came to be defined by its pinning to the grid. Propo-

nents of this model often cited its ability to link body-sites into a "geography" of culture that tempered the universalizing tendencies of ideology.

The sites, it is true, are multiple. But aren't they still combinatorial permutations on an overarching definitional framework? Aren't the possibilities for the entire gamut of cultural emplacements, including the "subversive" ones, precoded into the ideological master structure? Is the body as linked to a particular subject position anything more than a local embodiment *of* ideology? Where has the potential for change gone? (2–3)

For Massumi, moving the chess pieces feels a bit like not moving them at all. And insofar as the meta always signals the primacy of language itself, it always returns to this "oppositional framework" of the "grid." Instead, Massumi proposes a move to affect as an approach that reawakens the system as potential, as a means to think through this "oppositional framework" by signaling "unmediated experience" vis-à-vis bodies, sensations, and motion (Massumi 1). Affect stresses a certain spatiotemporal "continuity" that lives outside of ideology, mediation, history, intention, representation, and politics that are all part of the ideological grid (4). Thus, for an affect theorist, the Pink Tide and recent dictatorship are less important than what lives underneath, between, through, beyond, and before them. They are less important because they already exist, and insofar as they already exist they are a reflection of the grid, and are always already considered failures or closures. Instead, what lives underneath, between, through, beyond, and before them always embodies potential and the possibility of a better politics.

For this reason, Ruth Leys correctly notes that the force of affect is not located in the ideological or the political but rather is "independent of, and in an important sense prior to, ideology—that is, prior to intentions, meanings, reasons, and beliefs—because [affects] are nonsignifying, autonomic processes that take place below the threshold of conscious awareness and meaning" (437). Following the logic of affect, where the dictatorial aesthetics and criticism are crucially committed to addressing an ideological conflict, and where the postdictatorial criticism is concerned with language as a (de)construction of society, in this new moment, affect frees itself of both forms of criticism, since it "mov[es] attention away from considerations of meaning or 'ideology' or indeed representation to the subject's subpersonal material-affective responses, where, it is claimed, political and other influences do their real work" (451). In this way, the posthistorical world that Massumi responds and contributes to is one that will not be limited by these past political and historical constraints because affect resides in a space that is "independent of" or "prior to" oppositions registered in texts of the dictatorship, such as *Pedro y el Capitán* and *El beso de la mujer araña*, or of the postdictatorship, such as *Las cartas que no llegaron* or *Death and the Maiden*.

Affect theory is very much a critique as it is shaped by a posthistorical moment when criticism begins to consider capitalism as the only viable economic system on a global scale. From this vantage, then, affect theory positions itself in Latin America as a result of the failures of the Cold War and the failures that follow it, including the 2000 debt crisis and the rise (and fall) of the Left. (Again, they are failures because they are products of the grid.) Within Latin American cultural studies it is Alberto Moreiras's *Exhaustion of Difference* (2001) that announces the failure of the "aesthetic-historicist paradigm" that had come to define Latin Americanist thought (15). According to Moreiras, the paradigm maintains the "inside-outside relationship" that has been crucial to "cultural theories of modernity," including "master concepts" such as hegemony, identity, difference, and locational thinking more generally, which have now reached exhaustion (16). The critical objective thus becomes to "seek the undoing of the inside-outside polarity on which all aesthetic historicisms and all culturalist theories of modernity rest" (16). As such, Moreiras argues for what he calls "savage hybridity" that would deconstruct the limits of hegemony and civil society but still maintain a political, social, and historical reference in Latin America. The question then emerges as to how to critique these "master concepts" without giving them up entirely, which would, according to Moreiras, lead to the loss of "critical reason" or "irruptive and dividing force" (16, 17).

For an affect theorist, in contrast, Moreiras's logic, while initially productive, ultimately does not do enough, since it reaffirms the grid and quickly leads to "stasis" (Massumi 3). Instead, Jon Beasley-Murray proposes an affective approach that shifts away from deconstructive inertia and focuses on what is underneath, between, through, beyond, and before the grid. As Beasley-Murray explains, for example, although Moreiras's account critiques master concepts such as subalternism, hegemony, identity, and difference, he still holds on to the idea of the "inside and outside" (Beasley-Murray, *Posthegemony* xiv). Beasley-Murray continues: "Subalternism holds on to a distinction between inside and outside, and so perpetuates the fundamental binarism of both hegemony and civil society" (xiv). In short, Moreiras's approach still leans too heavily on language, or what Massumi calls the "grid" and Beasley-Murray calls the "game" (Massumi 2; Beasley-Murray, *Posthegemony* xiv).

Thus, the trouble with past social and cultural criticism, according to

Beasley-Murray, is that it treats master concepts such as hegemony as if they were real when they are, in fact, more like an "illusion" (*Posthegemony* ix). For this reason, one of the first interventions for Beasley-Murray is to declare that "there is no hegemony and never has been" (ix). Instead, he proposes a framework that deconstructs the false dichotomy of the inside and outside as well as stresses the affective world that lives beyond this illusion of binaries. This framework moves past this misconception to an affective world that "always takes place between bodies, at the mobile threshold between affective states as bodies either coalesce or disintegrate, as they become other to themselves" (*Posthegemony* 128). From this viewpoint, social order and social change are not so much promoted by language as they are by "affect and habit[, . . .] forms of (dis)organization beneath and beyond discourse, and so beyond the conceptual apparatus of cultural studies and civil society theory" (xvi).

And yet, it is for this reason, as Leys points out, that affect theory is interested less in the political than in the "nonsignifying, autonomic processes that take place below the threshold of conscious awareness and meaning" (437); that is, affect theorists locate potential in the materiality that lives in all objects, including artwork. As such, affect cannot be properly considered as another reiteration of the postmodern texts that have already been discussed, since affect functions less to blur the lines between art and reality than to imagine art, like all other objects, as illusions. The status of literature, within this affective framework, thus reveals a curious paradox, since literature's significance is found precisely in the realization of its inexistence. Or, like hegemony ("there is no hegemony and never has been" [*Posthegemony* ix]), what becomes most significant about literature is that *there is no literature and never has been.*[12]

For affect theory, the significance of literature rests not in its status as literature but in its materiality, which makes it an object like any other. This is why, if literature exists, it does so much as does anything else, including an "opera house" or even "gold, silver, copper, guano, rubber, chocolate, sugar, tobacco, coffee, coca" (Beasley-Murray, *Posthegemony* 129). Below, I explore how the reducibility of literature to gold, silver, or even coffee aims to make literature's status as a commodity more visible. For now, however, it warrants noting that from the perspective of affect theory, literature is relevant because, like anything else, it is an object of "capture" (Beasley-Murray, *Posthegemony* 128). And the idea of capture is paramount because it affords the dedifferentiation of art and nonart and because it highlights the innate fluidity that defines the idea of capture itself: what is captured can therefore also escape. According to Beasley-Murray, "something always escapes" (*Posthegemony* 7).[13] As a result, what makes affect theory politically appealing is that the escape (like the failure) is built into its approach. It always moves beyond stasis.[14]

As seen in chapters 4 and 5, the critique on the status of literature and autonomy in particular can be witnessed in the 1960s and 1970s. This desire is announced in Barthes's "The Death of the Author," which gives rise to "the birth of the reader," and the newfound sense in which literature is informed by our subject positions. This critique is also visible in *El beso de la mujer araña*, where, as Colás notes, metafiction in literature affords an ethical position in the reader: "The reader of the novel may no longer approach the text as autonomous. Instead of looking to fiction as pure escape, totally divorced from the 'real' world, the reader must wonder if that fiction somehow contains traces of that real world" (82). It is present also in Linda Hutcheon's postmodern reading of metafiction when she declares that "readers of metafiction are [. . .] made mindful of their active role in reading, in participating in making the text mean. They are the distanced, yet involved, coproducers of the novel" (13). Hutcheon, like Barthes and Colás, stresses that the reader, as much as the author, determines the meaning of the text(s).

As I have shown, the commitment to the reader is theoretically problematic. Nevertheless, there is still a desire to speak to a specific relationship between author, reader, and literary text; this is not the case with affect theory. That is, where Barthes, Colás, and even Hutcheon ascribe a certain importance to the reader, affect theory's insistence on the "illusion" of literature also means the "illusion" of the reader. Indeed, reading (and, more specifically, interpreting what you read), insofar as it is a cognitive activity, could be understood as a rather undesirable consequence of one's encounter with an object. Instead, what is significant for affect theorists is not literature but the materiality that unites all objects. For this reason, it is no longer the "reader" but rather the subject with a body and "the mobile threshold between affective states as bodies" that is essential (Beasley-Murray, *Posthegemony* 128). Thus, if Beasley-Murray is right that "what matters is how things present themselves to us, not what they may represent" (205), then the death of the author and the birth of the reader that marks the beginning of the postmodern moment now ends *not* with the rebirth of the author but rather with the death of both (205).[15] If one believes that it's the "things" that count, then one must also believe that literature cannot. Thus, the rise of affect theory marks the death not only of the author and the reader but also of aesthetic form.

But insofar as the idea of "how things present themselves to us" is paramount, one can begin to see how Zambra's novel becomes a kind of rejection of this affective account. As observed above, in *Bonsái* there is an

absence of any kind of explicit political message that marked the postdictatorial period and the relationship between text and "us." For example,
the novel does not conjure up, directly or indirectly, the politics that are
usually found in the *testimonio* genre or in the work of the Chilean neo-
avant-garde. Nor does it imagine a kind of antirepresentational approach
that seeks to transmit a certain politics of pain onto the reader. The novel
does not care, in other words, if we share the victim's pain; in fact, there is
really no victim in the novel. For this reason, it is indispensable to stress
the fundamental role the ordinary love story plays for the novel, since it
reveals that Zambra's text has less to do with the subject matter and how
it is meant to impact us than with the intention to make the subject matter secondary precisely so it distances us from that impact. In fact, the
(love) story allegorizes a kind of rejection of the reader who must witness
an event.

At the same time, while it is true that Julio and Emilia are readers who
also have identities, these identities seem secondary to the fact that they
are, first and foremost, readers who read literature. It is this connection to
literature that supersedes the question of who the reader is and, perhaps
more importantly, a politics that results from who the reader is. In *Bonsái*,
insofar as there are readers, there are no explicit politics attached to them.
Rather than telling us who we are, *Bonsái* wants to define, as Asecio Gómez notes, what it is as a work of literature, as "pure fiction, without the
marvelous, the fantastic or philosophical adornments" ("Similitudes").[16]
The entire point of the novel is not "the marvelous, the fantastic or philosophical" (all of which have been imagined as foundations for so many
identitarian readings of Latin American literature). The point instead is
structural, which can be seen not only in the definition of the bonsai as
ceasing to be a bonsai "once outside its flowerpot" (Zambra, *Bonsái* 75) but
also in the insistence that *Bonsái* has no interest in "reality" but rather
in an aesthetic world that is "simply invented" (Asecio Gómez). From this
position, the desire of *Bonsái* becomes to create an aesthetic object that
stands apart from anything and everything else that lives within and in
relation to it. As argued below, *Bonsái*, and metafiction in particular in the
text, is concerned with carving out an aesthetic world in relation not only
to this materiality but also to the commodification of this materiality.

Capitalism and Form Today

It is common within contemporary cultural criticism to note that everything, including art—indeed, the most significant aspect of art—has been

fully subsumed under capital. As Fredric Jameson argued almost thirty years ago, "What has happened is that aesthetic production today has become integrated into commodity production generally" (*Postmodernism* 4).[17] In Latin America, this integration of art into the market occurred via (or was accelerated by) political shock treatment in the form of authoritarian rule. The emphasis on the market as the primary objective of authoritarian rule is found in Idelber Avelar's claim that the dictatorships sought "the physical and symbolic elimination of all resistance to the implementation of market logic" (*Untimely* 1). Market logic has permeated both policies (including human rights policies) and the aesthetic sphere. But even if everything is understood as a commodity today, the differentiation of the aesthetic in *Bonsái* reveals an interest in understanding this novel, and literature more generally, as not simply a commodity. That is, the text is interested in ways of thinking of art as different from "silver, copper, guano, rubber, chocolate, sugar, tobacco, coffee, coca," or any commodity that may accrue value (Beasley-Murray, *Posthegemony* 129).

For market logic, what is fundamental about art is that, first and foremost, it is a commodity (and not the artist's intention or what the work of art means). Accordingly, as a commodity, what becomes equally important about one's relationship to art is not one's status as a beholder but one's status as a consumer. This is precisely Nicholas Brown's contention in his essay "The Work of Art in the Age of Its Real Subsumption under Capital." For Brown, once art is understood primarily as a commodity, the question of what the author intends the work to mean is rendered irrelevant. What counts instead is that the consumer purchases the product. The consumer's preference and his or her money interests become essential. This does not mean, of course, that objects can no longer be distinguished from one another. It doesn't mean, that is, that one person's intention to produce a chair and another person's intention to produce a videogame no longer exist. Rather, it means that as a commodity, whatever those intentions are, they are ultimately secondary to the consumer's own interest in that object. In other words, the market is indifferent to whether the consumer treats the chair as wood to burn or as an object to sit on.

But insofar as consumers' interests are primary, the (commodified) artwork becomes homologous with affect theory's insistence on the centrality of our experience (and irrelevance to the artwork's intended meaning). Or to return to Beasley-Murray's claim about affect theory: "What matters is how *things* [emphasis added] present themselves to us, not what they may represent" (205). Today, this interest in one's experience turns works of art into "things" that are primarily categorized as a commodity.

As I suggested above, for affect theory, whether it is literature, or a film, or an "opera house," or even "gold, silver, [or] guano" matters little, since potential is found in our own interest in the object above all. Accordingly, the importance of affect theory today should be considered in relation less to the death of intention, literature, or even the reader than to the birth, rise, and triumph of the consumer.

Affect theory, of course, has no problem ceding the point that it emerges in late capitalism or that it is a response to postmodernism. Indeed, the critique of the grid that is central to affect criticism only becomes visible in relation to this most recent stage in capital and the political and critical "stasis" of language in the postmodern period. For Beasley-Murray or Massumi, in other words, the political potential of affect theory is made available in the neoliberal moment when capital finally triumphs. But these critics would also note that affect theory is a critique of the triumph of the consumer and the commodification of all objects, since affect is that which escapes both.

But if it does escape, it doesn't seem to get very far. If, on the one hand, the turn to affect is symptomatic of late capitalism, on the other, it undermines any politics that disagrees with the triumph of capital insofar as it makes any disagreement—or any agreement for that matter—an endorsement of the grid. As Leys reminds us, affect makes all political and ideological disagreements irrelevant by insisting that all disagreements—including disagreements between competing aesthetic judgments or political beliefs—are reflections of the position one occupies on the grid. Thus, by reducing all politics and all objects as illusions of the grid or a game, that is, by reducing any political, intentional, and representational articulation, as a reaffirmation of that same grid, political potential is forever trapped between capitalism and affect. Which is just to say that if everything escapes, then nothing really does.

It is important to end this chapter by maintaining that *Bonsái* is not about escape and capture, but rather about form and disagreement. And this commitment to form and disagreement is important because it marks a break with the framework of neoliberalism and affect, that is, with the framework of the commodity form and its materiality. For this reason, the metafictional purpose of this novel to establish a distinction between "pure fiction" and the world outside of that fiction—that is, the desire to produce an account of what makes art different from other objects—becomes not only aesthetically but also politically relevant. Aesthetically, it is relevant because it is a claim toward autonomy (constitutive of the author's intent) in the face of a world in which everything is for sale and consumer preference reigns. Politically, it is relevant because it provides a space, much like Bolaño's *Estrella distante* and Botero's *Abu Ghraib*, in which to think of a structure that is something more than a commodity. But where *Estrella distante* and *Abu Ghraib* are still very much invested in the politics of human rights (or at least undoing them), *Bonsái* has moved beyond that investment. Or, said differently, the claim to autonomy in *Bonsái* is a stronger structural critique of capital insofar as what it responds to is less the political morality of capital than the structure of capital itself.

The point here is not that *Bonsái* is an anticommodity. Nor is it a nostalgic call for a return to a period of art for art's sake.[18] We do, in fact, live in a world where capitalism thrives. And it is because of (and a response to) the triumph of capital that the question of autonomy is different than it was in the past. That is, the political intervention of aesthetic autonomy today is only made available in the aftermath of neoliberalism's triumph and as a cultural response to affect theory that solidifies rather than problematizes neoliberalism—a theory that wants to treat all "things" as the same and thus all aesthetic judgments (because they are products of the grid) as politically inconsequential. In opposition to this account, *Bonsái*'s commitment to drawing awareness to its status as literature is a declaration that art is not simply a commodity but *means* something else. It is a declaration that art is constitutive of "intentions, meanings, reasons, and beliefs" and disagreements over aesthetic judgments and politics (Leys 437). For this reason, *Bonsái* is a rejection of the idea of the grid that eliminates this same space. The idea, in other words, is not so much to deny art's relation to the market, but rather to assert that the intended *meaning* of the work of art—unlike, say, "silver, copper, guano, rubber, chocolate, sugar, tobacco, coffee, coca"—is not that of a commodity. This assertion of meaning—that is, the assertion of understanding art as irreducible to the commodity form—is also a turn away from the neoliberal vision that is centered on the consumer and his or her interest. What this also means is that if anticapitalism is a project worth fighting for within Latin American cultural studies today, that fight must begin with a rejection of affect theory and with the assertion of aesthetic form.

The Victim, the Frame

In the foregoing pages I have attempted to map the rise and fall of the postdictatorial era; this fall, however, should not necessarily be considered negative, for it offers a sense of freedom that transcends the limits of the postdictatorial imagination. The framing of this period, which spans from redemocratization to the first decade of the twenty-first century, undoubtedly has to do with the decline of socialism on the world stage and the prominence of human rights in present-day politics. It also has to do with events that join the 2000 debt crisis, the emergence of the Pink Tide, and the structural adjustments to (and solidification of) neoliberalism in relation to this emergence. In the previous pages, I have argued for the examination of this period in relation to the coterminous appearance and eventual exhaustion of certain postmodern theories and the subsequent rise of affect theory. More specifically, I have argued against aesthetic deframing, which has also been crucial to the postdictatorial period; instead, I have suggested a reconsideration of the aesthetic frame—exemplified in the works of Botero and Bolaño—as responses not simply to this vanishing frame but also, and more importantly, to this moral conception within neoliberalism. The argument of the previous chapter was that Zambra's *Bonsái*, a text that never directly mentions the dictatorship, makes the case for the end of the postdictatorship most forcefully, but it makes it, as some may suggest, at the expense of the dictatorship itself. Nevertheless, we are reminded of the introduction to this book and my reading of Pablo Larraín's *No* as a contemporary film that speaks to the dictatorship without speaking to its moralism.

And *No* does so by insisting on the frame as a way of turning away from the utopian world of human rights that permeates the contemporary moment. The aesthetic project in *No* thus makes visible an anticapitalist critique that can also be found in other works discussed in this book. Larraín's film is meant to be primarily a critique of present-day neoliberalism, but it also introduces a kind of absorptive technique (vis-à-vis the U-matic) that seems more interested in creating an aesthetic space than in provoking a response in the viewer. To be sure, as I pointed out in my reading of Botero's *Abu Ghraib* in chapter 4, that response is no doubt there. Nevertheless, absorption in painting (but not only in painting) is the attempt to create aesthetic unity (i.e., aesthetic meaning) by also denying the presence of the beholder. This absorptive quality is paramount to *Pedro y el Capitán* when Benedetti insists on *not* representing torture because it will overwhelm the audience and impede them from understanding the historical reasons behind the torture. This turn away from torture is undoubtedly grounded in an aesthetic claim that wishes to construct a wall that will divide the play from the lives of the audience members. This absorptive space, as I have demonstrated throughout, is something that vanishes in human rights and in neoliberal aesthetics more generally. In effect, the political morality of neoliberalism is theatrical—even radically so.

What this means is that much of the aesthetic work since at least the 1980s figuratively—and sometimes literally—insists on the viewers' presence. Once again, one only has to think of the difference between the negation of the viewer in Benedetti's play (and the insistence on anticapitalist ideology) and the mirror scene at the end of Dorfman's play (and the complete absence of this ideology). In the last scene, as indicated in the stage notes, a mirror drops down in front of the audience, which not only directly concedes their presence, but also, it is presumed, is meant to make the audience somehow complicit with this future. The aesthetic wall crumbles as audience members are assaulted with a human rights mirror forever reflecting back at them. And, of course, this complicity and assault is no different in the logic of blood and ghosts that we saw in chapter 3, as it comes to us in spite of what we think or do. The theatricality of human rights and neoliberalism not only makes us complicit but demands that we see the world through its lens, a demand that is absent in *Pedro y el Capitán*, *Abu Ghraib*, *Estrella distante*, and *No*.

It is also absent in a more radical way in Zambra's *Bonsái*, which, nevertheless, like *No*, is more concerned with contesting a world in which neoliberalism has triumphed and affect has increasingly become the conceptual and critical apparatus of that triumph.[1] *Bonsái* doesn't explicitly engage with the recent past. *No*, of course, does. If one of the central claims made vis-à-vis *Bonsái* has been that the postdictatorship is now exhausted, another claim that I have *not* made—and am not making now—is that we should stop talking about the torture, disappearances, and deaths that these military regimes have committed. The point of the book, in other words, has been not that we should ignore these past abuses, but rather that we should understand the historical reasons that brought about these abuses, including, but, of course, not limited to, an ideology that attempted to contest economic exploitation.

This is a historical claim, but it is obviously also a political claim. The political point has been that the socialist project that is intrinsic to understanding this past has been ignored not only to the benefit of human rights victims (and human rights logic more generally) but also to the detriment of an ever-growing number of neoliberalism's economic victims. In this way, insofar as *No* makes the connection between these economic victims and the recent past visible, it also challenges an affective apparatus that has sought to render them invisible. I would like to conclude with one last point about the limits of the aesthetic at the end of the postdictatorial era. I have suggested here that while the postdictatorship has been synonymous with the morality of neoliberalism, and this morality has also created its aesthetic project—an aesthetics of the vanishing frame—the return of the aesthetic frame presents an intervention on neoliberal freedom. The consideration of the aesthetic frame surely means very little if we are concerned with directly changing present-day politics, but it is quite relevant if we are concerned with imagining a sense of freedom that is not simply reduced to the politics of neoliberalism. The insistence on the frame today—unlike any other time in the last forty years—is where that intervention and conversation is taking place both in Latin America and elsewhere. And this conversation begins when the vanishing frame reappears again.

Notes

Introduction

1. This is, of course, why Stanley Fish famously asked: "Is there a text in this class?" The answer to Fish's question—if we accepted the primacy of experience—is that whether it is a text (or whether it is something else) would be entirely determined by who we are.

2. I subscribe to John Beverley's idea that "the postmodernism debate in Latin America has to do above all with its connection to the ongoing process of democratization in the hemisphere and, contingently, to the need for a revision (or replacement) of the discourse of the Latin American Left in the wake of the defeat of both the armed struggle strategy represented by *guerrilla foquismo* and the 'peaceful road to socialism' represented by Allende's coalition-building electoral politics (and the problematization of Cuba as a model for an achieved socialist society)" (*Against Literature* 109). This debate in Latin America must also be linked to the general crisis of socialism on the world stage.

3. Throughout *The Vanishing Frame*, I will leave book titles in the original Spanish; when citing these texts, however, I will use the published English translation and page numbers. *Death and the Maiden* was first published in English, so I continue to use the original English title and text.

4. See, for example, Beverley's essay "The Neoconservative Turn in Latin American Literary and Cultural Criticism."

5. To be sure, some important scholars today have brought the question of exploitation to the forefront. See, for example, Ericka Beckman's *Capital Fictions* (2013) and Fornazzari's *Speculative Fictions* (2013).

6. Sarlo continues by noting that cultural studies largely disregards the "specific qualities" of art, "a question which is simplified under a purely institutional perspective (literature would be that which the literary institution defines as literature in each historic moment and each cultural space)" ("Cultural" 119). Sarlo herself has often (and perhaps, at times, deservedly) been regarded as an elitist who wishes nostalgically to return to a moment when literature still maintained a relationship to bourgeois national discourse. But this accusation does not re-

solve the crucial theoretical and political point registered in this historical shift from literary to cultural studies. Sarlo's aesthetic point is not necessarily meant to be read as a return; instead, the point is to recognize that the emphasis on the "social world" ignores the aesthetic object from which a political intervention can take place. Sarlo puts it this way: "Literature is socially meaningful because something, difficult for us to capture, endures in texts and can be activated once more once the text's social functions have been exhausted" ("Cultural" 119). From the position of *The Vanishing Frame*, the concern can be posed another way: in the desire to replace questions about the "specific qualities" of art with questions about its commodification, critics gain a foothold to witness a limitless neoliberal horizon but lose a critical space to question (or look beyond) that horizon. All we see—past, present, and future—is neoliberalism. To be sure, the ontological pursuit in Sarlo's essay is framed as a response less to the commodification of the aesthetic than to the "great public debates" of the 1980s and 1990s that focused on "traditional relativism or traditional multiculturalism" (123–124). But her point also makes evident the need to insist that the political potential of aesthetic autonomy needs to be understood in relation to the contemporary historical moment.

7. All translations are mine unless otherwise noted.

8. For an extended conversation on the relationship between autonomy and modernization, see Di Stefano and Sauri's "'La furia de la materia': On the Non-Contemporaneity of Modernism in Latin America" and Emilio Sauri's "Autonomy after Autonomy, or, The Novel beyond Nation: Roberto Bolaño's 2666."

9. The disregard for questions about the "specific qualities" of art can be considered in relation to the contemporary conversation on relative autonomy, which insists that a work of art is both a commodity and not a commodity (Sarlo, "Cultural" 119). What is stressed in these conversations, however, is art's circulation on the market as a marker of its commodification. In *The Vanishing Frame*, I am less interested in how it circulates than in how aesthetic autonomy today seeks to resist the reduction of art to a commodity.

10. Rama's and Ramos's readings, which reveal a certain uninterest in the status of the work of art as art in nineteenth-century literature, can surely be understood as symptomatic of the period in which both Rama's and Ramos's works are produced, a period, as just noted above, that stresses the social over the aesthetic. Nevertheless, it would be a mistake to reduce the status of the work of art in the nineteenth century to simply a tendency of cultural studies in the twentieth century. One can see that the unquestioned status is essential to the emergence of the historical avant-garde. Indeed, it is precisely the fact that the aesthetic object goes largely unquestioned at the turn of the twentieth century that makes the historical avant-garde's attack on the work of art not only provocative but productive. The political force of the historical avant-garde can only be understood as a response to a certain irrelevance in examining the distinction between art and nonart in the period that preceded it.

11. The question of institutionalization cannot simply be reduced to the historical avant-garde; indeed, it is also fundamental to national projects that take place, for example, in Mexico and Cuba.

Chapter 1: From Revolution to Human Rights

1. For an introduction to the "torture debate," especially in the wake of Abu Ghraib and Guantánamo, see Sanford Levinson, *Torture* (2004), and Thomas Hilde's *On Torture* (2008). For the intersection of human rights and Latin America, see the *PLMA* issue *Human Rights in Latin America* (2006), edited by Marianne Hirsch, and Ana Forcinito and Fernando Ordóñez's special issue *Human Rights and Latin American Cultural Studies* (2009) in the Hispanic Issues Series.

2. Following the 1973 coup, Benedetti fled into exile and soon after began writing the novel *El cepo*, which would eventually become the play *Pedro y el Capitán*. Published and staged in Mexico in 1979 by El Galpón, a famous theater group from Uruguay also in exile, the play would go on to garner critical acclaim and enjoy a very successful run. El Galpón would also stage the play in Uruguay immediately following the country's return to democracy in 1985.

3. Avelar's claim centers on an analysis of Roman Polanski's adaptation of Ariel Dorfman's play *Death and the Maiden*. Although his criticism of Benedetti's play is limited to a scant footnote, he maintains that both the film and Benedetti's text share the same "naïve" representation of torture (*Letter* 164n6). A similar critique of the torture can be found in Erin Graff Zivin's *Figurative Inquisitions* when she notes, for example, that Gillo Pontecorvo's *Battle of Algiers* produces the logic of torture even though the film tries to critique it because it posits the idea that information can be extracted: "That is, although the *Battle of Algiers* takes a (political or moral) stand against the violation of these prisoners' rights, the idea of torture itself remains intact because it is still shown to extract the truth: the infliction of violence elicits a name, which is added to a chart that maps the structure of the FLN in order to eliminate its leadership" (10).

4. Avelar places the idea of torture within a larger "modern epistemic structure," which reveals, among other things, that "civilization," "democracy," and "truth" are not the "opposite of torture," but rather that torture is already constitutive of these forms (*Letter* 41). While Avelar's contribution to a genealogy of torture and its relationship to Western civilization is appreciated, my concern is that this "modern epistemic structure" neither accounts for nor desires to engage with the question of liberal democracy beyond these modern limits. Despite his wish to address shifts in the discourse of torture, including the question of torture in the Southern Cone, Avelar's critique can only situate this discourse within a monolithic trajectory of Western liberal democracy and its barbarism (i.e., torture, dictatorships, human rights abuses, sexism, etc.). Following Avelar's logic, then, Benedetti's text and Pedro's confessional "truth," at their most radical, are only further evidence of the Janus-like quality of liberal democracy that constantly "lies to us" about this barbaric essence (41). In other words, Avelar's framework cannot imagine a form of social equality that goes beyond the very limits of liberal democracy and torture. For a more sustained engagement with human rights and torture, also see Avelar's essay "Unpacking the 'Human' in 'Human Rights.'"

5. In *Terremoto y después*, Mario Benedetti argues that behind the "repression and torture" of subversives are "strong economic motivations": "The government represses and tortures with the pretext of subversion, but let's not allow the din of the war to deafen us; let's not allow the hood of disinformation to obfuscate real-

ity. Behind the repression and the torture there are strong economic motivations. We all know that today repression is not due to subversion" (108). Eduardo Galeano echoes this point when he insightfully asserts that "in Uruguay people were in prison so that prices could be free" (qtd. in Weschler 147). Alexandra Barahona de Brito puts it this way: "Apart from the immediate aim of extracting a confession of crimes as a means of interrogation, [torture's] final aim was the destruction of political opposition to the system" (47).

6. The techniques employed in Benedetti's play clearly overlap with the techniques used by the Uruguayan military regime. The most brutal techniques utilized by the military were electric shock, dragging prisoners behind a horse, and the submarine. This last technique, also known as waterboarding, involved submerging the prisoner in a tank of water in order to suffocate and provoke the sensation of drowning (Aldrighi 64). The *picana* was another form of torture; it used a cattle prod to shock prisoners. The most widely used technique, the *plantón*, forced prisoners to stand for long periods of time without moving.

7. Clara Aldrighi states that "the Civil War in Uruguay took the form of a bellicose conflict between the State and the guerrillas, within the same political community, nation [. . .]" (143). In the postdictatorship, it is common, especially among those on the Left—in particular, the urban guerrillas, the Tupamaros— to reject the claim that it was in fact a civil war. But a quick glance at historical documents from this period proves that both the Tupamaros and the Uruguayan state defined the conflict in these terms. See, for example, Tupamaro communiqués that were published in the late 1960s and early 1970s. See "Tupamaro Communiqués 1–5," http://www.rodolfowalsh.org/spip.php?article2288.

8. In his excellent chapter on the Tupamaros and the "aestheticization" of their armed "operations" (51), Luis Camnitzer rightly notes that the Tupamaros were different from other urban guerrilla movements because they developed strategies of "armed propaganda" that "would not only avoid alienating the public but would also instantly make them attractive and persuasive in the eyes of the people" (46). Nevertheless, it is essential to stress that class warfare was always pertinent to their campaign and that this more "theatrical" element was less present in their later attacks. Furthermore, their interest in political action made them different from the traditional leftist political parties. The Uruguayan politician Wilson Ferreira Aldunate highlighted this difference when he described the guerrilla movement and the communists as "los tupamaros y los tapamuros" (qtd. in Campodónico 179). Los Tapamuros—a play on the name of the revolutionary group—literally means "wall coverers," referring to the Communist Party's inclination to cover the city walls with propaganda but to do little more. This tendency, as Miguel Ángel Campodónico correctly declares, was completely contrary to the Tupamaros, who saw political action as essential for social change.

9. The repression, nevertheless, continued. In the years that followed, totalitarian measures only intensified as the military soon began arresting all leftist "subversives," including members of the Communist Party (Partido Comunista de Uruguay; PCU) and left-leaning politicians in the traditional Colorado and Blanco Parties. "The victims of repression were mostly members of left-wing organizations. Of those detained by the security forces 62 per cent were active militants, 18 per cent were political leaders, and 9 per cent trade unionists. The first wave of

judicially processed detainees (1972–1974) primarily affected members of the Tupamaros, the second (1975–1977), members of the Communist Party" (Barahona de Brito 47).

10. US Representative Edward Koch had labeled Uruguay "the torture chamber of Latin America" after "the testimony of Ferreira Aldunante at the US Congress Committee for International Relations in Washington in June 1976," which also resulted in "the passing of the Koch amendment which placed an arms sale embargo on the country" (Barahona de Brito 83–84).

11. Exiles' shift toward a human rights framework in the mid-1970s marked a watershed moment in the political history of Uruguay, since a human rights position was virtually nonexistent prior to this period. As Barahona de Brito notes, "The human rights movement in Uruguay was a late development and an isolated *decidor de la verdad* (speaker of the truth). It was weak, fragmented, and had little power to influence the parties. Until 1981 human rights activism occurred only in exile" (Barahona de Brito 83). The virtual absence of human rights activism can be traced back in part to Uruguay's strong secular foundation, in which the Catholic Church—a primary promoter and organizer of human rights groups—was relatively weak and had almost no presence inside the traditional political parties. This absence slightly differed from the political situation in Argentina and Chile, where human rights organizations were already established in the political culture prior to their respective coups, which, of course, made it easier to mobilize campaigns immediately after the coups. At the same time, it is important not to overestimate this presence. Although human rights movements in Chile and Argentina existed, they were by no means a powerful political force in any of these countries. As Kathryn Sikkink has noted, "Human rights as a central foreign policy issue, and human rights groups as an important type of social movement, are relatively recent phenomena. Prior to 1973, most human rights organizations did not yet exist or were relatively small" (63). Nor does this mean that there was an absence of international human rights norms in these Southern Cone countries prior to the 1970s, but "they were not implemented in practice. Human rights did not constitute an important foreign policy category, nor was the term used frequently by social movements to frame their concerns or demands" (Sikkink 63). Indeed, Latin America played a role in the post–World War II debate over human rights, and Latin American states "championed the inclusion of human rights language in the United Nations charter and passed their own American Declaration of Human Rights even before the UN Declaration had been signed" (Sikkink 63).

12. This logic is precisely at play in Uruguay with AI's shift from "Prisoners of Conscience" (PoC) to their new "campaign against torture." AI had employed the term "PoC" in order to identify "individuals who have been persecuted for their conscientiously-held beliefs." The term, however, could only be applied "provided that they [individuals] have not used or advocated violence" (http://www.prisonersofconscience.org/about-poc/). This, of course, left AI in a predicament when dealing with torture in the Southern Cone, since most of the tortured subjects were members of revolutionary guerrilla groups, who believed and participated in armed warfare. The "campaign against torture" overcame this dilemma, since it shifted the discourse away from the individual and his or her acts and reasons and focused precisely on the regimes that employed torture as an inter-

rogation method. Many considered the campaign to be a huge success; AI was even awarded the Nobel Peace Prize in 1977 for its effort to stop torture. No doubt AI made a strategic decision in exposing these abuses to a wider audience. Yet, the point here is what was displaced in the shift from the PoC to the "campaign against torture." Even though PoC excluded an individual Tupamaro, its definition made those political reasons crucial to the individual's inclusion or exclusion. The "campaign against torture," on the other hand, could include every political prisoner regardless of his or her individual reasons, since the conversation shifted away from the individual to the act of torture. In other words, unlike the PoC, the "campaign against torture" rendered political consideration irrelevant and ideology invisible.

13. In the 1970s, human rights networks "focused [their] efforts on a range of rights narrower than that included in the human rights documents of the UN— especially on the so-called rights of the person, including the freedom from execution, torture, and arbitrary imprisonment" (Sikkink 63).

14. In her book *Left in Transformation*, Vania Markarian argues that the Uruguayan Left "adopts" the language of human rights "not to replace such a comprehensive framework for political action, but as a means of pressing very concrete goals in response to burning developments in the region" (6). For Markarian, the appropriation of human rights language is not understood, however, as a radical departure from their leftist ideology, since she maintains that the Left continued to fight for the "common cause." Markarian also notes that the appropriation of human rights language was met with strong resistance from the Left because it seemingly depoliticized its beliefs. Nevertheless, Markarian's work is less concerned with mapping out the future political consequence of this appropriation than it is with demonstrating how the Uruguayan Left came to "adopt" this language in the period of authoritarian rule. While my present chapter is highly indebted to Markarian's insightful historical analysis of the Uruguayan Left's appropriation of human rights language, it ultimately argues another point. In my chapter, I attempt to show the consequences of this shift, which sees the Left's commitment to human rights language not as a means to maintain a "radical ideology," but rather as a means to evacuate this ideology.

15. Part of the problem was that when revolutionaries used the term "victim" in the past, it meant something radically different. For revolutionaries, Markarian explains, the term "was [. . .] reserved to the exploited and underprivileged" (61). The point here is significant, since it underscores that for a revolutionary it was not torture that turned someone into a victim, but rather his political situation as an "exploited and underprivileged" subject within the economic structure. From the revolutionary perspective, what was unjust about the political system was not that it made you into a tortured person, but rather that it made you into a poor one. In effect, the (poor) victim was never considered bound to his or her victimhood, since those who decided to become revolutionaries "have decided to stop being [. . .] mere victims of the distant decisions of the government" (Markarian 61). The term "victim" for the Tupamaros is understood as an effect of class exploitation; it stressed the subject's "decision" to either accept the reality that the government imposed or fight against a bourgeois state that "exploited." Said differently, the shift from a "mere victim" to a revolutionary was constitu-

tive of a choice to act, to fight for socialism. Thus, for the Left, the human rights groups' definition of the term "victim" not only made (state) violence primary, but also, and more importantly, redefined the political prisoners as passive, since it rendered the logic to "stop being" a victim completely unavailable.

16. For a discussion about the centrality of the body in creating "humanitarian narratives" in eighteenth- and nineteenth-century literature, see Lynn Hunt's *Inventing Human Rights* (2007) and Thomas Laqueur's 1989 essay "Bodies, Details, and the Humanitarian Narrative."

17. This quote is taken from Ivan Morris's 1976 letter to the editors, "Torture in Uruguay," in the *New York Review of Books*. Morris urges readers to write "letters or postcards" to the Uruguayan president Bordaberry "to end torture," while stressing that AI is an "impartial, non-political, humanitarian organization" ("Torture"). Amnesty International, in other words, defined itself as nonpartisan, and Morris's "non-political" message makes it clear that their mission was not partial to the concerns of one political group or movement. Morris explains, "Political prisoners in Uruguay represent all political parties," and it was AI's mission to defend the rights of not only "Communist," but also the "right-of-centre Blanco (White) Party, and include workers, students, doctors, former parliamentarians, lawyers, teachers, and trade unionists" ("Torture"). Morris emphasizes that the organization considered itself nonpartisan and that political prisoners' beliefs were inconsequential to the organization's defense of their rights; that is, political prisoners merited equal humane treatment regardless of the political beliefs that they held (i.e., humanitarian).

18. It may be true that the text marks an important transition from Benedetti's revolutionary commitment to a humanitarian one, a commitment that certainly becomes apparent in his 1982 novel *Primavera con una esquina rota*. Stephen Gregory's book *Intellectuals and Left Politics in Uruguay, 1958–2006* presents an insightful analysis of Benedetti's trajectory as an intellectual in Uruguay since the 1970s, as well as a genealogy of the figure of the Uruguayan intellectual more broadly since the late 1950s.

19. Reflecting on the emergence of "human rights issues" in the 1970s, Sikkink points out that "what happened [. . .] was essentially the 'creation' of the human rights issue as an important and shared category to express the concerns of groups in both the south and the north" (63). The idea here is that human rights language was successful because it provided a "shared category" where common concerns could be expressed. What this implies is that the "creation" of this "shared category" was integral to successfully culling different "groups in both the south and the north," but in particular, in the United States and Europe, where the shared "category [. . .] found an echo in policy circles" (63). Sikkink's observation thus reveals that human rights became a strategic point of contact between the US government and human rights groups and victims. This should be noted, since in the period prior to repression in Uruguay and the Southern Cone, diplomatic ties between these Southern Cone countries and the US government had become strained due to a rise in communist sentiment after the Cuban Revolution. For the United States, Latin America was a hotbed of communism and was perceived as a threat to capitalism; the US government not only supported these coups in the 1970s but did so precisely because it sought to destroy the threat that

communism posed. These coups were effective in eradicating this communist threat through torture, repression, and killings; but insofar as human rights issues focused on torture, repression, and killings, they, too, collaborated in making communism irrelevant. From this perspective, then, what is important about the emergence of a "shared" human rights language is not only that it came at the expense of a "revolutionary discourse" but more importantly that it came at the expense of anticapitalist politics. But if this shift is understood as strategic in the period of repression, in the period of democratization it would become a definitive element of leftist politics. In this way, the force of a "shared" category of human rights was not and should be considered as not simply the elimination of torture but also the elimination of an ideology that sought to contradict the logic of capital. From this standpoint, the appropriation of a human rights language does not just signify a more "humanitarian" world that bridges a difference between the north and the south, but rather becomes an important technology through which the opposition between competing ideologies vanishes.

20. Or, as Sikkink suggests, "Whereas previously the movement had focused on documenting and denouncing abuses by military governments, it now called on emerging democratic regimes to hold accountable the perpetrators of past human rights abuses" (66).

21. One exception to the overall shift to the center can be found in the political group the Proletarios. However, they would disband by the mid-1990s, and since their dismantling, the crucial commitment of radical leftist politics has been to human rights justice and not to economic justice. For an interesting analysis of the Tupamaros in this period, see Adolfo Garcé's *Donde hubo fuego*.

22. http://www.uruguaychamber.com/press_11.php.

23. And this trend did not exclude the presidency of the ex-Tupamaro José "Pepe" Mujica. See my essay "From Shopping Malls to Memory Museums" for an analysis of the Mujica years of presidency.

24. In the years that followed the rise of the Pink Tide, there had been a return to conversations about revolutionary politics. At its most radical in Uruguay we find the Proletario, and the ex-Tupamaro Jorge Zabalza, who, in Federico Leicht's 2007 book *Cero a la izquierda: Una biografía de Jorge Zabalza*, critiques this Left's commitment to neoliberal politics. In Argentina, this conversation about revolution began in the mid-1990s with David Blaustein's film *Cazadores de utopias*, Miguel Bonasso's *Cámpora: El presidente que no fue*, and Eduardo Anguita and Martín Caparrós's *La voluntad* and extends to the present day with debates surrounding the publication of Héctor Jouvé's *testimonio* in *La intemperie*. I welcome these debates as a break with conventional human rights discourse; nevertheless, I wonder if they serve more as a platform to discuss issues such as the ethics of political violence, heroism, and "immolation for the common cause" or the *guerrillero arrepentido* than as a proper critique of class politics. For example, as María Sondéguer points out, the very title of Beatriz Sarlo's 1996 article "Cuando la política era joven" seems to suggest that Sarlo reduces guerrilla action and violence to nothing more than an error of youth. We can see something similar in the emergence of an overvalued and highly romanticized vision of violence and armed struggle that defines itself in opposition to what has been described as Sarlo's "posture of disillusion" (Beverley, "Rethinking" 48). I believe that Pilar Calveiro

is exactly right when she argues that "the recovery of militant politics for 'imitation,' the exaltation of 'heroic' lives that are not subject to a critique accomplishes subtraction: it impedes analysis, the valuation of what is right and wrong, and with them, the possibility of revising practice and, by extension, acting. In sum, it's another form of political subtraction" (13).

25. This logic can be found throughout her introduction to the 2009 English translation of the text. Indeed, in the introduction, she frames the text within a global context of torture in which "the globalization of torture makes time and place irrelevant" (iii).

Chapter 2: Disability and Redemocratization

1. Part of this lack of awareness is a reflection of the predominant medical model that equates disability with an "individual deficit" (Shakespeare 216). And one can understand the rise of disability studies as a response to this medical model vis-à-vis a social model, one that explains the "social exclusion" of disabled people by insisting that disability, much like gender, is socially constructed. From this position, according to Tom Shakespeare, the "medical model approaches are reactionary" (216).

2. The point is that they sought to entirely banish socialism from society. Poblete, for example, was a labor unionist, who, it is assumed, was disappeared for his beliefs and activities. To imagine, instead, that he was disappeared solely because of his disability is to render the political beliefs for which Poblete fought irrelevant. For a further discussion, see my essay "Disability and Latin American Cultural Studies."

3. MIR (Movimiento de Izquierda Revolucionaria/Revolutionary Left Movement) in Chile; MR8 (Movimento Revolucionário 8 de Outubro/Revolutionary October 8th Movement) in Brazil.

4. Unlike Plato's allegory that saw disability as a critique of democracy, Cristina Peri Rossi's *La nave de los locos* and Carlos Liscano's *El furgón de los locos* present good literary examples of how disability today is used to argue for a more inclusive and pluralistic society.

5. For Boom writers, as in the case of the military regimes, disability is deployed through an ableist lens, as a metaphor to cast a negative light on a national reality. For example, disability, as in the case of *Cien años de soledad*, represented the end of the bourgeois nation-state, a break with a decaying and decadent world, and a gesture toward a new political horizon. This is not to equate the Boom authors, complicit as they were with the commercialization of culture, with the bloody dictatorships, but to emphasize that they shared certain strategies of representation when it came to disability.

6. If Paulina's response to Gerardo's accusation that she is "sick" is "But can't one be sick and recognize a voice?" (23), the Hollywood film answers with a definitive "Yes, a disabled person can recognize a voice." The play, instead, answers with a "maybe." And this "maybe" registers a political climate of instability that marks the future of democracy in Chile.

7. These limitations include the fact that some of the same people who had

power during the military regime continued to hold power in the transition to democracy—a point that Paulina makes when she notes that a judge who, during the dictatorship, had told a wife that her disappeared husband had gone with "alguien más atractiva" (someone more attractive) was now in charge of bringing about "justice" in the democratic period (10). This quote is found in the Spanish edition.

8. Although the transition was different in each country, in each case the incorporation of human rights was central to the success of redemocratization. Argentina in the period of transition went for a more radical approach of trying officials, while in Uruguay a truth commission was completely forgone.

9. If the commission had tried and incarcerated these perpetrators, the question of who was out and who was in would look radically different and would effectively eliminate the drama. The story of Paulina would be less about revenge because of national uncertainty than about perhaps finding her place as a result of national stability.

10. In Geraldo's defense—and the defense of politicians and activists on the Left like him—the claim has often been made that the transition to democracy also meant compromising many ideals, since authoritarian rulers were always quick to threaten the nation with another coup if they were tried and convicted, which did in fact happen in Argentina. This tendency can be found to varying degrees in all the transitions in the Southern Cone, where new governments seemed to side ultimately with the military regime. Ksenija Bilbija and Leigh A. Payne note: "The democratic governments that replaced the dictatorships sometimes have proven to be more forceful than perpetrators in imposing the 'silence is golden' rule. Concerned about opening up deep ideological conflict, returning the country to violence or authoritarian rule, or governing across a deep memory schism, democratic governments may attempt to suppress traumatic memory, usually to no avail" (17). As I will demonstrate, however, in the following chapters, if that desire was real, it eventually turned into a staunch defense of neoliberalism on the part of the Left.

11. The neoliberal economist Gary Becker already makes this point in his text *The Economics of Discrimination* when noting that to stay competitive in a capitalist market it makes little sense to discriminate.

12. For hysteria and anorexia, see Susan Bordo's *Unbearable Weight*.

13. In the published Spanish edition, Gerardo is "la sociedad, no ella" ("society, not her"; 49).

14. In the Spanish version, this political commentary is much more explicit: "porque ahí tú usas fuerza física superior para imponer tu punto de vista" (38; English: "because then you use your superior physical force to impose your point of view").

15. In Spanish, that the "country reconciles." In English, it is "so the country can shut the door" (13).

16. The point here is not to deny that there were tortured victims who had no direct political involvement with the socialists or the communists. There were, in fact, a number of people who were tortured who didn't claim ending inequality as part of their project. Nevertheless, part of my critique of *Death and the Maiden* is to recognize that the play shares a general tendency in the postdictatorial period

to treat dictatorships that sought to exterminate socialism as dictatorships that sought to exterminate people without beliefs; in so doing, they also eliminate an entire historical and political project that served to end economic inequality.

17. This doesn't mean that the "communists" are never mentioned in the play (59). For example, in his "confession," Roberto mentions that he started working for the military regime because he wanted to fight the communists, but the fight is completely depoliticized because it is understood more as a vendetta for killing his father. But even if his objective had been purely ideological (which it wasn't), this objective would quickly disappear, as his confession primarily focuses on how torturing "turned into excitement" and that he "began to really truly like what [he] was doing" (59). The idea here is not that some torturers were sadists (some certainly were), but rather that the insistence on sadism functions to make the question of ideology irrelevant.

18. It seems, unfortunately, that this critique of stereotypes for Avelar is only limited to gender and not to disability itself, since, at one point, he crudely characterizes Gerardo as "almost mentally retarded" (*Letter* 53).

19. Antebi also articulates this anti-identitarian form of disability politics when she notes that disability is "open to practices through which new and shifting identities may be articulated" (8).

20. For another version of the logic of neoliberalism and its disruption, see Masiello's *Art of Transition*. Masiello notes that "if neoliberalism, as a celebration of free-marketeering, paints a sheen of apparent neutrality on social contradiction, erasing strands of memory that bound individuals to their past and suppressing discussion of 'value,' literature and art instead cultivate tension, revealing the conflicts between unresolved past and present, between invisibility and exposure. [. . .] In this way, cultural texts interrupt the comfortable 'flow' of the postdictatorship regimes, so easily given to the sale of 'difference' yet so often indifferent to the depths of experience" (3).

21. See, for example, Shoshana Felman and Dori Laub's *Testimony*, in which they argue that representation performs another injustice on victims of torture when it falsely provides the idea that pain can be represented.

22. Eltit puts it this way: "The narratives of these witnesses show how much the tragedy brought about by the 1973 coup is definitively revealed to be irreparable. I mean there is no possibility of a juridical or a financial reparation that might cover much less objectify the multiple and complex dimension of the human debacle exercised during the seventeen years of military control of the country" (171).

Chapter 3: Making Neoliberal History

1. *Las cartas que no llegaron* was a bestseller in Uruguay (now in its tenth edition) and quite successful internationally. It has been published in ten different countries, including two editions in Spain and translations into English and German. Director Pablo Dotta is now adapting it into a film.

2. Detained on May 19, 1972, Rosencof spent the first eight months in jail being interrogated and tortured; these first months he required hospitalization on four separate occasions as a result of the military's brutality. He was then trans-

ferred to the ironically named Libertad (Freedom) prison, where he stayed until the 1973 coup in Chile. At that point, the military classified Rosencof, along with eight other high-profile Tupamaros (including the future president José "Pepe" Mujica), as *rehenes* (hostages); he was then told they would be executed if their organization participated in any more acts of violence. Over the next twelve years, the "hostages" were regularly transferred to undisclosed military barracks throughout Uruguay. In a translator's note to Rosencof's *Conversations with My Sandal*, Louise B. Popkin describes the conditions for Rosencof this way: "During most of the [time] he was forced to endure filth, extreme temperatures, and humidity in a tiny cell two by two meters, as well as hunger and thirst so great that he sometimes had to drink his own urine to stay alive; he was denied virtually all human contact" (*Conversations* 67).

3. Unlike most Latin American nations, Uruguay had enjoyed a relatively stable democracy for most of the twentieth century. Until the early 1950s it was still considered a so-called model country, maintaining a sound middle class, a literacy rate of 95 percent, and universal health care. It was around this period that Uruguay was called the Switzerland of Latin America. By the mid-1950s, this stability was coming undone, as the ill effects of failed ISI (import-substitution industrialization) policies could no longer be contained. It was around this period that Rosencof met the future Tupamaro leader Raúl Sendic while covering a 1956 rice-workers' strike in Uruguay's interior. Rosencof's main role in the group was as a writer and propagandist. His most famous text from this period was *La rebelión de los cañeros* (The rebellion of the sugarcane workers; 1969), which depicts the life and work of Raúl Sendic leading up to the organization of the Tupamaros. Rosencof was also a key contributor to the creation of Costa Gavras's *State of Siege*.

4. This was the typical language of Tupamaro communiqués that circulated between 1967 and 1971. The book does, however, mention words like "socialism" (15) and "bourgeois" (16), but they appear largely in the first section of the book, which is told from the perspective of a child narrator, who has no idea what these words mean, and they have little connection to why he is in prison.

5. It is important to recognize that Rosencof's previous works were more straightforward accounts of the dictatorship; see, for example, *Memorias del calabozo* (Memories of the dungeon; 1987), which he wrote with Eleuterio Fernández Huidobro. The argument can thus be made, as Anna Forné does, that these earlier political writings paved the way for him to explore more personal events (54). While this may be true, the point of departure for my discussion is less an account of the possible reasons why he did write the book than what he did, in fact, write. There are many ways one can tell one's life story; this chapter is concerned with exploring the story that is represented in *Las cartas que no llegaron*.

6. The appearance of this phrase in *Las cartas que no llegaron* presents a radical break with traditional Tupamaro philosophy in more ways than one. To divorce the qualifier "class" from the "enemy" not only delivers a very vague, nondescript "enemy" but also eliminates, in drastic fashion, precisely what it means to be a Tupamaro. It also cannot go unnoticed that the traditional guerrilla's strategic call for "armed action" is now transformed into an indistinguishable, passive victim of an action done "against us" (*Las cartas* 1). The point of this redescription of Tupamaro rhetoric into a more ambiguous, and subsequently more inclusive, "en-

emy" is that the "enemy" is now intrinsically tied to Rosencof being Jewish. Ultimately, for Rosencof, this "enemy" will collapse into the figure of Hitler.

7. For Rosencof, this is not simply a literary device. In a biography published the same year as *Las cartas que no llegaron*, Rosencof asks, "Por qué no puede haber memorias que también se hereden?" (Why not have memories that can also be inherited?) (Campodónico, 342). As will be discussed later, treating memories as if they were in fact physical traits will become essential to grasping how history functions in *Las cartas que no llegaron*.

8. For an analysis of a childhood perspective and the importance of the imagination in *Las cartas que no llegaron*, see Colvin's "Memory and Fantasy: The Imaginative Reconstruction of a Lost Past in *Las cartas que no llegaron*." Colvin also argues that perspective is always fragmented and thus is closer to Nora's idea of memory that "takes root in the concrete, in spaces, gestures, images, and objects" (Nora 9). Anna Forné's article explores these objects, including photos, letters, and words, or what she calls (and titles her article) "the materiality of memory," to construct this uneven, nonlinear past.

9. Criticism has often insisted on this link. In her essay "Nuestra Shoá: Dicta-duras, Holocausto y represión en tres novelas judeorioplatenses," Ran notes the link between the Holocaust and the dictatorships; in her essay, however, she is interested not in critiquing the conflation between the two, but in stressing how both horrors in fiction can avoid being a "cliché" (16). She also examines other postdictatorial texts that bridge the Holocaust and the dictatorships, including Manuela Fingueret's *Hija del silencio* (1999) and Sergio Chejfec's *Lenta biografía* (1990). We can also add to this list Lucía Puenzo's *Wakolda* (2013), Edmundo Paz Soldán's *El delirio de Turing* (2003), Jorge Volpi's *En busca de Klingsor* (1999), and Roberto Bolaño's *El Tercer Reich* (2010) and *La literatura nazi en América* (1996). Not all these novels and films subscribe to the same aesthetic and political project as Rosencof's text.

10. I cite an online edition of Huntington's essay.

11. My argument is a critique not of Rosencof but of *Las cartas que no llegaron*. This means that the evacuation of a story about the Tupamaros should not be read as an attempt on Rosencof's part to disassociate or to disavow himself from his past. But it also shouldn't be read as what Gustavo Lespada calls autobiographical "autonomía," or poetic license. Lespada declares in his essay that "the risk of the critic to confuse autonomy with the social-historical referent is not possible, due to the enormous autobiographical component" (1). To make this observation is to miss the point being made here. To distinguish between an "autobiography" or even "fiction" and independent "history" is to completely overlook Rosencof's intention to imagine—regardless of the book's testament to truth or fiction—that the Holocaust and his imprisonment are intrinsically linked by what it means to be Jewish.

12. See Ran's essay on the question of anti-Semitism, especially in Argentina. For an analysis of anti-Semitism in Uruguay, see Clara Aldrighi, María Magdalena Camou, Miguel Feldman, and Gabriel Abend, *Antisemitismo en Uruguay: Raíces, discursos, imágenes (1870–1940)* (Montevideo: Ediciones Trilce, 2000).

13. See, for example, Miguel Bonasso's *Campora: El presidente que no fue* (1997)

and *Diario de un clandestino* (2000) and Eduardo Anguita and Martín Caparrós's *La voluntad* (1997, 1998).

14. At the same time, this documentary has been strongly criticized for its exaggerated focus on who the Carris really were, which extends well beyond the ideological project that defined the Montoneros. For example, in her reading of the documentary in *Tiempo pasado*, Beatriz Sarlo points to the film's interest in the every-day trivialities of Carri's parents' lives and stresses that the documentary does not provide any new insight on the Argentine dictatorship, but rather, at its best, solely serves the emotional interests of the family directly affected. What is problematic for Sarlo is that if one wants to know more about the dictatorship, little can be learned about the recent past in *Los rubios*; that is, finding out whether Carri's parents cheated when they played sports or how they behaved generally tells us absolutely nothing about the historical imbrications of the dictatorships. Furthermore, once the fundamental idea shifts from the history of the dictatorship to finding out who her parents really are, it matters very little whether this information is political (they were, in fact, Montonero guerrillas) or personal (they cheated when playing sports); everything becomes relevant in the discovery of who you are.

Despite Sarlo's criticism, this commitment to the discovery of who they are continues to be a pressing concern for an entire generation of activists, including, or especially, for the children of the *desaparecidos*. *Los rubios* reflects an interesting moment in relation to the recent dictatorships when those who are now writing books and directing films about the dictatorships are *not* those who directly experienced torture, imprisonment, and trauma.

15. A "specter," according to Jacques Derrida, is a "revenant," a ghost that cannot be explained through an eschatological history; the specter does not have an origin or a destination and is always already coming back, suspended in an infinite process of mourning. It is for this reason that the specters of the past haunt the present and bring different demands for justice (*Specters* 46).

16. This logic is also at the heart of Derrida's own account of how he came to the idea of specters as it relates to Marx, which he states, is intimately connected to "those of us" who lived through this experience in the 1950s; that is, the specter is grounded in his "generation" and "resonates like an old repetition" (*Specters* 15).

17. To be sure, Marx spoke of the specter in the *Communist Manifesto*, but the specter stood for communism, not a politics of constant deferral. For Marx, in other words, the project is about communism, not about an undetermined open project to come.

18. See her chapter "Obstinate Memory" in *The Decline and Fall of the Lettered City: Latin America in the Cold War*.

19. Ksenija Bilbija and Leigh A. Payne, in *Accounting for Violence*, challenge this idea of memory by noting that memory projects, including books and films, sell well in the market. In the introduction of the book, Bilbija and Payne set out to produce a type of taxonomy of the memory industry, and thus to extend Avelar's comment that "every corner of social life has been commodified" (*Untimely* 1). For them, this commitment to mapping out memory as a commodity does not necessarily mean that it can't be a form of resistance. Both critics note, for example,

that the memory market has an "activist component" that allows for a specific message to be disseminated (27). Thus, the question for them rests less on trying to find a project that stands outside of capitalism than on trying to distinguish between good memory projects and bad ones. But how do you discern between a project that "cheapens memory goods" and "derails progress toward building a human rights culture" and one that focuses on "victims" and ultimately tries not to "repeat" this horrific past (3)? For Bilbija and Payne, valid memory projects do not "sell out" memory at the victim's expense (3). What is important about their approach is that it incorporates commodity into the equation. Nevertheless, it leaves human rights ideology completely untouched, suggesting an opposition between neoliberalism and "human rights culture."

20. Sarlo has suggested a similar idea in her reading of Primo Levi in *Tiempo pasado*. The same can be said of Margarita Saona's masterful book on memory in Peru, where the argument is made that insofar as there still exists a question of radical injustice with regard to the recent past, memory still serves a purpose to bear witness and speak to that past.

Chapter 4: The Reappearance of the Frame

1. It is not my objective to endorse an indexical reading of photography (à la Sontag); mediation still informs the photos of Abu Ghraib. Rather, the objective is to show how the logic of indexicality has been paramount to an understanding of contemporary Latin American postmodern theory vis-à-vis the *testimonio*.

2. Randall Williams, Christian Gundermann, and Slavoj Žižek have also critiqued aspects of human rights discourse.

3. For more details on Botero's oeuvre, see Sillevis. For an interesting essay arguing against the idea of Botero as a politically engaged artist, see Barnitz.

4. Painting also has an indexical component, but it is related to the brush and the paint, not to the object that is seen in the painting.

5. A point that the narrator of César Aira's novel *Un episodio en la vida del pintor viajero* (*An Episode in the Life of a Landscape Painter*; 2002) gets exactly right when he notes that the job of the landscape painter would be replaced by a photographer in the twentieth century. For a brilliant essay on the question of indexicality in photography, see Michaels's "Photographs and Fossils."

6. It is undoubtedly true that the ontology of digital photography is different than that of analogue photography. Nevertheless, photography still continues to maintain a level of factuality that is absent in paintings, and this sense of factuality still guides most people's relationship to photography, despite the emergence of digital photography. Manipulation, on the other hand, has been as central to the history of analogue photography as it has to digital photography.

7. This does not mean that the US Army did not know about the abuses that were occurring in Abu Ghraib. Indeed, the Taguba Report, a fifty-three-page document that was completed in late February 2004 and subsequently leaked, had already documented much of what had taken place.

8. For an intriguing discussion on the abuses that occurred in Abu Ghraib prison and their relationship to the photos, see Errol Morris's documentary *Stan-*

dard Operating Procedure and his book *Believing Is Seeing: Observations on the Mysteries of Photography.*

9. See, for example, the works of Ebony and Danto.

10. It should be noted that the Abu Ghraib photos were shown in New York's International Center of Photography in September 2004 and also in the Andy Warhol Museum in Pittsburgh. This reveals, perhaps indirectly, that intentionality is another equally significant aspect that must be considered when approaching these photos. Chapter 5 explores intentionality as the primary marker to determine the status of the work of art. For further discussion on the intersection of indexicality, photography, and art, see both Fried's *Why Photography Matters as Art as Never Before* and Michaels's book *The Beauty of a Social Problem.*

11. Juan Carlos Botero's claim is made about several pieces in Botero's *Abu Ghraib*. Although I disagree with his reading of Botero's paintings, I have cited him here because his claim perfectly embodies the political gesture of theatrical art.

12. See Agosín's collection for a good overview of human rights fiction in Latin America.

13. I agree with Williams and Moreiras insofar as the *testimonio* becomes crucially linked with identity politics in this period and also evacuates an emancipatory politics because of it. This chapter is meant not as an exhaustive investigation of the *testimonio*, but rather as a critique of the antirepresentational approaches of the *testimonio*, especially in the work of Beverley and Yúdice. See also Colás's "What's Wrong" and Larsen and Sklodowska for critiques of antirepresentational accounts of the *testimonio*.

14. See, for example, Beverley's essay "The Neoconservative Turn in Latin American Literary and Cultural Criticism."

15. As Barthes notes, photography does bear an indexical relationship to the object it represents, though this does not make it the object itself. The "emanation of the referent" is not the referent itself, even though you cannot have that emanation (photograph) without the referent. For this reason, it cannot lie, or at least it cannot lie about the fact that it was there; and this is why Valeria de los Ríos claims that "photography is testimonial" (75).

16. Furthermore, indexicality also provides a possible excuse for what is now known as the Rigoberta Menchú controversy. The controversy revealed that Menchú had lied about certain details of her *testimonio*. Beverley defended the *testimonio* and Rigoberta Menchú by suggesting that the *testimonio* couldn't lie because the overall history of genocide and atrocities is true, and because the *testimonio* as a form directly captures the life of the community. And the way that this was achieved was by imagining the *testimonio* as an indexical mechanism that must capture this event rather than as a work whose subject intends to (mis)represent this event. The point of treating the *testimonio* as an indexical mechanism, in other words, is that it makes it *impossible* for Menchú to represent (or misrepresent) because the *testimonio* just registers what is already there (e.g., Peirce's smoke). We can observe this question most clearly in the episode surrounding the anthropologist David Stoll's accusation that certain elements of Rigoberta Menchú's *I, Rigoberta Menchú* were misleading (if not entirely false). Stoll, who had been carrying out fieldwork in Guatemala, noted several discrepancies in Menchú's *testimonio*; the most apparent dealt with inconsistencies surrounding the death of

Menchú's brother. Beverley—whom Stoll had described as "an authority on testimonio"—defended the veracity of Menchú's book tooth and nail despite evidence suggesting otherwise (Stoll 226). Noting Beverley's wholehearted commitment to the *testimonio* in general and Menchú's text in particular, Stoll remarks that Beverley treated the *testimonio* like "a fundamentalist interprets the Bible." Of course, what Stoll meant by this was not simply that the only truth for a fundamentalist was the Bible, but that Beverley had failed to be objective despite the reliability of his findings. And for this reason, Stoll continues, Beverley "seemed to be arguing against interpreting [the *testimonio*]" (Stoll 226–227). Instead of the biblical nature of the *testimonio*, what Beverley insists on is the indexicality of the form. For this reason, Beverley can't imagine that Menchú lied because indexicality doesn't lie; it just is. For more details on this episode, see Arturo Arias's *The Rigoberta Menchú Controversy* or Stoll's own account in his book *Rigoberta Menchú and the Story of All Poor Guatemalans*.

17. One can begin to see how the question of the frame—or at least an attack on the frame—now becomes central for contemporary theory. For example, Judith Butler has addressed the problem of the frame in her recent work on human suffering. More specifically, Butler's work is concerned with questions such as "Who counts as human? Whose lives count as lives? [. . .] What makes for a grievable life?" (*Precarious* 20). Butler believes that the visibility of human vulnerability is at the center of "non-military political solutions," but hegemonic forces such as the United States deny or limit this vulnerability by either ignoring or manipulating how these people are seen (*Precarious* 29). In this way, Butler understands violence (and mourning of those who die from violence) as a symptom of visibility and recognition; she also understands that "non-military political solutions" begin with questioning how these precarious lives are depicted or framed. Butler explains that "the frame works both to preclude certain kinds of questions, certain kinds of historical inquiries, and to function as a moral justification for retaliation [. . .] It seems crucial to attend to this frame, since it decides, in a forceful way, *what we can hear*, whether a view will be taken as explanation or as exoneration, whether we can hear the difference and abide by it" (*Precarious* 4–5). The frame, for Butler, decides who is human, and for this reason it not only reflects but also *is* power and ideology; and it is for this same reason that the frame must be not just critiqued but eliminated. If the frame produces a problem, by Butler's account, the solution becomes the attempt to move beyond the frame in order to achieve a world that no longer divides between those we see (and mourn) and those we don't see and continue to ignore. Critical work, for her, always points to where the frame or representation fails so that we, too, can bear witness. Recalling the work of Emmanuel Levinas, Butler notes: "For representation to convey the human, then, representation must not only fail, but it must show its failure. There is something unrepresentable that we nevertheless seek to represent, and that paradox must be retained in the representation we give" (*Precarious* 144). From this position, then, questioning the frame and representation more generally becomes essential to producing a politics that also brings us closer to being human. For Butler, behind the frame one sees both grievable lives and that the problem is precisely one of witnessing and experiencing. Whether Butler's account is meant as a critique of human rights that limit those who are seen or as a

better version of human rights that will include all humans, it insists that we fail to witness these events as well as that the frame prompts this failure (which Butler portrays as central to the political problem). Butler has also written specifically about Abu Ghraib; see *Frames of War: When Is Life Grievable?*

18. By the 1990s, in fact, many countries across Latin America had implemented new constitutions that incorporated language for groups that had largely been excluded. See Van Cott for further discussion.

19. Castañeda's book lays the foundation for this project in the early 1990s.

Chapter 5: Anti-intentionalism and the Neoliberal Left

1. See, for example, Moretti's chapter on detective fiction. It is also interesting to note that Borges imagined the detective story as the realization of this autonomy.

2. Many of these concerns are discussed in Beverley, Oviedo, and Aronna's *The Postmodernism Debate in Latin America*.

3. Emerging in 1979 from within *La escena de avanzada* or the Chilean neo-avant-garde, CADA is composed of five members: the artists Lotty Rosenfeld and Juan Castillo, the sociologist Fernando Balcells, the writer Diamela Eltit, and the poet Raúl Zurita. For more details on the *avanzada* movement, see Richard's *Márgenes e instituciones*, Camnitzer, and Neustadt.

4. The polemic surrounding the political value of social realism and avant-garde art is in no way new. Within the Latin American context, Idelber Avelar, Beatriz Sarlo, and Nelly Richard have all scrutinized the realist form. From their perspective, what is wrong with social realism is that it reproduces rather than undermines market logic. Others have argued that avant-garde art is an elitist aesthetic that can only be appreciated by the bourgeoisie and the intellectual class. Inside Chile, this debate takes place between Hernán Vidal and Richard regarding CADA. See both Vidal's essay and Richard's response in *The Postmodernism Debate in Latin America*.

5. The story of the fascist poet first appears in *La literatura nazi en América* (*Nazi Literature in the Americas*; 1996). It also should not be lost on the reader that both novels, *La literatura nazi en América* and *Estrella distante*, register postcoup class dynamics insofar as both names, Wieder and Ruiz-Tagle, also clearly conjure up the triumph of the country's German immigrant elite and Creole landed oligarchy.

6. When addressing intentionality, I am drawing from Paul de Man's essay "Form and Intent in the American New Criticism." As de Man suggests, "intentionality is neither physical nor psychological in its nature, but structural, involving the activity of a subject regardless of its empirical concerns, except as far as they relate to the intentionality of the structure" (25). In his later work, de Man would famously disavow this commitment to intentionality; see, for example, his essay "The Purloined Ribbon."

7. For an excellent reading of Bolaño's work, especially of *Amuleto*, although differing from mine, see Draper's "Demanding." Draper sees Bolaño doing the opposite of autonomy by challenging "the usual figures historically articulated by

aesthetics and politics. By this I mean either the ideal of autonomy or art for art's sake, with the figure of the activist artist who transmits a message, or the notion of a vanguard as the group of forerunners who lead or guide the masses" ("Demanding").

8. Jennerjahn's insightful essay centers primarily on the historical avant-garde in *La literatura nazi en América*. Jeremías Gamboa Cárdenas instead focuses on *Estrella distante*, noting that Wieder's literary reincarnation as the barbaric writer Jules Defoe—who wants not only to create nonpoems by nonpoets but also to abolish literature altogether—is also clearly inspired by the historical avant-garde. In this way, Gamboa Cárdenas suggests that Wieder's artwork follows "certain declarations and fantasies from the most nihilistic movements of the historical avant-garde: the erosion without restrictions of the division between art and life as a way of dismantling the aestheticization of modern art and the admiration of crime as one of the fine arts" (217–218).

9. For Williams, Wieder's artwork reveals that the political potential behind the *avanzada*'s "claim to newness in representation" had already been rendered politically irrelevant by the coup and the "military's break with representation" ("Sovereignty" 135). What Williams means is that the *avanzada*'s neo-avant-garde project is entirely compatible with the logic of Pinochet's "state of exception," a claim that Wieder himself makes when he declares that his most spectacular happening would "show the world that the new regime and avant-garde art were not at odds" (135; Bolaño, *Estrella* 77). By locating his analysis as a response to the neo-avant-garde, Williams concludes that while *Estrella distante* "might point to the limits of the *avanzada* movement, it nevertheless remains 'ensconced' in the same politics that Bolaño himself ascribes to this Chilean literary movement" (Williams, "Sovereignty" 138). In other words, despite his efforts to critique the neo-avant-garde, for Williams, Bolaño's text fails to provide a political solution that moves beyond aesthetic and political compatibility, leaving a politics of the Right untouched. Franklin Rodríguez has taken a similar stance that gestures toward a certain exhaustion of past aesthetics and politics and declares, like Williams, that Bolaño provides no political "remedy" (217).

10. The original citation comes from Germán Bravo's "Las nuevas escrituras" in *Utopía(s)* (353).

11. Like the project of the various avant-garde movements, postmodernism can be understood as attempting to elide art and life. However, an important difference, and one that this chapter insists on, is how postmodernism's point of departure is not necessarily aesthetics, but rather the oppositional framework that supports Western thought, including art and life. In other words, art is symptomatic of a more global project. This point is radically different from the historical avant-garde, which is primarily understood as an aesthetic project. As Peter Bürger notes, the political impetus of the historical avant-garde is found in destroying the bourgeois institution that separated art from the "praxis of life," calling into question "the coherence and autonomy of the work" in a bourgeois society (56, 55). In short, while aesthetic form is central to the avant-garde, this is not necessarily the case with postmodernism. Indeed, postmodernism is deeply suspicious of the very existence of the category of art.

12. Josefina Ludmer argues in her "Literaturas postautónomas" that a moment has been reached in which old binaries such as realism and the avant-garde no longer carry the political value they once held, and thus, all wars between aesthetic camps prove to be irrelevant. In *Estrella distante*, this process can be witnessed in two rival poets, the Latin American realist Juan Stein and the European Diego Soto with his elitisms, whose whereabouts and importance as writers slowly vanish after the coup. Despite the attempt of Bibiano—a fellow poetry workshop classmate—to recuperate symbolically these aesthetico-political projects by tracking down the two poets, Stein and Soto disappear into a history of hearsay, loss, and mourning. Unlike the successful search to find Wieder (and aesthetic form), the attempt to locate a politics in realism or the avant-garde fails.

13. Ludmer argues that we have reached the end of the cycle of literary autonomy of which Bolaño's fiction is representative. Although Ludmer localizes this postautonomous literature primarily in contemporary Argentinean urban fiction, its traits seem to merely rearticulate what Fredric Jameson had already defined as postmodernism in 1984, traits that are clearly apparent in the turn toward high theory by critics and artists alike around the same period. Indeed, the two founding postulates of postautonomous literature according to Ludmer—that the economic is the cultural and the cultural is the economic; that reality is fiction and fiction is reality—are also foundational to Jameson's understanding of the aesthetic in late capitalism. If one takes Jameson's postulates as true, then Ludmer's account of postautonomy seems to be merely a further rearticulation of the postmodern project being outlined here; in other words, the absence of autonomy is already crucial to a discussion taking place in the 1980s and 1990s surrounding the *testimonio* and the neo-avant-garde.

14. One is reminded of Bürger's point: "Shocking the recipient becomes the dominant principle of artistic intent" (18).

15. According to Derrida, this commitment to the free-floating signifier—or iterability—is a political device that undermines the social, ethical, political "force" that adheres to all meanings and interpretations (*Limited* 102). By destabilizing the fixed meaning that hegemonic force imposes, a politically progressive position emerges that reveals that thought can no longer be constrained by "oppositional limits" (102).

16. As Sontag declared almost forty years earlier: "Today is such a time, when the project of interpretation is largely reactionary, stifling. Like the fumes of the automobile and of heavy industry which befoul the urban atmosphere, the effusion of interpretations of art today poisons our sensibilities. In a culture whose already classical dilemma is the hypertrophy of the intellect at the expense of energy and sensual capability, interpretation is the revenge of the intellect upon art. Even more. It is the revenge of the intellect upon the world. To interpret is to impoverish, to deplete the world—in order to set up a shadow world of 'meanings.' It is to turn the world into this world. ('This world'! As if there were any other.) The world, our world, is depleted, impoverished enough. Away with all duplicates of it, until we again experience more immediately what we have" (*Against* 4–5).

17. Here, again, I return to the question of disability. Tobin Siebers notes, for example, that disability requires that we reconsider intentionality. For this rea-

son, Siebers writes that artists with severe cognitive disabilities such as Judith Scott challenge the question of intentionality: "Traditionally, we understand that art originates in genius, but genius is really at a minimum only the name for an intelligence large enough to plan and execute works of art—an intelligence that usually goes by the name of 'intention.' Defective or impaired intelligence cannot make art according to this rule. Mental disability represents an absolute rupture with the work of art. It marks the constitutive moment of abolition, according to Michel Foucault, that dissolves the essence of what art is" (69).

18. In an interview with Avelar, Richard has argued the need to maintain the continuity between art and heteronomy; nevertheless, her commitment to imagining the object as determined by one's response rather than one's interpretation functions to render the aesthetic object irrelevant (Avelar, "La escena" 265). What defines the object for Richard, in other words, is determined primarily by the beholder's experience and not by the author's intention.

19. From this position, the *testimonio* shares with the neo-avant-garde the same kind of antirepresentational investment in what Shoshana Felman and Dori Laub have suggested as the point where the "breakdown" or the "breakage of words" occurs (*Testimony* 39). And while this "breakdown" would certainly count as a failure for Pedro in his quest to persuade the Capitán that he is wrong (see chap. 1), for Felman and Laub, it is in the moment of the "breakdown" that the "singular pain" or "trauma" can be transmitted to the reader. In other words, the breakdown of representation counts as a triumph for both the *testimonio* and, especially, the neo-avant-garde, as Richard reads it.

20. The original in Spanish is: "[El] valor de puro afecto [es] un antivalor, sin duda, puesto que lo propio suyo sería sustraerse a cualquier intercambio" (Avelar, "Alegoría" 25).

21. This lack of commitment to human rights is what Vidal sees as problematic in Richard's work. It's not necessarily human rights that Richard finds problematic, however, but rather political realism more generally. See Richard's "Reply" in the special issue, *The Postmodernism Debate in Latin America* in *boundary 2*.

22. For a version of how this commitment to difference at the expense of disagreement plays out in the North American context, see Michaels's seminal book *The Shape of the Signifier*.

23. It is true that Beverley ultimately comes to accept that the *testimonio* form is an exhausted project (see, for example, his article "The Real Thing"). Nevertheless, the political logic that defined the *testimonio* continues to survive even in Beverley's most recent book, *Latinamericanism after 9/11* (2011). Beverley notes that in the wake of 9/11, La Marea Rosada, and the triumph of neoliberalism, Latin Americanists must reconsider the very question of Latin Americanism, which, at the same time, requires understanding how "globalization and neoliberal political economy have done, more effectively than ourselves, the work of cultural democratization and dehierarchization" (*Latinamericanism* 21). But rather than abandon the project because it is deeply compatible with neoliberalism—and perhaps turn instead to questions of economic equality—Beverley believes that the objective of Latin Americanists today should be to double down on "cultural democratization and dehierarchization" and reclaim the project for the Left. See Hatfield for an outstanding dismantling of Beverley's argument.

Chapter 6: Literary Form Now

1. In his essay "Objective Form," Roberto Schwarz examines the Brazilian critic Antonio Candido's essay on *Memórias de um sargento de milícias* to suggest that the novel must be considered primarily at the level of form. Indeed, the brilliance of Candido's essay can be located, according to Schwarz, in the argument that the novel's form registers the structural determinations that are taking place in Brazil in the nineteenth century. For Schwarz, Candido's assertion of form must be read "against the background of the novel" (191). Schwarz puts it this way: "[. . .] What has to be done is to read the novel against its real background and study reality against the background of the novel—more on a formal level than in relation to its content, and in a creative way" (191). In this chapter I attempt to approach Zambra's *Bonsái* in a similar fashion. Thus, one way to imagine the omission of human rights and the assertion of form would be to say that Zambra's *Bonsái* is simply uninterested in the discourse of human rights and the postdictatorship; another way—and the way that it is being argued here—is that both this assertion and omission must be understood as a response to the waning belief that human rights present a true alternative to the structural determinations of capital in neoliberal Chile.

2. The epilogue is taken from one of Yasunari Kawabata's novels.

3. One should also consider Darío, Onetti, and Carver, who are read by Julio and Emilia, against a larger economic project and social dynamic. More to the point, one can understand their works as the desire to capture capitalist transformations at other points in time. In her superb book *Capital Fictions*, Ericka Beckman, for example, insightfully argues that at the turn of the twentieth century, Rubén Darío's *Azul* functioned to create a fiction of "consumption of European styles, referents, and objects," which ultimately endorses the idea that capitalism, despite its devastating impact on the majority of Latin America, was not only desirable but natural (47). Thus, *modernismo* becomes a capital fiction of the Export Age in that it promotes the thought that economic liberalization and modernization are a "natural and normal facet of social life" (x). I'm grateful to Beckman's book, as it offers a critical opening to understand Zambra's *Bonsái* not only in relation to past modernization projects but also as a response to the more recent "hypercommoditized logic of neoliberalism" (viii).

4. To be sure, Bolaño's *Estrella distante* and Zambra's *Bonsái* both seek to capture the radical alteration of economic structures in Chile through the lives of rather unsuccessful artists. In *Bonsái*, however, this precarious situation of unemployment directly gives rise to the creation of a novel. It should also be noted that Bolaño still very much identifies with the fall of a past socialist project in Latin America, which, in turn, is registered in the downtrodden workers and lumpenproletariats that are found in his texts. Unlike Bolaño, as Marcela Valdes suggests, "Zambra's characters are mostly downwardly mobile bourgeoisie. (At one point, *Bonsai* even refers to working-class beachgoers as *lumpen*, or riffraff.)" ("Seed"). But this omission of working-class figures can also be connected partially to an intensifying neoliberal project reflected in a new creative class whose interests shift away from representations of workers to middle-class subjects. For further discussion on the relationship between the creative class and neoliber-

alism, see Brouillette's *Literature and the Creative Economy* and Sánchez Prado's *Screening Neoliberalism*.

5. Colás's reading of Piglia's *Respiración artificial* (1980) is very insightful; however, I ultimately disagree with it. Colás sets out to show how this utopian vision found in Puig is altered after the Proceso de Reorganización Nacional. Unlike both Benedetti and Puig, who went into exile, Piglia remained in Argentina, a point that undoubtedly informs the structure of *Respiración artificial*, a novel that fully embraces a codified language of metafiction, parody, fragmentation, and gaps. What Colás wants to point to is how Piglia's use of this codified language becomes a form of postmodern resistance to the "pure" official history imposed by the junta. *Respiración artificial*, for Colás, provides an "impure" history that challenges the Proceso's essentialist account of history" (*Postmodernity* 172). In brief, while the Proceso insisted on purity, *Respiración artificial* resisted that concept by presenting purity as a "myth" (*Postmodernity* 94). Nevertheless, even though it is a critique of the inside and outside binary as "myth," it still posits a geographical, historical, and political utopian space that is outside of official history. That is, while metafiction may critique the myth of "official history," it also signals, much like Benedetti's *Pedro y el Capitán*, an autonomous space that remains outside of it. The binary, in other words, still remains in place. For an interesting reading on how Piglia deploys autonomy throughout his work, see Torres Perdigón.

6. If the dictatorship's repression not only gives rise to but also in a certain sense justifies this particular form of codified writing, this is not the case for the period of transition and, especially, for the period of democracy. In democracy—which Colás only briefly alludes to in the final chapter in his examples of the *testimonio*, the Madres de Plaza de Mayo, and other new social movements—these literary devices still hold a position of resistance. As he indicates throughout the book, part of the problem for the purity of leftist politics of the 1960s was that it was unreachable and quite destructive. Such was the case with the Montoneros, whose political absolutism blinded them to Perón's true intentions. What Piglia's text anticipates and what postmodern resistance does is correct this more "modernist" approach by stressing the impurity of politics and aesthetics (*Postmodernity* 169). New social movements such as the Madres do not naïvely follow dogmas, as did the revolutionary groups of the 1960s and 1970s; instead, they "resisted[,] because the history they embodied was not a history to be learned and slavishly followed, but one generated as the process of a group of subjects' confronting the present as the future of the past and as the past of the future" (*Postmodernity* 172). These new social movements that exist in transition and democracy incorporate the lived experiences that the dictatorship had disappeared, and they become, for Colás, models for change.

The emphasis on lived experience challenges the sense of "unity" that the Left in previous periods insisted on but also makes political change happen (*Postmodernity* 171). Ideological "unity" is both unnecessary and part of the problem (171). To support this claim he cites Judith Butler: "The insistence in advance on coalitional 'unity' as a goal assumes that solidarity, whatever its price, is a prerequisite for political action. But what sort of politics demands that kind of advance purchase on unity? Perhaps a coalition needs to acknowledge its contradictions and take action with those contradictions intact. Perhaps also part of what dialogic understanding entails is the acceptance of divergence, breakage, splinter, and fragmentation as part of the often torturous process of democratization. [. . .] Without the presupposition or goal of 'unity,' which is [. . .] always instituted at a conceptual level, provisional unities might emerge in the context of concrete actions that have purposes other than the articulation of identity" (qtd. in Colás, *Postmodernity* 171).

By accepting "divergence, breakage, splinter, and fragmentation," coalitions and social movements can divert the downfalls of past political movements without losing "oppositional impulses of an earlier generation" (*Postmodernity* 172). In this way, what Colás finds significant about the Madres is "their flexibility extended to forming coalitions with different prodemocracy and human rights groups" (*Postmodernity* 171). But as I demonstrated in the first three chapters, what is notable about these newer movements and their "provisional unities" is not the process, per se, or even their losing "impulses," but rather their evacuation of the political project of class equality. Instead, the process becomes the politics. That is, attempting to include those who were excluded is transformed into the primary politics of postdictatorship. In other words, despite whatever these movements like the Madres "resist," they continue to be compatible with capitalism. What we witness, then, is a whole series of mechanisms in politics and literature designed to replace the narrative of class conflict with neoliberal narratives of democracy, coalitions, and human rights.

7. This, of course, doesn't mean that *Los rubios* is not interested in official history. Indeed, the film directly examines official history when the actress playing Carri is watching videos of the former Montoneros who were the compañeros of Carri's parents. In this sense, the film is counteracting the "official history" of the Montoneros organization and exposing some of its inner contradictions.

8. As Patricia Waugh suggests in *Metafiction* (1984), though metafiction is at least as old as the genre of the novel itself, it becomes especially relevant in the postmodern period as an aesthetic and a political project. She defines metafiction as "a term given to fictional writing which self-consciously and systematically draws attention to its status as an artifact in order to pose questions about the relationship between fiction and reality" (2). Unlike Gass's account above that stresses the status of fiction, Waugh's postmodern definition calls into question this division, since it reveals that "the reality we live day by day is similarly constructed [to fiction]" (18). From this postmodern definition, Waugh believes that metafiction smudges the lines between reality and fiction in order to highlight a "dissatisfaction with traditional values" (6), values that have been treated as true, total, and eternal. Rather than insisting on an aesthetic space, metafiction, according to her, primarily functions to problematize binaries as a critique of Western ideology.

9. Morales Gamboa does believe Zambra's text is postmodern. However, he differs from these other critics in an important way. He believes that postmodernism can still maintain literary autonomy despite eliminating the distinction between art and nonart. But, as I argued in the last chapter, the opposite is true. If postmodern cultural production is the attempt to undermine, or deconstruct, the division between binaries, including the binaries between art and life, then it is also the elimination of literary autonomy. This is why, as just noted, Silva

rightly suggests following Hutcheon and García Canclini, who argue that post-modern novels challenge "the concepts of autonomy and transcendence" (11). If everything is a text, then nothing is. In this way, postmodernism can be defined not by its autonomy, but rather by its desire to be postautonomous.

10. This becomes a point of criticism for James Wood in his *New Yorker* piece: "The self-reflexive fictionality, in its multiple iterations, appears obsessive, and strikes one as an elaborate way to make a point already familiar in much post-modern work of the past forty years: that life resembles a fiction, and that fiction resembles another fiction, too" (*New Yorker*). Instead, Wood prefers Zambra's later works, whose "metafictional mediation" deals more with "a political culture of actual disappearance." From this position, it should be added that where this may be the situation in North America and Europe, it has not been in Latin America. Instead, what Wood wants ("a political culture of actual disappearance") is exactly what has dominated Latin America for the last forty years, which *Bonsái* breaks with while Zambra's later works, such as *Formas de volver a casa* (*Ways of Going Home: A Novel*; 2011), will return to.

11. If these governments were not able to prosecute all perpetrators of human rights violations, at the very least, the shift in power from violators to their victims was a symbolic victory.

12. It is a paradox because even if literature is an illusion, affective critics treat it as if it were real. What is more, they treat it as a mechanism to imagine a political potential. For example, in her reading of Bolaño's *Amuleto*, Susana Draper suggests, following Martin Heidegger, that art is linked to a "'measure' that corresponds to the incommensurable (that which affects, inhabits, or questions thought). Its power resides in the effort [of] power to interpellate us from the non-measurable, and thus from what becomes incommensurable to our present, and to question, test, and critique it" ("Demanding"). For Draper, literature—and representation more generally—is productive insofar as it affords the possibility to move beyond it. Furthermore, this incommensurability "from within literature" also offers a "promise" that negates a politics of the recent past and, instead, demands "the impossible" of a future politics, demands that we see past and present politics in a different manner altogether. Literature thus becomes a means of locating what Massumi calls "potential" (1). And this same sense of potential can be located in Beasley-Murray's work when he asserts that reading for affect in literature can lead to the "emergence of individuals and multitudes" ("History, Affect, Literature").

13. My critique of affect theory in no way is meant to be exhaustive. I focus on Beasley-Murray's *Posthegemony* in particular not only because it is superbly written and argued but also because it is one of the first and most comprehensive works in Latin American theory and criticism to deal with affect. For other important works on affect in Latin American theory and criticism, see, for example, Ludmer, the collection edited by Moraña and Sánchez Prado, and Reber's excellent *Coming to Our Senses*.

14. But again, if it does move beyond stasis, it must do so by treating literature as an illusion. To treat literature otherwise would transform it from an object of capture to an object of complete closure. Said differently, to treat literature, and art more generally, as such is also to return to the inside and outside postmodern

world of the grid and deconstruction, of language, and, ultimately, of political stasis. According to the logic of affect, potential can be located only when literature
becomes the illusion it has always been.

15. It is important to stress here that despite differences—differences discussed in a *Nonsite* piece titled "Making It Visible" that I wrote with Emilio
Sauri—Moreiras fully understands that the loss of the object is also the death
of critical thought. From this position, it can be argued that what affect theory
achieves is, in fact, the loss of the object from which critical thought can emerge.

16. The question of "pure fiction," for Asecio Gómez, is juxtaposed with the
possible world of Macedonio Fernández. In "Tantalia," she argues that aesthetic
autonomy does something more philosophical but also more possible. *Bonsái* instead has no desire to be either philosophical or possible: "If Fernández's characters are characters in that they inhabit a possible reality, Julio and Emilia are fictional constructions through the metafictional device of parody, and they inhabit
a world that is not impossible, but simply invented" ("Similitudes").

17. Jameson also puts it this way: "The image is the commodity today, and
that is why it is vain to expect a negation of the logic of commodity production
from it, that is why, finally, all beauty today is meretricious and the appeal to it by
contemporary pseudo-aestheticism is an ideological manoeuvre and not a creative
resource" (*Cultural Turn* 135).

18. To say nothing of the romantic roots of philology that Moreiras has de-
tailed; see *Exhaustion*.

Coda

1. One could add to this list of artists the work of César Aira, Pedro Mairal,
and Sergio Chejfec. In his excellent reading of Chejfec's *La experiencia dramática*,
Stephen Buttes convincingly argues that the Argentine writer sets out "to critique
contemporary finance capitalism" by mobilizing an antitheatrical literary project
that seeks to separate our lived experiences—experiences that include the intersection between debt and the digital world—with a representation of said experiences. Buttes puts it this way: "Chejfec establishes for literature an important
'critical potentiality,' one that asserts that it isn't enough to simply see and experience the everyday as we watch it take place on a computer screen. Whether on
the screen or not, debt and its manifestations in its ordinary, mundane, temporal
operation must be represented; it must be narrated; and however partially it may
happen, it must be understood" ("Towards an Art"). For another equally insightful account of the relationship between aesthetic form and economics (more specifically, poverty), see Buttes's essay "Re-fictionalizing the Argentine Dream: Poverty and the Return to Literature in *La virgen cabeza*."

Works Cited

Agosín, Marjorie. *Ashes of Revolt: Essays on Human Rights*. Fredonia, NY: White Pine Press, 1996.

Aira, César. *Un episodio en la vida del pintor viajero*. Santiago: Lom Editorial, 2002.

Aldrighi, Clara. *La izquierda armada: Ideología, ética e identidad en el MLN-Tupamaros*. Montevideo: Trilce, 2001.

Aldrighi, Clara, María Magdalena Camou, Miguel Feldman, and Gabriel Abend. *Antisemitismo en Uruguay: Raíces, discursos, imágenes (1870–1940)*. Montevideo: Ediciones Trilce, 2000.

Alem-Walker, Beatriz. "El teatro como guardián y precursor de la memoria colectiva en tres obras de autores uruguayos." PhD diss., Texas Tech U, 2005.

Anguita, Eduardo, and Martín Caparrós. *La voluntad: Una historia de la militancia revolucionaria en la Argentina*. Barcelona: Norma, 1998.

Antebi, Susan. *Carnal Inscriptions: Spanish American Narratives of Corporeal Difference and Disability*. New York: Palgrave Macmillan, 2009.

Arias, Arturo, ed. *The Rigoberta Menchú Controversy*. Minneapolis: U of Minnesota P, 2001.

Aristaráin, Adolfo, dir. *Time for Revenge*. Actor Federico Luppi. Buenos Aires: Aries, 1982. Film.

Asecio Gómez, Monserrat. "Similitudes y diferencias: La relación entre *Bonsái* de Alejandro Zambra y 'Tantalia' de Macedonio Fernández como una construcción paródica." Proyecto Patrimonio, 2010. http://letras.mysite.com/az280910.html.

Avelar, Idelber. "Alegoría y postdictadura: Notas sobre la memoria del mercado." *Revista de Crítica Cultural* 14 (June 1997): 22–27.

———. "La escena de avanzada: Photography and Writing in Postcoup Chile—A Conversation with Nelly Richard." In *Photography and Writing in Latin America*, edited by Marcy E. Schwartz and Mary Beth Tierney-Tello, 259–270. Albuquerque: U of New Mexico P, 2006.

———. *The Letter of Violence: Essays on Narrative, Ethics, and Politics*. New York: Palgrave Macmillan, 2004.

———. "Unpacking the 'Human' in 'Human Rights': Bare Life in the Age of Endless War." In *Human Rights in Latin American and Iberian Cultures*, edited by Ana

Forcinito, Raúl Marrero-Fente, and Kelly McDonough, 25–36. *Hispanic Issues On Line* 5.1 (2009). http://hdl.handle.net/11299/182854.

———. *The Untimely Present: Postdictatorial Latin American Fiction and the Task of Mourning.* Durham, NC: Duke UP, 1999.

Badiou, Alain. "La ética y la cuestión de los derechos humanos." *Acontecimiento* 19–20 (2000): N.p. www.reflexionesmarginales.com/pdf/19/Documentos/2.pdf.

Barahona de Brito, Alexandra. *Human Rights and Democratization in Latin America: Uruguay and Chile.* Oxford: Oxford UP, 1997.

Barnitz, Jacqueline. "New Figuration, Pop, and Assemblage in the 1960s and 1970s." In *Latin American Artists of the Twentieth Century*, edited by Waldo Rasmussen, 122–133. New York: Museum of Modern Art, 1993.

Barrios de Chungara, Domitila. *Si me permiten hablar . . . : Testimonio de Domitila, una mujer de las minas de Bolivia.* Edited by Moema Viezzer. Mexico City: Siglo Veintiuno, 1977.

Barthes, Roland. *Camera Lucida: Reflections on Photography.* Translated by Richard Howard. New York: Hill and Wang, 1981.

———. "The Death of the Author." In *Image—Music—Text*, 142–149. Translated by Stephen Heath. New York: Fontana Press, 1978. Originally published in 1967.

Beasley-Murray, Jon. "History, Affect, Literature." *Posthegemony: Something Always Escapes!*, blog entry, 12 January 2014.

———. *Posthegemony: Political Theory and Latin America.* Minneapolis: U of Minnesota P, 2011.

Becker, Gary. *The Economics of Discrimination.* Chicago: U of Chicago P, 1957.

Beckman, Ericka. *Capital Fictions: The Literature of Latin America's Export Age.* Minneapolis: U of Minnesota P, 2013.

Benedetti, Mario. *Pedro and the Captain.* Translated by Adrianne Aron. Tiburon-Belvedere, CA: Cadmus Editions, 2009. Originally published as *Pedro y el Capitán*. Madrid: Santillana, 1979.

———. *Primavera con una esquina rota.* Mexico City: Editorial Nueva Imagen, 1982.

———. *Terremoto y después.* Montevideo: Arca Editorial, 1973.

Benson-Allott, Caetlin. "An Illusion Appropriate to the Conditions: *No* (Pablo Larraín, 2012)." *Film Quarterly* 66.3 (Spring 2013): 61–63.

Bergero, Adriana, and Fernando Reati, eds. *Memoria colectiva y políticas de olvido: Argentina y Uruguay, 1970–1990.* Rosario: Beatriz Viterbo Editora, 1997.

Berliner, David. "The Abuses of Memory: Reflections on the Memory Boom in Anthropology." *Anthropological Quarterly* 78.1 (December 2005): 197–211.

Beverley, John. *Against Literature.* Minneapolis: U of Minnesota P, 1993.

———. *Latinamericanism after 9/11.* Durham, NC: Duke UP, 2011.

———. "The Margin at the Center." In *Testimonio: On the Politics of Truth*, 29–44. Minneapolis: U of Minnesota P, 2004.

———. "The Neoconservative Turn in Latin American Literary and Cultural Criticism." *Journal of Latin American Cultural Studies: Travesia* 17.1 (2008): 65–83.

———. "The Real Thing." In *Testimonio: On the Politics of Truth*, 63–78. Minneapolis: U of Minnesota P, 2004.

———. "Rethinking the Armed Struggle in Latin America." *boundary 2* 36.1 (2009): 47–59.

Beverley, John, José Oviedo, and Michael Aronna, eds. *The Postmodernism Debate in Latin America*. Durham, NC: Duke UP, 1995.

Beverley, John, and Marc Zimmerman. *Literature and Politics in the Central American Revolutions*. Austin: U of Texas P, 1990.

Bilbija, Ksenija, and Leigh A. Payne. "Introduction: Time Is Money: The Memory Market in Latin America." In *Accounting for Violence: Marketing Memory in Latin America*, edited by Ksenija Bilbija and Leigh A. Payne, 1–40. Durham, NC: Duke UP, 2011.

Blaustein, David, dir. *Cazadores de utopias*. Buenos Aires: Instituto Nacional de Cine y Artes Audiovisuales, 1996. Film.

Bolaño, Roberto. *Distant Star*. Translated by Chris Andrews. New York: New Directions, 2004. Originally published as *Estrella distante*. Barcelona: Anagrama, 1996.

———. *El Tercer Reich*. Barcelona: Anagrama, 2010.

———. *La literatura nazi en América*. Barcelona: Seix Barral, 2005.

———. *2666*. Translated by Natasha Wimmer. New York: Farrar, Straus and Giroux, 2008.

Bonasso, Miguel. *Cámpora: El presidente que no fue*. Buenos Aires: Planeta, 2012.

Bordo, Susan. *Unbearable Weight: Feminism, Western Culture, and the Body*. Berkeley: U of California P, 1993.

Borges, Jorge Luis. "Pierre Menard, Author of Don Quixote." In *Ficciones*. Translated by Anthony Bonner. New York: Grove Press, 1962. Originally published as "Pierre Menard, autor del Quijote" in 1939.

Bosteels, Bruno. "Politics, Infrapolitics, and the Impolitical: Notes on the Thought of Roberto Esposito and Alberto Moreiras." *CR: The New Centennial Review* 10.2 (Fall 2010): 205–238.

Botero, Juan Carlos. "The Art of Fernando Botero." *Working Papers: Center for Latin American Studies, University of California, Berkeley* 31 (May 2012): 1–27. clas.berkeley.edu/sites/default/files/shared/docs/papers/Botero.pdf.

Bravo, Germán. "Las nuevas escrituras." In *Utopía(s)*. Santiago: División de Cultura del Ministerio de Educación, 1993.

Brinkema, Eugenie. *The Forms of the Affects*. Durham, NC: Duke UP, 2014.

Brogna, Patricia. *Visiones y revisiones de la discapacidad*. Mexico City: Fondo de Cultura Económica, 2009.

Brouillette, Sarah. *Literature and the Creative Economy*. Stanford: Stanford UP, 2014.

Brown, Nicholas. "The Work of Art in the Age of Its Real Subsumption under Capital." *Nonsite.org* (13 March 2012): N.p. nonsite.org/editorial/the-work-of-art-in-the-age-of-its-real-subsumption-under-capital.

Bürger, Peter. *Theory of The Avant-Garde*. Trans. Michael Shaw. Minneapolis: U of Minnesota P, 1984.

Burgos, Elizabeth. *Me llamo Rigoberta Menchú y así me nació la conciencia*. Buenos Aires: Siglo Veintiuno, 1985. First edition, Havana: Casa de las Américas, 1983.

Butler, Judith. *Frames of War: When Is Life Grievable?* New York: Verso, 2010.

———. *Precarious Life: The Powers of Mourning and Violence*. London: Verso, 2006.

Buttes, Stephen. "Re-fictionalizing the Argentine Dream: Poverty and the Return to Literature in *La virgen cabeza*." *A Contracorriente* 14.3 (Spring 2017): 200–

219. acontracorriente.chass.ncsu.edu/index.php/acontracorriente/article/view
/1557.

———. "Towards an Art of Landscapes and Loans: Sergio Chejfec and the Politics of Literary Form." *Nonsite.org* 13 (2014): N.p. nonsite.org/article/towards-an -art-of-landscapes-and-loans.

Calveiro, Pilar. *Política y/o violencia: Una aproximación a la guerrilla de los años 70.* Buenos Aires: Norma, 2005.

Camnitzer, Luis. *Conceptualism in Latin American Art: Didactics of Liberation.* Austin: U of Texas P, 2007.

Campodónico, Miguel Ángel. *Las vidas de Rosencof.* Montevideo: Fin de Siglo, 2000.

Carri, Albertina, dir. *Los rubios.* Buenos Aires: Primer Plano Film Group, 2003. Film.

Castañeda, Jorge. *Utopia Unarmed: The Latin American Left after the Cold War.* New York: Vintage, 1994.

Casullo, Nicolás. *Pensar entre épocas: Memoria, sujetos y crítica intelectual.* Buenos Aires: Norma, 2004.

Chávez, Daniel. "Uruguay: La izquierda en el gobierno: entre la continuidad y el cambio." In *La nueva izquierda en América Latina,"* edited by César A. Rodríguez Garavito, Patrick S. Barrett, and Daniel Chávez, 149–187. Madrid: Catarata, 2008.

Chejfec, Sergio. *Lenta biografía.* Buenos Aires: Puntosur, 1990.

Colás, Santiago. *Postmodernity in Latin America.* Durham, NC: Duke UP, 1994.

———. "What's Wrong with Representation? *Testimonio* and Democratic Culture." In *The Real Thing: Testimonial Discourse and Latin America,* edited by Georg M. Gugelberger, 161–171. Durham, NC: Duke UP, 1996.

Colvin, Andrea. "Memory and Fantasy: The Imaginative Reconstruction of a Lost Past in *Las cartas que no llegaron.*" *Mester* 36.1 (2007): 38–52.

Costa-Gavras, Constantin, dir. *State of Siege.* Santiago: Reggane Films, 1972. Film.

Cronan, Todd. *Against Affective Formalism: Matisse, Bergson, Modernism.* Minneapolis: U of Minnesota P, 2013.

Currie, Mark. *Metafiction.* New York: Routledge, 1995.

Danto, Arthur C. "The Body in Pain." *The Nation.com,* 9 November 2006: N.p. https://www.thenation.com/article/body-pain/.

Dargis, Manohla. "Try Freedom: Less Filling! Tastes Great!" *New York Times,* 14 February 2013.

De la Campa, Román. *Latin Americanism.* Minneapolis: U of Minnesota P, 1999.

De los Ríos, Valeria. "Cartografía salvaje: Mapa cognitivo y fotografías en la obra de Bolaño." *Taller de letras* 41 (2007): 69–81.

De Man, Paul. "Form and Intent in the American New Criticism." In *Blindness and Insight: Essays in the Rhetoric of Contemporary Criticism,* 20–35. Minneapolis: U of Minnesota P, 1983.

———. "The Purloined Ribbon." *Glyph* 1:39 (1977): 28–49.

Derrida, Jacques. *Limited Inc.* Evanston, IL: Northwestern UP, 1988.

———. *Specters of Marx: The State of the Debt, The Work of Mourning, and the New International.* Translated by Peggy Kamuf. New York: Routledge, 1994.

———. *The Truth in Painting.* Translated by Geoffrey Bennington and Ian McLeod. Chicago: University of Chicago P, 1979.

"Discapacidad y Dictadura: Entre Ayer y Hoy." *RNMA Argentina*. 23 Mar. 2009. rnma.org.ar/nv/index.php?option=com_content&task=view&id=583.

Di Stefano, Eugenio. "Cuerpo, crisis y discapacidad: La familia en *El obsceno pájaro de la noche*." In *Memorias de JALLA 2004 Lima: Jornadas Andinas de Literatura Latinoamericana*, edited by Carlos M. García-Bedoyan, 415–421. Lima: Univ. Nacional Mayor de San Marcos, 2005.

———. "Disability and Latin American Cultural Studies: A Critique of Corporeal Difference, Identity and Social Exclusion." *Canadian Journal of Disability Studies* 4.2 (2015): N.p. cjds.uwaterloo.ca/index.php/cjds/article/view/209.

———. "From Shopping Malls to Memory Museums: Reconciling the Recent Past in the Uruguayan Neoliberal State." In *Reconciliation and Its Discontents*, edited by Txetxu Aguado and Annabel Martín. Special Issue of *Dissidences* 4.8 (2012): N.p. digitalcommons.bowdoin.edu/cgi/viewcontent.cgi?article=1039&context=dissidences.

Di Stefano, Eugenio, and Emilio Sauri. "'La furia de la materia': On the Non-Contemporaneity of Modernism in Latin America." In *The Contemporaneity of Modernism: Literature, Media, Culture*, edited by Michael D'Arcy and Mathias Nilges, 148–164. New York: Routledge, 2015.

———. "Making It Visible: Latin Americanist Criticism, Literature, and the Question of Exploitation Today." *Nonsite.org* 13 (2014): N.p. http://nonsite.org/article/making-it-visible.

Donoso, José. *El obsceno pájaro de la noche*. Barcelona: Seix Barral, 1970.

Dorfman, Ariel. *Death and the Maiden*. New York: Penguin, 1992. First edition, London: Nick Hearn Books, 1990.

———. *La muerte y la doncella*. New York: Siete Cuentos, 2001.

Dove, Patrick. *Literature and "Interregnum": Globalization, War, and the Crisis of Sovereignty in Latin America*. Albany, NY: SUNY P, 2016.

Draper, Susana. *Afterlives of Confinement: Spatial Transitions in Postdictatorship Latin America*. Pittsburgh: U of Pittsburgh P, 2012.

———. "Demanding the Impossible: Literature and Political Imagination (*Amuleto*, 1968 in the Nineties)." *Nonsite.org* 13 (2014): N.p. nonsite.org/article/demanding-the-impossible.

Ebony, David. *Botero: Abu Ghraib*. Munich: Prestel, 2006.

Eltit, Diamela. *El padre mío*. Santiago: Francisco Zegers Editor, 1989.

Felman, Shoshana, and Dori Laub. *Testimony: Crises of Witnessing in Literature, Psychoanalysis and History*. New York: Routledge, 1992.

Fernández Huidobro, Eleuterio, and Mauricio Rosencof. *Memorias del calabozo*. Montevideo: Tae, 1987.

Fernández-Savater, Amador. "Jon Beasley-Murray: 'La clave del cambio social no es la ideología, sino los cuerpos, los afectos y los hábitos.'" *El diario.es*, 20 February 2015: N.p. www.eldiario.es/interferencias/Podemos-hegemonia-afectos_6_358774144.html.

Fingueret, Manuela. *Hija del silencio*. Buenos Aires: Planeta, 1999.

Fish, Stanley. *Is There a Text in This Class?: The Authority of Interpretive Communities*. Cambridge, MA: Harvard UP, 1982.

Forcinito, Ana, and Fernando Ordóñez, eds. *Human Rights and Latin American Cultural Studies*. Hispanic Issues Series. *Hispanic Issues On line* 4.1 (2009).

Fornazzari, Alejandro. *Speculative Fictions: Chilean Culture, Economics, and the Neoliberal Transition*. Pittsburgh: U of Pittsburgh P, 2013.

Forné, Anna. "La materialidad de la memoria en *Las cartas que no llegaron* de Mauricio Rosencof (Uruguay, 1930–2000)." *Historia Crítica* 40 (2010): 44–59.

Franco, Jean. *Cruel Modernity*. Durham, NC: Duke UP, 2013.

———. *The Decline and Fall of the Lettered City: Latin America in the Cold War*. Cambridge, MA: Harvard UP, 2002.

———. *An Introduction to Spanish-American Literature*. Cambridge: U of Cambridge P, 1994.

Fried, Michael. *Absorption and Theatricality: Painting and Beholder in the Age of Diderot*. Chicago: U of Chicago P, 1988. First edition, Chicago: U of Chicago P, 1980.

———. "Art and Objecthood." In *Art and Objecthood: Essays and Reviews*, 148–172. Chicago: U of Chicago P, 1998.

———. *Why Photography Matters as Art as Never Before*. New Haven, CT: Yale UP, 2008.

Fukuyama, Francis. "The End of History?" In *The Geopolitics Reader*, edited by Gearóid Ó Tuathail, Simon Dalby, and Paul Routledge, 107–114. London: Routledge, 2006.

Gamboa Cárdenas, Jeremías. "¿Siameses o dobles? Vanguardia y postmodernismo en *Estrella distante* de Roberto Bolaño." In *Bolaño Salvaje*, edited by Edmundo Paz Soldán and Gustavo Faverón-Patriau, 211–236. Barcelona: Candaya, 2008.

Garcé, Adolfo. *Donde hubo fuego: El proceso de adaptación del MLN-Tupamaros a la legalidad y a la competencia electoral (1985–2004)*. Montevideo: Fin de Siglo, 2006.

García Márquez, Gabriel. *Cien años de soledad*. Buenos Aires: Editorial Sudamericana, 1967.

Garland Thomson, Rosemarie. *Extraordinary Bodies: Figuring Physical Disability in American Culture and Literature*. New York: Colombia UP, 1997.

Gilio, Maria Esther. *The Tupamaro Guerrillas*. Translated by Anne Edmondson. New York: Saturday Review Press, 1972.

Graff Zivin, Erin. *Figurative Inquisitions: Conversion, Torture, and Truth in the Luso-Hispanic Atlantic*. Evanston, IL: Northwestern UP, 2014.

Gregory, Stephen. *Humanist Ethics or Realistic Aesthetics*. New South Wales, Australia: La Trobe U, 1991.

———. *Intellectuals and Left Politics in Uruguay, 1958–2006: Frustrated Dialogue*. Eastbourne BN, UK: Sussex Academic P, 2009.

Gugelberger, Georg M., ed. *The Real Thing: Testimonial Discourse and Latin America*. Durham, NC: Duke UP, 1996.

Gundermann, Christian. *Actos melancólicos: Formas de resistencia en la postdictadura argentina*. Buenos Aires: Beatriz Viterbo, 2007.

Hamrit, Jacqueline. *Authorship in Nabokov's Prefaces*. Newcastle upon Tyne, UK: Cambridge Scholars, 2014.

Harlow, Barbara. *Resistance Literature*. New York: Routledge, 1997. First edition, New York: Methuen, 1987.

Hatfield, Charles. *The Limits of Identity: Politics and Poetics in Latin America*. Austin: U of Texas P, 2015.

Hersh, Seymour M. "Torture at Abu Ghraib." *New Yorker.* The YGS Group, 10 May 2004: N.p. www.newyorker.com/magazine/2004/05/10/torture-at-abu-ghraib.

Hilde, Thomas. *On Torture.* Baltimore: Johns Hopkins UP, 2008.

Hirsch, Marianne, ed. *Human Rights in Latin America.* Special issue of *PMLA* 121.5 (October 2006): 1662–1674.

———. "Surviving Images: Holocaust Photographs and the Work of Postmemory." *Yale Journal of Criticism* 14.1 (2001): 5–37.

Howe, Alexis. "Yes, No, or Maybe? Transitions in Chilean Society in Pablo Larraín's *No.*" *Hispania* 98.3 (2015): 421–430.

Hunt, Lynn. *Inventing Human Rights.* New York: W. W. Norton, 2007.

Huntington, Samuel P. "The Clash of Civilizations?" *Foreign Affairs* 72.3 (Summer 1993): 22–49.

Hutcheon, Linda. *Narcissistic Narrative: The Metafictional Paradox.* Ontario: Wilfrid Laurier UP, 1980.

Huyssen, Andreas. "Present Pasts: Media, Politics, Amnesia." *Public Culture* 12.1 (Winter 2000): 21–38.

Jameson, Fredric. *The Cultural Turn.* London: Verso, 1998.

———. *Postmodernism, or, The Cultural Logic of Late Capitalism.* Durham, NC: Duke UP, 1991.

Jara, René. Prologue to *Testimonio y literatura*, edited by René Jara and Hernán Vidal, 1–6. Minneapolis, MN: Institute for the Study of Ideologies and Literature, 1986.

Jennerjahn, Ina. "Escritos en los cielos y fotografías del infierno: Las 'Acciones de arte' de Carlos Ramírez Hoffman, según Roberto Bolaño." *Revista de Crítica Literaria Latinoamericana* 28.56 (2002): 69–86.

Kanzepolsky, Adriana. "El linaje vacío o *Las cartas que no llegaron* de Mauricio Rosencof." *Astrolabio: Revista Virtual del Centro de Estudios Avanzados de la Universidad Nacional de Córdoba* 4 (2010): N.p. revistas.unc.edu.ar/index.php /astrolabio/article/view/252.

Labanyi, Jo. "Doing Things: Emotion, Affect, and Materiality." *Journal of Spanish Cultural Studies* 11.3–4 (2010): 223–233.

Laqueur, Thomas. "Bodies, Details, and the Humanitarian Narrative." In *The New Cultural History*, edited by Lynn Hunt, 176–204. Berkeley, CA: U of California P, 1989.

———. "Botero and the Art History of Suffering." *Working Papers: Center for Latin American Studies, University of California, Berkeley* 18 (August 2007): 1–10. clas.berkeley.edu/sites/default/files/shared/docs/papers/artViolenceWebBook .pdf.

Larraín, Pablo, dir. *No.* Santiago: Fabula, 2012. Film.

Larsen, Neil. *Reading North by South: On Latin American Literature, Culture, and Politics.* Minneapolis: U of Minnesota P, 1995.

Leicht, Federico. *Cero a la izquierda: Una biografía de Jorge Zabalza.* Montevideo: Letraeñe, 2007.

Lespada, Gustavo. "Las manifestaciones del silencio: Lo inefable en *Las cartas que no llegaron* de Mauricio Rosencof." *Everba* (Spring 2003): N.p. eter.org/everba /spring03/lespada.html.

Levinson, Sanford, ed. *Torture: A Collection.* Oxford: Oxford UP, 2004.

Leys, Ruth. "The Turn to Affect: A Critique." *Critical Inquiry* 37.3 (2011): 434–472.

Liscano, Carlos. *Truck of Fools: A Testimonio of Torture and Recovery.* Translated by Elizabeth Hampsten. Foreword by David William Foster. Nashville: Vanderbilt UP, 2004. Originally published as *El furgón de los locos.* Montevideo: Planeta, 2001.

Ludmer, Josefina. "Literaturas postautónomas." *CiberLetras: Revista de Crítica Literaria y de Cultura* (17 July 2007): N.p. www.lehman.cuny.edu/ciberletras/v17/ludmer.htm.

Markarian, Vania. *Left in Transformation: Uruguayan Exiles and the Latin American Human Rights Network, 1967–1984.* London: Routledge, 2005.

Martín-Cabrera, Luis. *Radical Justice: Spain and the Southern Cone beyond Market and State.* Lewisburg, PA: Bucknell UP, 2011.

Marx, Karl, and Friedrich Engels. *The Communist Manifesto.* London: Pluto Press, 2011.

Masiello, Francine. "Art and Violence: Notes on Botero." *Working Papers: Center for Latin American Studies, University of California, Berkeley* 18 (August 2007): 11–23. clas.berkeley.edu/sites/default/files/shared/docs/papers/artViolenceWebBook.pdf

———. *The Art of Transition: Latin American Culture and Neoliberal Crisis.* Durham, NC: Duke UP, 2001.

Massiah, Ernest. "Disability and Inclusion: Data Collection, Education, Transportation and Urban Development." In *Social Inclusion and Economic Development in Latin America*, edited by Mayra Buvinić, Jacqueline Mazza, and Ruthanne Deutsch, 61–86. Washington, DC: Inter-American Development Bank, 2004.

Massumi, Brian. *Parables for the Virtual: Movement, Affect, Sensation.* Durham, NC: Duke UP, 2002.

Michaels, Walter Benn. *The Beauty of a Social Problem: Photography, Autonomy, Economy.* Chicago: U of Chicago P, 2015.

———. "The Force of a Frame: Owen Kydd's Durational Photographs." *Nonsite* 11 (14 March 2014): N.p. nonsite.org/feature/the-force-of-a-frame.

———. "Photographs and Fossils." In *Photography Theory*, edited by James Elkins, 431–450. New York: Routledge, 2006.

———. *The Shape of the Signifier: 1967 to the End of History.* Princeton, NJ: Princeton UP, 2004.

Mitchell, David, and Sharon Snyder. *Narrative Prosthesis: Disability and the Dependencies of Discourse.* Ann Arbor: U of Michigan P, 2000.

Morales Gamboa, Fernando Emilio. "*Bonsái*: Alejandro Zambra." *Letras Hispanas* 3.2 (Fall 2006): 170–172.

Moraña, Mabel, and Ignacio Sánchez Prado, eds. *El lenguaje de las emociones: Afecto y cultura en América Latina.* Frankfurt: Verlag Vervuert, 2012.

Moreiras, Alberto. "Afterword: Pastiche Identity, and Allegory of Allegory." In *Latin American Identity and Constructions of Difference*, edited by Amaryll Beatrice Chanady, 204–238. Minneapolis: U of Minnesota P, 1994.

———. *The Exhaustion of Difference: The Politics of Latin American Cultural Studies.* Durham, NC: Duke UP, 2001.

Morello-Frosch, Marta. "El diálogo de la violencia en *Pedro y el capitán* de Mario Benedetti." *Revista de Crítica Literaria Latinoamericana* 9.18 (1983): 87–96.

Moretti, Franco. *Signs Taken for Wonders: Essays in the Sociology of Literary Forms.* Rev. ed. New York: Verso, 1988.

Morris, Errol. *Believing Is Seeing: Observations on the Mysteries of Photography.* New York: Penguin, 2011.

———, dir. *Standard Operating Procedure.* New York: Sony Pictures Classics, 2008. Film.

Morris, Ivan. "Torture in Uruguay." *New York Review of Books,* 18 March 1976. www.nybooks.com/articles/1976/03/18/torture-in-uruguay/.

Moyn, Samuel. *The Last Utopia: Human Rights in History.* Cambridge, MA: Harvard UP, 2010.

Neustadt, Robert. *(Con)Fusing Signs and Postmodern Positions: Spanish American Performance, Experimental Writing, and the Critique of Political Confusion.* New York: Routledge, 1999.

Nora, Pierre. "Between Memory and History: Les Lieux de Mémoire." *Representations* 26, Special Issue: Memory and Counter-Memory (Spring 1989): 7–24.

Nouzeilles, Gabriela. "Postmemory Cinema and the Future of the Past in Albertina Carri's *Los Rubios.*" *Journal of Latin American Cultural Studies: Travesia* 14.3 (2005): 263–278.

Onell, Roberto. "*Bonsái* de Alejandro Zambra." *Taller de Letras* 39 (2006): 163–166.

Page, Joanna. "Memory and Mediation in *Los rubios*: A Contemporary Perspective on the Argentine Dictatorship." *New Cinemas: Journal of Contemporary Film* 3.1 (2005): 29–40.

Parada Lezcano, Mario. "Libros." *Cuadernos Médico Sociales* 44.4 (2004): 292–296.

Paz Soldán, Edmundo. *El delirio de Turing.* La Paz: Alfaguara, 2003.

Peirce, Charles Sanders. *Collected Papers.* Vol. 2. Edited by Charles Hartshorne and Paul Weiss. Cambridge, MA: Harvard UP, 1960.

Pérez, Carolina. "Dictadura y discapacidad: Una historia sin punto final." *Diario UChile,* 9 September 2013: N.p. http://radio.uchile.cl/2013/09/09/dictadura-y -discapacidad-una-historia-sin-punto-final/.

Peri Rossi, Cristina. *La nave de los locos.* Barcelona: Planeta, 1984.

Piglia, Ricardo. *Respiración artificial.* Buenos Aires: Pomaire, 1980.

Polanski, Roman, dir. *Death and the Maiden.* United Kingdom: Capitol Films, 1994. Film.

Poniatowska, Elena. *La noche de Tlatelolco: Testimonios de historia oral.* Mexico City: Biblioteca Era, 1971.

Puenzo, Lucía, dir. *Wakolda.* Buenos Aires: Historias Cinematográficas Cinemania, 2013. Film.

Puig, Manuel. *Kiss of the Spider Woman.* Translated by Thomas Colchie. New York: Vintage, 1980. Originally published as *El beso de la mujer araña.* Barcelona: Seix Barral, 1976.

Quayson, Ato. *Aesthetic Nervousness: Disability and the Crisis of Representation.* New York: Columbia UP, 2007.

Rama, Ángel. *Rubén Darío y el modernismo.* Caracas: Ediciones de la Biblioteca de la Universidad Central de Venezuela, 1973. First edition, Caracas: Ediciones de la Biblioteca de la Universidad Central de Venezuela, 1970.

Ramos, Julio. *Desencuentros de la modernidad en América Latina.* Caracas: Fundación Editorial El perro y la rana, 2009. First edition, Mexico City: Fondo de Cultura Económica, 1989.

Ran, Amalia. "Nuestra Shoá: Dictaduras, Holocausto y represión en tres novelas judeorioplatenses." *Letras Hispanas* 6.1 (2009): 17–28.

Reber, Dierdra. *Coming to Our Senses: Affect and an Order of Things for Global Culture.* New York: Columbia UP, 2016.

Richard, Nelly. *Cultural Residues: Chile in Transition.* Translated by Alan West-Duran and Theodore Quester. Minneapolis: U of Minnesota P, 2004.

———. *The Insubordination of Signs: Political Change, Cultural Transformation, and Poetics of the Crisis.* Translated by Alice A. Nelson and Silvia R. Tandeciarz. Durham, NC: Duke UP, 2004.

———. *Márgenes e instituciones: Arte en Chile desde 1973.* Santiago: Francisco Zegers Editor, 1987.

———. "Reply to Vidal (From Chile)." *boundary 2* 20.3, Special issue, *The Postmodernism Debate in Latin America* (Autumn 1993): 228–231.

Robben, Antonius C. G. M. "How Traumatized Societies Remember: The Aftermath of Argentine's Dirty War." *Cultural Critique* 59 (Winter 2005): 120–164.

Rodríguez, Franklin. "Unsettledness and Doublings in Roberto Bolaño's *Estrella distante*." *Revista Hispánica Moderna* 63.2 (December 2010): 203–218.

Romney, Jonathan. "The Future Is No." *Sight and Sound* 23.3 (2013): 28–32.

Rosencof, Mauricio. *Conversations with My Sandal.* Translated by Louise B. Popkin and Julia Ackerman. *The Kenyon Review* 13.3 (Summer 1991): 67–73.

———. *La rebelión de los cañeros.* Montevideo: Fin de Siglo, 2009.

———. *The Letters That Never Came.* Translated by Louise B. Popkin. Albuquerque: U of New Mexico P, 2004. Originally published as *Las cartas que no llegaron.* Montevideo: Alfaguara, 2000.

Rosencof, Mauricio, and Eleuterio Fernández Huidobro. *Memorias del calabozo.* Montevideo: Tae, 1987.

Rosenfeld, Lotty. *Una milla de cruces sobre el pavimento.* Santiago: Ediciones C.A.D.A., 1980.

Sánchez Prado, Ignacio M. *Screening Neoliberalism: Transforming Mexican Cinema, 1988–2012.* Nashville: Vanderbilt UP, 2014.

Saona, Margarita. *Memory Matters in Transitional Peru.* New York: Palgrave Macmillan, 2014.

Sarlo, Beatriz. "Cuando la política era joven." *Punto de Vista* 20.58 (August 1997): 15–19.

———. "Cultural Studies and Literary Criticism at the Crossroads of Values." *Journal of Latin American Cultural Studies* 8.1 (1999): 115–124.

———. *Tiempo pasado: Cultura de la memoria y giro subjetivo: Una discusión.* Buenos Aires: Siglo Veintiuno, 2005.

Sauri, Emilio. "'A la pinche modernidad': Literary Form and the End of History in Roberto Bolaño's *Los detectives salvajes*." *MLN* 125.2 (2010): 406–432.

———. "Autonomy after Autonomy, or, The Novel beyond Nation: Roberto Bolaño's *2666*." *Canadian Review of Comparative Literature* 42.4 (December 2015): 396–409.

Schwarz, Roberto. "National by Imitation." In *The Postmodernism Debate in Latin*

America, edited by John Beverley, José Oviedo, and Michael Aronna, 264–281. Durham, NC: Duke UP, 1995.

———. "Objective Form: Reflections on the Dialectic of Roguery." Translated by John Gledson. In *Literary Materialisms*, edited by Mathias Nilges and Emilio Sauri, 185–199. New York: Palgrave Macmillan, 2013.

Shakespeare, Tom. "The Social Model of Disability." In *The Disability Studies Reader*, edited by Lennard Davis, 214–221. 4th ed. New York: Routledge, 2013.

Siebers, Tobin. "Disability Aesthetics." *Journal of Cultural and Ritual Theory* 7.2. (Spring/Summer 2006): 62–73.

Sikkink, Kathryn. "The Emergence, Evolution, and Effectiveness of the Latin American Human Rights Network." In *Constructing Democracy: Human Rights, Citizenship, and Society in Latin America*, edited by Elizabeth Jelin and Eric Hershberg, 59–84. Boulder, CO: Westview, 1996.

Sillevis, John. *The Baroque World of Fernando Botero*. New Haven, CT: Yale UP, 2007.

Silva, Macarena. "La conciencia de reírse de sí: Metaficción y parodia en *Bonsái* de Alejandro Zambra." *Taller de Letras* 41 (2007): 9–20.

Siraganian, Lisa. *Modernism's Other Work: The Art Object's Political Life*. Oxford: Oxford UP, 2012.

Sklodowska, Elzbieta. "Spanish American Testimonial Novel: Some Afterthoughts." In *The Real Thing: Testimonial Discourse in Latin America*, edited by Georg M. Gugelberger, 84–100. Durham, NC: Duke UP, 1996.

Sontag, Susan. *Against Interpretation and Other Essays*. New York: Farrar, Straus and Giroux, 1966.

———. "Regarding the Torture of Others." *New York Times Magazine*. New York Times, 23 May 2004: N.p. www.nytimes.com/2004/05/23/magazine/regarding -the-torture-of-others.html.

Sosnowski, Saúl. "Political Exclusion/Literary Inclusion: Argentine and Uruguayan Writers." In *Latin American Literary Culture: Subject to History*. Vol. 3 of *Literary Cultures of Latin America: A Comparative History*, edited by Mario J. Valdés and Djelal Kadir, 522–525. Oxford: Oxford UP, 2004.

Stoll, David. *Rigoberta Menchú and the Story of All Poor Guatemalans*. Boulder, CO: Westview, 1999.

Timerman, Jacobo. *Prisoner without a Name, Cell without a Number*. Translated by Toby Talbot. Madison: U of Wisconsin P, 1981.

Torres Perdigón, Andrea. "Reflexividad y narratividad en Ricardo Piglia: De Macedonio a Fitzgerald." *Kamchatka: Revista de Análisis Cultural* 1 (April 2013): 133–153.

"Tupamaro Communiqués 1–5." *Equipo de Investigaciones Rodolfo Walsh*. Rodolfo walsh.org. www.rodolfowalsh.org/spip.php?article2288.

"Uruguay Sets Course to Become Gateway to Mercosur Bloc." *Journal of Commerce* (14 May 1999). Uruguayan-American Chamber of Commerce in the USA. www .uruguaychamber.com/press_11.php.

Valdes, Marcela. "Seed Projects: The Fiction of Alejandro Zambra." *The Nation*, 17 June 2009. https://www.thenation.com/article/seed-projects-fiction -alejandro-zambra/.

Valenzuela, Luisa. "Cambio de armas." In *Cambio de armas*. Buenos Aires: Norma, 1982.

Van Cott, Donna Lee. "Constitutional Reform in the Andes: Redefining Indigenous-State Relations." In *Multiculturalism in Latin America: Indigenous Rights, Diversity and Democracy*, edited by Rachel Sieder, 45–73. London: Palgrave Macmillan, 2002.

Van Horn, Rob, and Philip Mirowski. "The Rise of the Chicago School of Economics and the Birth of Neoliberalism." In *The Road from Mont Pèlerin: The Making of the Neoliberal Thought Collective*, edited by Philip Mirowski and Dieter Plehwe, 139–178. Cambridge, MA: Harvard UP, 2009.

Vidal, Hernán. "Postmodernism, Postleftism, and Neo-Avant-Gardism: The Case of Chile's *Revista de Crítica Cultural*." In *The Postmodernism Debate in Latin America*, edited by John Beverley, José Oviedo, and Michael Aronna, 282–306. Durham: Duke UP, 1995.

Volpi, Jorge. *En busca de Klingsor*. Barcelona: Seix Barral, 1999.

Waugh, Patricia. *Metafiction: The Theory and Practice of Self-Conscious Fiction*. New York: Routledge, 1984.

Weschler, Lawrence. *A Miracle, A Universe: Settling Accounts with Torturers*. New York: Viking Penguin, 1991.

Wilkinson, Amber. "Man in the No." *Eye for Film*, 8 February 2013. www.eyeforfilm.co.uk/feature/2013-02-07-pablo-larrain-talks-about-his-oscar-nominated-film-no-feature-story-by-amber-wilkinson.

Williams, Gareth. *The Other Side of the Popular: Neoliberalism and Subalternity in Latin America*. Durham, NC: Duke UP, 2002.

———. "Sovereignty and Melancholic Paralysis in Roberto Bolaño." *Journal of Latin American Cultural Studies* 18.2–3 (2009): 125–140.

———. "Translation and Mourning: The Cultural Challenge of Latin American Testimonial Autobiography." *Latin American Literary Review* 21.41 (1993) 79–99.

Williams, Randall. *The Divided World: Human Rights and Its Violence*. Minneapolis: U of Minnesota P, 2010.

Wood, James. "Story of My Life: The Fictions of Alejandro Zambra." *New Yorker*, 22 June 2015.

Yúdice, George. "*Testimonio* and Postmodernism." In *The Real Thing: Testimonial Discourse in Latin America*, edited by Georg M. Gugelberger, 42–57. Durham, NC: Duke UP, 1996.

Zambra, Alejandro. *Bonsai*. Translated by Carolina de Robertis. New York: Melville House, 2008. Originally published as *Bonsái*. Barcelona: Anagrama, 2006.

———. *Formas de volver a casa*. Barcelona: Anagrama, 2011.

———. "La vanguardia melancólica." *No Retornable*, 4 September 2013. www.no-retornable.com.ar/v1/dossier/zambra.html.

———. *No leer: Crónicas y ensayos sobre literatura*. Santiago: Universidad Diego Portales, 2010.

Zamora, Daniel. "When Exclusion Replaces Exploitation: The Condition of the Surplus-Population under Neoliberalism." *Nonsite* 10 (13 September 2013): N.p. nonsite.org/feature/when-exclusion-replaces-exploitation.

Žižek, Slavoj. "Against Human Rights." *New Left Review* 34 (July–August 2005): 115–131.

———. *Looking Awry: An Introduction to Jacques Lacan through Popular Culture*. Cambridge, MA: MIT Press, 1991.

Index